KT-582-986

Newham London

ADULTS
S7

9/5/12		

24 hour automated telephone renewal line
0115 929 3388
Or online at www.newham.gov.uk

This book must be returned (or its issue renewed)
on or before the date stamped above

By the same author

Fiction

In the Secret State

A Loss of Heart

The Fabulous Englishman

Mainland

The Psychological Moment

Suspicion

Non-fiction

The Story of English (*with William Cran and Robert MacNeil*)

My Year Off: Rediscovering Life After a Stroke

Wodehouse: A Life

For Children

The World is a Banana

The Brontosaurus Birthday Cake

Globish

*How the English Language Became
the World's Language*

ROBERT MCCRUM

PENGUIN BOOKS

PENGUIN BOOKS

Published by the Penguin Group
Penguin Books Ltd, 80 Strand, London WC2R ORL, England
Penguin Group (USA) Inc., 375 Hudson Street, New York, New York 10014, USA
Penguin Group (Canada), 90 Eglinton Avenue East, Suite 700, Toronto, Ontario, Canada M4P 2Y3
(a division of Pearson Penguin Canada Inc.)
Penguin Ireland, 25 St Stephen's Green, Dublin 2, Ireland (a division of Penguin Books Ltd)
Penguin Group (Australia), 250 Camberwell Road, Camberwell, Victoria 3124, Australia
(a division of Pearson Australia Group Pty Ltd)
Penguin Books India Pvt Ltd, 11 Community Centre, Panchsheel Park,
New Delhi – 110 017, India
Penguin Group (NZ), 67 Apollo Drive, Rosedale, Auckland 0632, New Zealand
(a division of Pearson New Zealand Ltd)
Penguin Books (South Africa) (Pty) Ltd, 24 Sturdee Avenue, Rosebank, Johannesburg 2196,
South Africa

Penguin Books Ltd, Registered Offices: 80 Strand, London WC2R ORL, England

www.penguin.com

First published by Viking 2010
Published in Penguin Books 2011

1

Copyright © Robert McCrum, 2010
All rights reserved

The moral right of the author has been asserted

The permissions on page 295 constitute an extension of this copyright page

Printed in England by Clays Ltd, St Ives plc

ISBN: 978-0-141-02710-4

www.greenpenguin.co.uk

For my mother,
Christine McCrum,
who gave me English:
with love and thanks

For certainly our language now used varyeth far from that which was used and spoken when I was born. For we Englishmen have been born under the domination of the moon, which is never steadfast, but ever wavering and waxing one season.

William Caxton, Prologue to *Enydos*

In all pointed sentences, some degree of accuracy must be sacrificed to conciseness.

Samuel Johnson, 'The Bravery of the English Common Soldiers'

They spell it Vinci and pronounce it Vinchy; foreigners always spell better than they pronounce.

Mark Twain, *The Innocents Abroad*

The United States themselves are essentially the greatest poem.

Walt Whitman, *Leaves of Grass*

The great enemy of clear language is insincerity. When there is a gap between one's real and one's declared aims, one turns as it were instinctively to long words and exhausted idioms, like a cuttlefish squirting out ink

George Orwell, *Shooting an Elephant*

Contents

PART FIVE: GLOBALIZERS

Prologue: 'Crazy English'

The twenty-first century has revealed a world more intertwined than at any time ... Will we stand for the human rights of the dissident in Burma, the blogger in Iran or the voter in Zimbabwe? Will we give meaning to the words 'never again' in Darfur?

Barack Obama, speaking in Berlin, 24 July 2008

1

The Renmin University of China, also known as the People's University, in Beijing has about 36,000 students, studying everything from politics to social anthropology. The university, one of several in the capital, is based to the north-west of the city, on Zhongguancan street in Haidian district. Its alumni are typical of the post-Mao Zedong generation. Every Friday evening, quite informally, several hundred gather in the so-called 'English Corner' to hold 'English conversation'. This extraordinary scene, reiterated on campuses across China today, is a popular routine that says a lot about the aspirations of contemporary Chinese – and the state of the nation. This is, after all, an authoritarian, one-party regime in which dissent is ruthlessly crushed, and its enemies imprisoned, beaten up or sent into exile. However, here in the twilight, on a cool March Friday, under the shady pine trees of a little square, there are hundreds of young Chinese in running shoes, jeans and puffa jackets chatting together, in English, about anything and everything, including asides about Tiananmen Square. I remember the Soviet Union before glasnost and perestroika in which the atmosphere was menacing and fearful; surveillance everywhere; and the state inflexibly vigilant. This feels different. Perhaps these Chinese have been cunningly infiltrated by informers, or perhaps everyone is exercising heroic self-censorship about the topics that matter, but the mood is unquenchably relaxed, friendly and inspired by a common purpose, which is to learn better English.

As a tall westerner, I stand out in this crowd like Gulliver, and it is not difficult to start up a conversation. When I begin with 'I'm from London', about a dozen students crowd round at once. Everyone's interested, there's a murmur of 'London' across the group. One brave soul strikes up with 'Where in Lon-don?' I explain that my home is near Notting Hill. Oh yes, they have all heard of *Notting Hill*. Now the conversation, initially a stilted Q & A, goes quickly forward: movies, film stars, Hollywood, America ... So then, I ask: 'Has anyone been to America ... or London?' No, not yet; but they all seem to want to. I hand out Chinese business cards with an email address. We get on to the US presidential race. 'Hillary' is a hard name for the locals to get their tongues round, but, apart from a few stumbles, the level of conversation is remarkably high. The group's interest is really to ask about the UK, about football, Victoria Beckham, BBC television and so forth. Eventually, I move on to another circle, which is learning basic language skills by rote.

The instructor stands by a blackboard, as much like a bookie at a racetrack as a foreign language teacher, and reads out a line of English: 'I'm sorry I misjudged you, Mr Prescott.' The group repeats it: '*I'm sorry I misjudged you, Mr Prescott.*' Someone hands me a flyer with some Chinese characters beneath the slogan 'Never Let Spoken English Become Your Limitation'. The teacher intones another line: 'If you hate this job, why don't you quit?' '*If you hate this job,*' repeats the group with the furrowed concentration of a prayer meeting, '*why don't you quit?*' 'Jobs aren't that easy to come by,' says the teacher. '*Jobs aren't that easy to come by,*' repeats the class. Less than a 'conversation', this seems more like boot camp, but no one's complaining. They are here to join the English-speaking world, and will submit to whatever extraordinary adjustment it takes. After all, Mandarin (more than 1,000 million speakers) outnumbers the global figure for English by more than two to one, and the marketing of China's quest for English suggests that even the Chinese recognize it as slightly eccentric. One of the more popular ways of learning English in China is through a course entitled 'Crazy English', where the emphasis is on learning to speak the language before writing it down: 'To shout loud, you learn.' But the process is not as bizarre as one might think and the way that the English language has travelled and changed through time and space throws up many examples of contemporary craziness.

'Globalization' is a word that first slipped into its current usage during the 1960s; and the globalization of English, and English literature, law, money and values, is the cultural revolution of my generation, before and after the 'credit crunch'. Combined with the biggest IT innovations since Gutenberg, it continues to inspire the most comprehensive transformation of our society in five hundred, even a thousand years. This is a story I have followed, and contributed to, in a modest way, ever since I wrote the BBC and PBS television series *The Story of English*, with William Cran and Robert MacNeil, in the early 1980s. When Bill Gates was still an obscure Seattle software nerd, and the latest cool invention to transform international telephone lines was the fax, we believed we were providing a snapshot of the English language at the peak of its power and influence, a reflection of the Anglo-American hegemony. Naturally, we saw our efforts as ephemeral. Language and culture, we knew, are in flux. Any attempts to pin them down would be antiquarianism at best, doomed at worst. Besides, some of the experts we talked to believed that English, like Latin before it, was already showing signs of breaking up into mutually unintelligible variants. *The Story of English* might turn out to be a last hurrah.

We were, of course, dead wrong. The global power and influence of Anglo-American language and culture in the broadest sense were about to hit another new high. When the Cold War ended, after the Berlin Wall came down and once the internet took off in the 1990s there was an astonishing new landscape to explore and describe. Sometimes during these years the spread of Anglo-American culture seemed like the fulfilment of the ambition expressed by America's Founding Fathers to play a role 'among the Powers of the Earth' derived, as they put it, from 'the Laws of Nature'. The world had become a planet composed of some 193 countries, all enjoying a greater or lesser familiarity with English and Englishness. Was this the end of Babel? A hundred years ago, one description of this phenomenon might have been 'Anglo- or America-philia', but that will not wash today. Anglo-American culture has so many contemporary faces. It can conjure up elderly gentlemen of Germanic demeanour in brogues and tweed jackets, or a certain kind of American WASP taking tea and crumpets in Fortnum and Mason. Or it can be found in the angry *banlieues* of Paris where, echoing the universal tongues of rap music and football, many of the kids are called 'Steeve', 'Marky', 'Britney' or even 'Kevin'. Again, it can convey the enthusiasm for English of, for example, DJ Static (aka Mike Lai), a Montreal rapper who came to Canada from Hong Kong as a boy of eleven and learned English by repeating the lyrics of hip-hop songs. Or it can describe the excitement of English-language students in Japan who, in the spring of 2009, were filmed by the BBC solemnly repeating extracts from the speeches of Barack Obama as part of their training. There is also the demotic energy of English in, for instance, contemporary Los Angeles, which is both the multicultural capital of Hispanic California and simultaneously the headquarters of a global movie business, the American dream factory. Cross the Pacific and the perspective changes again. There, you will find Nury Vittachi, aka 'Mister Jam', a journalist and novelist of Australian descent now based in Hong Kong, who describes the lingua franca of the Far East as 'Englasian' – a mostly English vocabulary set into Chinese and Hindi syntax. 'Throw away your dictionaries,' writes Vittachi. 'The unwritten language Englasian really is threatening to supplant English as the business language of Asia.' Still others speak of 'Panglish', the global tongue.

At the dawn of a new millennium the phenomenon of English seems more vivid and universal than ever before. Like a Jackson Pollock of language, countless new variants are adding to the amazing technicolor texture of the overall picture: urban patois like 'Jafaikan'; or local Asian hybrids like Konglish (English in South Korea) and Manglish (Malay and English); or contemporary slang like 'cheddar', 'phat' and 'noob', for 'money', 'wonderful/great' and 'somebody new/ignorant'. Yet, even at its zenith, this has been a fleeting moment, with a tragic reckoning: the 9/11 attack on the twin towers, the Iraq

War and the polarization of the global community in the 'War on Terror'. Overnight, the benign sensations of the 1990s were replaced by something much more chill, and menacing. Since 2001 the achievements of what might be seen as the American century have been swiftly obliterated.

During the presidency of George W. Bush American language and culture became associated with unilateral and often irrational policies of a wounded superpower, acts of aggression, masquerading as self-defence and motivated by rage, insecurity and fear. In former times this phase might have resulted in a retreat from the dominant language and culture of the moment. But this did not happen – for two main reasons. First, in 2008, after almost a decade of angry chauvinism, American democracy seemed to rediscover its purpose and elected Barack Obama. Secondly, so-called 'soft power' has its own trajectory; there was always an important distinction to be drawn between culture and foreign policy. Young Iranians could hate George W. Bush but idolize American pop stars, burn the Stars and Stripes but splash out on American-style jeans and computers. Moreover, English had developed a supranational momentum that gave it a life independent of its British, and more especially its American, roots. Already multinational in expression, English was becoming a global phenomenon with a fierce, inner multinational dynamic, an emerging lingua franca described by the historian Benedict Anderson as 'a kind of global-hegemonic post-clerical Latin'. For example, in the aftermath of the disputed Iranian election of June 2009, some protesters paraded before the world's press with placards like 'Get Away England'.

Today there is almost no limit to the scope of this subject. The world's varieties of English range from the 'Crazy English' taught to the Chinese-speaking officials of the Beijing Olympics, to the 'voice and accent' manuals issued by Infosys and Microsoft at their Bangalore headquarters. Thus, English today embodies a paradox. To some, it seems to carry the seeds of its own decay. In the heartlands of the mother tongue, there are numerous anxieties about its future: in the United States, language conservatives agonize about the Hispanic threat to American English. But simultaneously, and more stealthily – almost unnoticed, in fact – the real challenge to the English of Shakespeare and the King James Bible comes less from alien speech than from the ceaseless amendments made to English in a myriad daily transactions across the known world. Here, global English, floating free from its troubled British and American past, has begun to take on a life of its own. It will be one of the predictions of this book that the twenty-first-century expression of British and American English – the world's English – is about to make its own declaration of independence from the linguistic past, in both syntax and vocabulary.

In *The Prodigal Tongue*, 'dispatches from the future of English', Mark Abley has a telling passage about the 'Latvians and Macedonians, Indonesians and Peruvians, Israelis and Egyptians' who sign up for the official online forum of the rock group Coldplay. To these fans, writes Abley,

it doesn't matter that the band consists of three Englishmen and a Scot singing in a tongue that was once confined to part of an island off Europe's coast. Now, wherever on the planet these fans happen to live, music connects them. So does language. As long as they're willing to grope for words in the accelerating global language that Coldplay speaks, the forum gives all its members a chance to speak.

This is the interactive, ever-changing world of global English. At the beginning of the twenty-first century, rarely has a language and its culture enjoyed such an opportunity to represent the world. In crude numbers alone, English is used, in some form, by approximately one third of the world's population, and outnumbered only by the speakers of Chinese, approximately 350 million of whom also speak some kind of English.

2

This has many expressions. In an offshoot of 'crazy English', *Harry Potter and the Deathly Hallows* was pirated in several Chinese versions, blending storylines lifted from Tolkien and kung-fu epics, with titles like *Harry Potter and the Chinese Empire* and *Harry Potter and Leopard Walk up to Dragon*. At the same time, J. K. Rowling's triumphant coda to her series would also be launched, in English, from Reykjavik to Quito. This is what happened on the night of 21 July 2007 when a global fraternity of juvenile wizards mobbed bookstore checkouts across the world, with an immediate sale (3.5 million copies in the first week) of the English-language edition. In Germany, the *Guardian* reported, 'muggle', 'quidditch' and 'house elf' were becoming 'part of German schoolchildren's vocabulary'.

The world's appetite for English language and culture means that the Royal Shakespeare Company will tour its 'Complete Shakespeare' productions worldwide, Manchester United will plan its matches to suit Japanese television schedules and the House of Lords will rule on the use of torture in the 'War on Terror' using arguments whose roots lie in the debates surrounding Magna Carta. The same pressures mean that, in 2006–7, about 80 per cent of the world's home pages on the World Wide Web were 'in some kind of English', compared to German (4.5 per cent) and Japanese (3.1 per cent), while Microsoft publishes no fewer than eighteen versions of its 'English language' spellcheckers. The India of *Hobson-Jobson* has also found a new global audience. A film such as Mira Nair's *Monsoon Wedding* is typical of the world's new English culture. The Indian bridegroom has a job in Houston. The wedding guests jet in from Melbourne and Dubai and speak in a mishmash of English and Hindi. Writing in the *Sunday Times*, Dominic Rushe noted that Bollywood English is 'hard to reproduce in print, but feels something like this: "*Yudhamanyus ca vikranta uttanaujas ca viryanavan*, he lives life in the fast lane."' Every English-speaking visitor to India watches with fascination the facility with which contemporary Indians switch from Hindi or Gujarati into English, and then back into a mother tongue. In 2009 the film *Slumdog Millionaire* took this a stage further. Simon Beaufoy's script, a pot-pourri of languages, adapted from an Indian novel, was shot in Mumbai, with a British and Indian cast, by Scottish director Danny Boyle, but launched worldwide with an eye on Hollywood's Oscars, where it eventually cleaned up.

India illustrates the interplay of British colonialism and a booming multinational economy. Take, for instance, the 2006 Man Booker

Prize. First, the result was broadcast on the BBC World Service from Delhi to Vancouver. The winner was *The Inheritance of Loss* by Kiran Desai, an Indian-born writer who had attended writing classes in New York. So far removed from any English experience, though steeped in its literary tradition, was *The Inheritance of Loss* that, finally, the British critic John Sutherland was moved to describe Desai's work as 'a globalised novel for a globalised world'. The writer herself is emblematic of the world's new culture: educated in Britain and America, she wrote her novel in her mother Anita Desai's house in the foothills of the Himalayas, and boasts on her website of feeling 'no alienation or dislocation' in her transmigration between three continents.

The Inheritance of Loss is the literary representation of a contemporary experience. Desai says that her book 'tries to capture what it means to live between East and West, and what it means to be an immigrant'; it also explores 'what happens when a western element is introduced to a country that is not of the West'. She also asks, 'How does the imbalance between these two worlds change a person's thinking and feeling? How do these changes manifest themselves in a personal sphere over time?' Or, she might have added, in a linguistic and cultural sphere. By 2010 Britain's role in the world, no longer colonial, is to participate in the international rendering of English and its culture. Like an elderly relative at a teenage rave, the UK sponsors the consumption of English as a highly desirable social and cultural force, 'the worldwide dialect of the third millennium'.

Those are the words of Jean-Paul Nerrière, a French-speaking former IBM executive and amateur linguistic scholar. In 1995, M. Nerrière, who had noticed that non-native English-speakers in the Far East communicated more successfully in English with their Korean and Japanese clients than competing British or American executives, formulated the idea of 'decaffeinated English' and, in a moment of inspiration, christened it 'Globish'. His idea quickly caught on. In *The Last Word*, his dispatches from the front line of language change, journalist Ben MacIntyre writes, 'I was recently waiting for a flight in Delhi, when I overheard a conversation between a Spanish UN peacekeeper and an Indian soldier. The Indian spoke no Spanish; the Spaniard spoke no Punjabi. Yet they understood one another easily. The language they spoke was a highly simplified form of English, without grammar or structure, but perfectly comprehensible, to them and to me. Only now do I realise that they were speaking "Globish", the newest and most widely spoken language in the world.' For Nerrière, Globish starts from a utilitarian vocabulary of some 1,500 words, is designed for use by non-native speakers, and is currently popularized in two (French language) handbooks, *Découvrez le Globish* and *Parlez Globish*. As a concept, 'Globish' is now quite widely recognized across the European Union, and is often referred to by Europeans who use English in their everyday interactions.

In 2007, having read about Jean-Paul Nerrière in the *International Herald Tribune*, I interviewed him in Paris. He turned out to be a delightful Frenchman, with quixotic ambitions not only for global fraternity but also for the preservation of the French language. 'Globish', he told me over a *steak frites* in a little restaurant opposite the Gare du Nord, 'will limit the influence of the English language dramatically.' As I returned to London, I reflected that 'Globish' was more than just a new word for a dialect or an international communications tool. It was a description of a lingua franca, but with a difference. On further consideration, it was also a metaphor for the novelty of global English culture today.

3

Global capitalism is the mechanism of this transformation, which has also spread into the Export Processing Zones of Far East Asia, into the sweatshops of Bangkok and Shanghai, and into the hypermarkets of Japan and Korea. The world's English can be seen at work in a new non-alcoholic drink, Kidsbeer, marketed to children in Japan with the English slogan 'Even Kids Can't Stand Life Unless They Have A Drink'. All this goes hand in hand with the contemporary package deal: tourism and mass consumerism are opposite sides of the same coin. In their transactions, the language of Thomas Cook's employees, of Mastercard call centres and any Sheraton checkout desk will be conducted in the world's English. In the same revolution, we find that the Goethe Institute now advocates promoting German culture through the medium of a Europeanized English for which Globish, 'the worldwide dialect of the third millennium', is an apt description.

In this language laboratory, the world's English becomes the linguistic default position for the society that the journalist Thomas Friedman has described as 'flat'. The exercise of Globish also means that Taiwan Chinese read online reports of Falang Gong repression filed by *New York Times* reporters. Meanwhile, on the Chinese mainland itself, the novel *Wolf Totem* by Jiang Rong, which sold at least 4 million copies in Chinese (with perhaps 20 million pirated copies), was then translated into English, and launched not in London or New York, but *from Beijing*, into the international market. In this revolution, South Koreans protest against North Korean nuclear testing with slogans such as 'Stop The Nukes' and 'Give Us Peace Now'. At the *Observer*, the British newspaper with which I am associated, the editor-in-chief Alan Rusbridger recently codified his version of this perception into ten propositions, beginning with 'There is no such thing as Abroad', and 'Most of our readers are "foreign"'. The logic of Rusbridger's propositions is vividly illustrated by the English-language version of Al Jazeera, the Qatar-based Arab television station. In the words of the *Atlantic* magazine in October 2009, 'Al Jazeera is what the internationally minded elite really yearns for: a visually stunning, deeply reported description of developments in dozens upon dozens of countries simultaneously.' So, for example, the world's English became the medium through which Al Jazeera treated several recent items: the war in Somalia, the floods in Bangladesh, the threats to the Bedouin way of life in northern Sudan, Sikh violence in India, human-rights demonstrations in Guatemala, an election campaign in Lebanon, and a Pakistani army offensive the Swat valley. Using the world's English, a television station based in Doha can focus on every aspect of global affairs rather than, in the words of the *Atlantic*, 'the flash points of any imperial or post-imperial interest'.

The world's English plays a role in politics as well as media. During the crisis in Georgia of August 2008 President Mikheil Saakashvili exploited his fluency in English to dominate the international coverage of the crisis. Saakashvili presented a political narrative in which, in the words of the Russian spokesman, former defence minister Sergei Ivanov, 'a big Russian bear attacked a small, peaceful Georgia', when in reality it was Georgia that provoked the crisis by attacking the breakaway republic of South Ossetia. Especially through his CNN interviews, Saakashvili exploited some four days of unchallenged coverage on behalf of his pro-NATO, anti-Russian administration before Moscow responded in English. Moreover, in his propaganda offensive, the Georgian president was not alone. Many of his senior officials were relatively young, telegenic, media-savvy and fluent in American English. In the long term none of this may make much difference on the ground – Russian tank battalions still present a rather persuasive argument – but in the short term the Kremlin was forced to counter Saakashvili by dispatching a spokesman experienced in dealing with western media, and with a good grasp of American English. This was Sergei Ivanov, a seasoned Russian politician and the hard-driving confidant of Vladimir Putin. Another aspect of this defining moment was the reaction of the Russian stock market. When Soviet tanks rolled into Prague in 1968 there were no implications for Russia's economy. None. After the invasion of Georgia, as an illustration of the world's interconnections, the Russian market plunged. Today, language, culture, money and power are linked. In the words of the *New York Times*, 'the unipolar, American-dominated world that followed the cold war is dead. The rise of China, India and now Russia has ended that heady nanosecond of American ascendancy.'

So this book is the biography of a phenomenon, one that is both simple and unique. It argues that Anglo-American culture and its language have become as much a part of global consciousness as MS-DOS or the combustion engine. There is hardly a transaction in any city in today's world that is innocent of English, in some form. This fact becomes all the more fascinating when viewed alongside the argument, disputed by some, that the West's power is on the wane. The English language in its global expression has become a power in itself and is now as far removed from its original source as it is from

Caxton's printing press, which first fixed it in place. You could say that English plus Microsoft equals a new cultural revolution.

This raises a principal question addressed by this book: is this revolution a creature of globalization, or does global capitalism owe some of its energy and resilience to global English in all its manifestations, cultural as well as linguistic? Someone once said that a great language is a dialect – with an army and a navy. In 2010 the days in which language and culture can be sustained by land or sea power are long gone, but America's soft power is certainly an element in the forces we call globalization. Chicken or egg? I shall return to this question, at the end of the journey through time and space described here, in the Epilogue. What is not in doubt is that, in the twenty-first century, the phenomenon of the world's English is an everyday experience for millions the world over. In this arena, language becomes more than just an essential means of communication: it embodies a contemporary aspiration, expressing a willingness to innovate with new ideas, to adapt old uses and to enfranchise new people. Language, it cannot be stressed too strongly, is intrinsically neutral, but it is no contradiction to claim that English – by virtue of its origins and history – is unique. English has special characteristics derived from a peculiar, and quite extraordinary, set of circumstances. The short version is astonishing.

4

A foggy archipelago off the north-west coast of Europe – islands without silver or precious stones, with just a marginal linguistic connection to the mainland, and with virtually no direct access to the Mediterranean civilizations of Greece and Rome – becomes the subject of mystified curiosity and finally an object of fruitless occupation. After centuries of invasion and resistance, these islands are finally conquered and subdued by French forces, who subject their people to an administrative despotism that should have extinguished their native fire for good. And yet, cut off from the European mainstream, these people, their language and culture, flourish. Then within a few hundred years part of this archipelago has become England, an emergent nation whose people, still defiant and increasingly self-confident, call themselves 'the English'. After a slow start, these English become global adventurers, half-pirate, half-pastor, on an awesome scale. By the late eighteenth century seeds of English and Englishness have become planted successfully across the known world, from Botany Bay to Boston. Finally, a millennium after annihilation by the French, English life, laws and literature become a universal phenomenon dominating the world's attention for about 150 years. In the past the traditional view was that the waning of the British empire was followed by the rise of American power into the present day. In the words of the *Oxford Guide to World English*, 'American English has a global role at the beginning of the twenty-first century comparable to that of British English at the start of the twentieth – but on a scale larger than any previous language or variety of a language in recorded history.'

This book argues for a slightly different perspective. The linguistic historian Nicholas Ostler has written, in *Empires of the Word*, about the distinctive traits we can find in many linguistic traditions: 'the austere grandeur' of Arabic, 'Chinese and Egyptian's unshakeable self-regard; Sanskrit's luxuriating classifications and hierarchies; Greek's self-confident innovation; Latin's civic sense; Spanish rigidity; French admiration for rationality; and English admiration for business acumen'. To put this another way, every language becomes a vessel for thought and behaviour. So English is like a virus that has spread round the world, carrying with it a way of looking at, and expressing, new experiences. 'Globish' is just one name for that virus, and the history of the world's English becomes the pathology of a global culture. This is not, however, an abstract narrative; it concerns humanity. In the words of Henry Hitchings, author of *The Secret Life of Words*, 'English is, to an unusual degree, a place of strange meetings.'

Globish puts one small country's language on the side of the individual confronting demanding new challenges about his or her place in society. It is the suspenseful narrative of a people and their successive empires coming out of nowhere to create a culture that – against the odds – has achieved lasting global consequence. This Darwinian process, stretching over hundreds of years, involves millions of ordinary, and a few extraordinary, people. Inevitably, it is an imperfect story, with many loose ends and much unfinished business. But it is precisely the imperfections of English that are part of its enduring strength. Like British liberty itself, it is always work in progress. When social conservatives point to scare-headlines about the decline of, say, British or American literacy among Asian, Hispanic or African immigrant populations they overlook the fact that, for the simple purpose of communication, the world's English remains a brilliantly adaptable and highly efficient system. English dominance does not derive from some innate quality. The language does have some special characteristics, but it is emphatically not easier to learn than French, or German, or Spanish. 'Our marvellous native tongue' (the words are Auden's) takes its fire and colour from the people and events it describes, which is why, in the chapters that follow, *Globish* will have a strong historical theme.

Driven by the IT revolution, the world's English is also spreading at warp speed: electronic time is somehow faster than real time. There are, it has been estimated, some 175,000 new blogs created every day. That's two every second. In the more traditional world of books, many readers who are simultaneously dazzled and oppressed by mass communications feel overwhelmed by choice. In language, new words, phrases and expressions whizz into circulation and then drift off into oblivion. John Naughton, the *Observer*'s internet correspondent, has calculated that 'the indexed part [of the World Wide Web] hovers at around 40 billion pages' while the 'deep web' hidden from search engines is between 400 and 750 times bigger than that, perhaps 80 per cent of it in some kind of English. Universal access to this virtual library, and electronic browsing through its countless files, is the enthralling prospect of the immediate future. As I write, Google is just celebrating its one trillionth website. Dictionaries, even online dictionaries like the *OED*, struggle to keep up. In this chaos, it is sometimes difficult to find landmarks and easy to become discouraged about the strength and significance of a global culture. How to make sense? How to be heard? How to be understood? If you can see where the roots of global English and its predominantly American culture are planted, how and why they evolved and what contributed to its special character, you might feel more confident about the world we are in, and be at peace with it.

5

Writing merely of the English language, the celebrated American critic Ralph Waldo Emerson noted that it was 'the sea which receives tributaries from every region under heaven'. In the new millennium English and the numberless manifestations of its culture surround us like a sea; and like the waters of the deep, it is full of mysteries. Why do some Germans idolize Shakespeare? How did a football trophy sponsor peace among warring factions in Iraq? Why does a leading Japanese artist, Norio Ueno, copy English words and phrases into his otherwise abstract artworks? Constantly in a state of ungovernable flux, at the mercy of fashion, whim and caprice, the indefinable genius – the word is hardly too strong – of the English language has always been to adapt itself, like mercury, to every new contour.

Globish is a book about a phenomenon so obvious and all-pervading that it is sometimes taken for granted. It begins with the origins, and examines the basic elements of early English that remain so remarkably functional today. From the founders to the pioneers is just one perilous transatlantic crossing, a voyage that millions completed in hope, degradation or despair: the making of American and African-American English is a vital turning point. Subsequently, in Parts Three and Four, we see how the adventurous anglophone societies of Britain and the United States popularized, and then modernized, the English-speaking world, extending it to the point at which it became neither British nor American but a universal lingua franca, a global means of communication that is irrepressibly contagious, adaptable, populist and subversive.

As we embark on this journey from the icy swamps of pre-Roman Saxony to the shopping malls of Seoul, this is a good moment to concede the magic of a subject that gives new meaning to a faded old brown parchment (Magna Carta), a 900-page book bound in pigskin (Shakespeare's First Folio), a country house on a Virginian mountain-top (Monticello), a 272-word presidential speech (the Gettysburg Address), a pop song ('Buffalo Soldiers') and a scratchy black-and-white videoclip of men on the moon ('One giant leap for mankind . . .'). Everyone who reads these words and is connected to the moments associated with these landmarks is also enfranchised into a global society. No one, indeed, who lives a full life in the contemporary world, and responds intensely to it, can ignore the fractional degrees of separation between blogs and books; politics and dub poetry; football and fantasy; literature and manga novels; historians, biographers and movie-makers. By word of mouth, the world's English becomes the medium of this interconnectedness, and it raises profound questions about who we are, and the ways in which we conduct our lives. Linguistically speaking, as Penelope Lively puts it in her Booker Prize-winning novel, *Moon Tiger*, 'we are walking lexicons. In a single sentence of idle chatter we preserve Latin, Anglo-Saxon, Norse; we carry a museum inside our heads, each day we commemorate peoples of whom we have never heard.' The great quality of the English language in the contemporary world is that its transactions urge us cease-lessly to engage our imaginations, and express them, on a global scale. Can there be a more thrilling invitation?

PART ONE
Founders

1. In the Beginning

Four Invasions and a Cultural Revolution

I felt a curious thrill, as if something had stirred me, half wakened
from sleep. There was something very remote and strange and beautiful
behind those words, if I could grasp it, far beyond Ancient English.

                                                                J. R. R. Tolkien

1

Our story begins with a human sacrifice. Stranger than this, it starts in a
Danish swamp. Perhaps strangest of all, we owe this information about
the violent origins of the English-speaking world to the Roman historian Tacitus, the author of *Germania*, 'On the Origin and Character of
Germany'. The German tribes, wrote Tacitus, love freedom, their women
are chaste, and there is no public extravagance; the Tencteri excel in
horsemanship; the Suebi 'tie their hair in a knot', and so on. But no picture is perfect. There are, Tacitus continues, seven tribes about whom
there is 'nothing noteworthy' to say, except that they worship Nerthus,
the goddess Mother Earth, in 'a ceremony performed by slaves who are
immediately afterwards drowned in the lake'. One of these seven barbarous tribes was 'the Anglii', better known to history as the Angles.

Tacitus turns out to have been a good witness. Peat has a curious
property, and the savage rituals of the Anglii have not been entirely
forgotten. In 1950, two Danish peat-cutters, working in the neighbourhood of Tollund, unearthed the body of a man. But when the
police came, their response was to summon the local archivist, not
the coroner, and the investigation quickly took on a historical dimension. These *Moorleichen* (swamp corpses), unmistakably sacrificial
victims, still on display in Danish museums, are astonishingly well
preserved. One man has been strangled. Another's throat has been

cut: you can see the stubble on his chin. Amid those far-off horrors, speech was dumb in the presence of a cruel death, but if, by some rough magic, you could restore their speech, you would hear a language that distantly echoes our own. These leathery corpses are the remote ancestors of the English-speaking peoples, and the discovery of their remains is a reminder that, to this day, traces of the English language can sometimes be found in the most surprising places. The other lesson of this snippet from a Dark Age police blotter is that English was originally a foreign tongue. Albion, the ancient word for these islands off the north-west coast of Europe, comes from British roots, Celtic (*albio*) and Gaelic (*alba*), with connotations of 'whiteness' that may invoke Britain's white cliffs. Albion was a place of chalky giants, primitive sorcery, sun worship and sea monsters. Albion is where England and its story begin.

The making of a recognizable Englishness, the painful transition to Anglo-Saxon 'Englaland', is a history of four invasions and a cultural revolution. English, of course, is not unique. French, German and Russian all have obscure and violent origins. But English was slightly different, by virtue of its location. English was a mirror to its island state, an idiosyncratic mixture of splendid isolation and humiliating foreign occupation. On the positive side, the first invasion, by the Romans, connected the island to a European Latin tradition that would linger for more than a thousand years. The second, by the Anglo-Saxons, established an independent vernacular culture. The third invasion, by the Vikings, would inspire a strong sense of national identity. Each contributed to the mongrel character of English culture, a quality that plays well in a multicultural world. Meanwhile, the arrival of Christianity sponsored a cultural transformation whose influence persists to the present day. Finally, all of these upheavals would be trumped by the Norman Conquest, the mother of all invasions. Daniel Defoe, the author of *Robinson Crusoe*, summarizing the first millennium, described 'your Roman-Saxon-Danish-Norman English'. From 55 BC to AD 1066 the traditions of the place evolve, but there was never any doubt of the country's identity: it was an island (properly, an archipelago) whose inhabitants were never further than a hard day's ride from the sea.

The tides and climate of the sea shaped the making of English in countless ways. At the outset, the sea was not just the most effective natural defence known to man and a great natural highway, it also made the tribes it protected separate, proud, watchful and self-conscious. Islanders are not like other people; they have different psychic and physical horizons. It is no accident that the English were the first in Europe to produce a vernacular account of their exploits, the Anglo-Saxon Chronicle. But insularity does not automatically sponsor an appetite for trade. Plenty of island cultures, Japan for example, have cultivated isolation. However, in this story, trade and culture became intimately related. The sea did more than just define the English, it inspired them to become sailors, merchants, explorers and empire-builders. Language and culture reflected this experience and gave English its highly interactive character. The sea linked Liverpool to Dublin and Charleston, Whitby to London and New South Wales, and Bristol to Jamaica, Philadelphia and Calcutta. In the making of an English consciousness, it is impossible to overestimate the importance of the sea. There is, as the historian David Miles has put it, another way of looking at this: 'The outside world does not bounce off the white cliffs of Dover; rather it washes around them and into the inlets of the Thames, Ouse, Humber and Trent, the Tyne, Forth, Clyde, Dee, Mersey, Severn and Shannon.' All the climactic moments of British history – the Armada of 1588, the battle of Trafalgar in 1805, the battle of Britain, 1940 – owe their significance to one thing: the defence of the realm conducted around the approaches to the English Channel, southern, western or aerial. The first of these historical milestones occurred in the late summer of 55 BC when Rome's all-conquering general, Julius Caesar, launched a seaborne landing on the south coast.

2

Caesar shared Tacitus' verdict that the misty island to the north of Gaul was *pretium victoriae* (worth the conquest), but his assault on Britain was a fiasco. The Romans' invasion force had to anchor off Dover, conceding the advantage of surprise. The Britons, watching from the white cliffs, mobilized chariots and cavalry to shadow the fleet as it moved along the coast. When Caesar's legions finally struggled ashore, they endured a difficult month in hostile territory before retreating across the Channel to the comforts and security of Gaul. A second invasion, the following year, was scarcely more successful. Until the Romans could decide whether they were conquerors or colonizers, their invasions remained pointless and ill-conceived, but in AD 43 the emperor Claudius finally established Britannia as Rome's northernmost province. The benefits of the *pax Romana* brought roads, civic values and education to an agricultural and largely illiterate society. It also established an elite cadre of Romanized Britons who enjoyed a level of civilization (as can be seen, for example, at the splendid palace at Fishbourne, near Chichester) commensurate with life in Rome or any of its great Mediterranean colonies. Latin became established as the language of scholarship, law and government; educated Britons began to have access to Continental culture. The poet Martial, for instance, claimed that his work was read in remote Britannia. For about four hundred years, while Rome was strong, this settlement went largely unchallenged. When the legions withdrew (traditionally, in AD 410) this achievement was rapidly undone, as a new generation of European raiders turned its attention to the fertile islands across the water.

And out of the confused last decades of the Romans in Britain comes the legend of Camelot, one of the founding myths of English culture. Few can resist the appeal of King Arthur and his Knights of the Round Table. Scholars will always debate the origins of 'the once and future king', who was perhaps both a Celtic hero and a Roman *dux bellorum*, but one thing is certain: history or fantasy, Arthur has inspired a literature that transcends academic controversy, includes Tennyson, Wagner and Mark Twain, and continues to flourish as a potent popular legend. Merlin, Guinevere, Lancelot and the rest have become English archetypes, but Arthur – a patriot, and a noble champion of a doomed way of life – was actually British, not English, an important distinction. It was the Angles and Saxons, Germanic marauders introducing their values at the point of a sword, who represented the future – as the *Angelcynn*, or 'English-kind'.

3

According to their own record of events, the Anglo-Saxon Chronicle, these raiders from Saxony were a terrifying new enemy. 'Never', wrote the chronicler, 'was there such slaughter in this island.' Between 449 and 800 Roman Britannia was conquered, occupied and subdued. The Celts, driven north and west, fled from the invaders 'as from fire'. The Anglo-Saxons occupied former Romano-British settlements and established control of the most fertile parts of the island. In the course of 150 years they set up seven kingdoms (Northumbria, Mercia, East Anglia, Kent, Sussex, Essex and Wessex) in territory that roughly corresponds to present-day England and explains the tenacious survival of its ancient dialects. The dispossessed Britons became known as *wealas* (foreigners), the origin of *Welsh*. Saxon–Celt hostility went both ways. One fragment of an early Welsh folk song tells of a young man going with 'a heart like lead' to live in 'the land of the Saxons'. The conquerors were always 'Saxons', but gradually the terms 'Anglii' and 'Anglia' crept into everyday usage. About 150 years after the first sea-raids, the people came to be referred to as *Angelcynn* in the vernacular. Their language, which is known today as Old English, was *Englisc*. By 1000 the country would be generally known as *Englaland*, the land of the Angles. Despite the chasm between the English on the one side and the Scots, Welsh and Irish on the other, there was an important cross-fertilization that still makes a powerful contribution to contemporary English culture.

The lyrical spirit of the Celts imbues English speech and literature, from the earliest ballads to the poetry of George Mackay Brown and Seamus Heaney, with a quality unknown to the Saxon mind. Many of the finest writers in English – Swift, Burke, Burns, Scott, Stevenson, Wilde, Shaw, Beckett, Joyce, Dylan Thomas – are of Celtic origin. Their work tempers the plainness of the Anglo-Saxon tradition with wit, plangent melancholy and an indefinable sense of 'otherness'. The Welsh writer Jan Morris has identified this 'concept of unspecified yearning' peculiar to the Celts as *hiraeth*. 'Pathos is part of it,' she writes, 'but in a lyrical form to which I am sentimentally susceptible ... it is as though I have been taken, for a brief sententious glimpse, out of time to nowhere.'

Compared to the Britons, the Anglo-Saxons were pragmatic, with a can-do approach to life, reminiscent of gung-ho Americans. They came as raiders, and conquered as warriors, but settled as farmers and artisans. They were an agricultural people whose sinuous and complex art, visual as much as literary, seems to celebrate both the mystery of the world and its miraculous design. Their vocabulary is full of farming: *sheep*, *earth*, *plough*, *dog*, *wood*, *field* and *work* all derive from Old English. When the daily struggle of life in the field was over, they loved to celebrate with *glee*, *laughter* and *mirth*. Their language is the robust and charismatic heart of an extraordinary literary tradition.

Old English – Tolkien's 'Ancient English' – remains the cornerstone of English. All its basic building blocks – words like *the*, *is*, *you* – are Anglo-Saxon. It is impossible, without tortuous circumlocution, to write a contemporary English sentence without Anglo-Saxon vocabulary; and some Old English words, for instance *mann*, *hus* and *drincan*, hardly need translation. Everyone who speaks or writes any kind of English in the twenty-first century is using accents, grammar and vocabulary which, with several modifications, can be traced in a direct lineage to the Old English of the Anglo-Saxons. Popular lyrics, for instance, often echo the simplicity of the Nordic tradition. In the Beatles song 'Yesterday', only the word 'trouble' has an old French/Latin root, *troubler/turbidare*. In Sonnet 80, Shakespeare achieves a similarly brilliant effect with 'O how I faint when I of you do write'. When in 1940 Winston Churchill appealed to the hearts and minds of the English-speaking people, he did so with the plain bareness for which Old English is renowned: 'We shall fight on the beaches; we shall fight on the landing grounds; we shall fight in the fields and in the streets; we shall fight in the hills...' Churchill was inciting the emotions of an island people. After nearly two thousand years there was still plenty of rhetorical voltage to be found in allusions to beaches, cliffs and Germanic invaders.

The Anglo-Saxons were sophisticated in the arts of speech. Theirs was an oral culture, favouring understatement and wit. Their expression for allusion and bawdy wordplay is *wordum wrixlan* (to weave words together). Their love of innuendo – a distinguishing characteristic of

English, and one that will always commend it to DJs and comedians – is most clearly demonstrated in the pleasure they took in punning ambiguity, for example the Exeter Book of riddles. In a pagan world, with some lingering traces of Roman Christianity, people worshiped local deities and the gods or goddesses of old Germania. Their priests and sacred buildings (about which we know very little) celebrated a pastoral way of life with heathen rituals not far removed from those described by Tacitus. When Christianity arrived in the country in 597 it achieved a cultural revolution that transformed England and Englishness, and continues to shape the world's English: the global communion of the Anglican Church, for example, is as much African and American as English. The extraordinary impact of Christianity is reported by the Venerable Bede in his *History of the English Church and People*, a story that says as much about the fruitful collision of Latin and Old English as it does about the spread of God's word.

4

According to tradition, St Augustine's all-important mission in 597 was inspired by the man who would become Pope Gregory the Great. Walking in Rome's marketplace, he came upon some fair-haired boys being sold as slaves. He was told they came from the island of Britain, and were pagans. 'What a pity', said Gregory, 'that the author of darkness is possessed of men of such fair countenances.' And what was the name of their country? They were called Angles (*Anglii*). 'Right,' replied the holy man, 'for they have an angelic face; it is fitting that they should be co-heirs with the angels in heaven. What is the name', he asked, 'of the province from which they have been brought?' He was advised that they were natives of the province known to the Romans as Deira. 'Truly they are *de ira*,' is how Bede expresses the future pope's reply, 'plucked from wrath and called to the memory of Christ. And how', he went on, 'is the king of that province called?' They told him his name was Aella. Gregory, who appears to have had an incorrigible appetite for puns, replied: 'Alleluia, the praise of God the Creator must be sung in those parts.'

Gregory intended to undertake the mission to Britain himself, but in the end he sent Augustine and about fifty monks to Kent, a minor English kingdom. When the missionaries preached at the court of King Aethelbert, the king replied, 'Your words and promises are fair indeed; but they are new and uncertain, and I cannot accept them and abandon the age-old beliefs that I have held, together with the whole English nation.' Aethelbert, however, was a fair-minded man. 'But since you have travelled far, and I can see that you are sincere . . .' he went on, 'we will not harm you. We will receive you hospitably and take care to supply you with all that you need; nor will we forbid you to preach and win any people you can to your religion.' Augustine's mission went ahead unimpeded.

With the word of God came the building of churches and monasteries, the pillars of Anglo-Saxon culture. Bede, at his monastery in Jarrow, writes that not only were the great monk-teachers learned in 'sacred and profane literature', they taught poetry, astronomy and arithmetic. The new monasteries also encouraged vernacular writing, and some astonishing work in stone and glass, rich embroidery and magnificent illuminated manuscripts.

The cultural revolution of Christianity both enriched Old English with scores of new words (*apostle*, *pope*, *angel*, *psalter*) and, just as importantly, also introduced the capacity to articulate abstract thought. Before St Augustine it was easy enough to express the common experience of everyday life – *sun* and *moon*, *hand* and *heart*, *heat* and *cold*, *sea* and *land* – in Old English, but much harder to convey subtle ideas without the use of cumbersome and elaborate German-style portmanteaus like *frumweorc* (= creation), from *fruma*, beginning, and *weorc*, work.

In the long run, the role of the English Church would be as much cultural as religious. Souls might be saved but sentences would be transformed. The language of the King James Bible (and The Book of Common Prayer), braided into English, echoes through the poetry of George Herbert and William Blake, the novels of Dickens, the rhetorical cadences of Martin Luther King and, lately, Barack Obama. Listen, for instance, to Obama's account of his origins in his bestselling memoir, *Dreams from My Father*:

First there was Miriwu. It's not known who came before. Miriwu sired Sigoma, Sigoma sired Owiny, Owiny sired Kisodhi, Kisodhi sired Ogelo, Ogelo sired Otondi, Otondi sired Obongo, Obongo sired Okoth, and Okoth sired Opiquo. The women who bore them, their names are forgotten, for that was the way of our people.

Next to Shakespeare, there is no more influential text in the English tradition than the Bible. In the seventh century AD, however, the interplay of creativity and the word of God seemed so rare and miraculous that Bede actually cites a singular example of divine inspiration, the case of an illiterate Yorkshire poet, and the author of the earliest surviving poem in English, known as 'Caedmon's Hymn'.

This nine-line fragment of Old English vernacular was not the work of a monk or a scholar. Caedmon was a cowherd who could not sing. When, around the fireside, the harp was passed among the other herdsmen, Caedmon would make his excuses and depart, embarrassed by his tin ear. He remained aloof from the festive hearth until one evening, Bede reports, an angel came to him in a dream. 'Caedmon,' called the Angel, 'sing something.' 'I cannot,' replied the cowherd, 'for I do not know how to sing, and for that reason I left the gathering.' 'Still,' persisted the angel, 'you can sing.' 'What shall I sing about?' asked Caedmon. 'Sing about the creation of the world,' instructed the angel. And so Caedmon was inspired, and made his song. These beginnings of English poetry seem fanciful, but they echo the making of Ireland's Nobel laureate, Seamus Heaney. When he was growing up, a farmer's son in Co. Derry, the closest Heaney came to poetry was through traditional festival recitations. He found his vocation through a poetry-reading circle in Belfast and then, in a burst of inspiration, completed the poems 'Death of a Naturalist' and 'Tollund Man' (a poem about *Moorleichecn*), which announced the arrival of an important new poetic voice. Heaney says he harks back to the Anglo-Saxons, a society whose culture haunts the work of poets through the ages, from Milton to the present. W. H. Auden, indeed, once declared himself 'spellbound' by Old English poetry.

In the end, the Anglo-Saxon settlement proved as vulnerable as the Roman, and its obsession with the transitoriness of life came into its own. In the eighth century as much as the fifth, an island with the promise of minerals would always be attractive to invaders. For the next three hundred years the English experienced another foreign occupation in which their culture would be forced to adapt or face annihilation. In the words of Ralph Waldo Emerson, 'Mixture is a secret of the English island.' This time, the enemy from the sea was symbolic of a wider European phenomenon.

5

The mass movement of the Scandinavian peoples between the years 750 and 1050, one of the great migrations of European history, began as seasonal plunder-raids and ended as conquest and settlement. Collectively these people are known as the Vikings, a name thought to come either from the Norse *vik* ('a bay'), indicating 'one who frequents inlets of the sea', or from the Old English *wic*, a camp – the formation of temporary encampments was a prominent feature of Viking raids. Unlike the ethnic cleansing by the Anglo-Saxons, which obliterated virtually everything Celtic in English culture, the Viking settlers had a profound influence on the making of England. There was consanguinity between these Nordic peoples; it was often difficult to distinguish between invading Norseman and resident Saxon. At the time, however, the Vikings were notoriously destructive. In 793 the monasteries of Jarrow and Lindisfarne were sacked in successive seasons and plundered of gold and silver. By the middle of the ninth century almost half the country was in Viking hands. Now the Norsemen, or 'Danes', turned their forces against the jewel in the crown: the kingdom of Wessex.

Wars make leaders. The king of Wessex was a young man named Alfred. In the early history of Britain, where Arthur is a myth, Alfred is a historical hero, 'Angelonde's deorling', according to the twelfth-century priest Layamon. Arthur's historical existence is at best shadowy, Alfred's is well documented. But they have one thing in common: both Arthur and Alfred are remembered by apocryphal stories. In the making of English, fact and fantasy are sometimes inseparable. Alfred, of course, is the king who burned the cakes. This, as the historian David Horspool notes, is 'a moment in history that probably never happened'. As the story goes – the desperate king taking refuge in a cowherd's hovel, alone, almost destitute, and reduced to the condition of a common traveller – Alfred was sitting by the fireside, brooding on his fate, when the woman of the house asked him to mind some cakes she was baking over the embers. Then, as Charles Dickens narrates it in *A Child's History of England*, 'thinking deeply of his poor unhappy subjects whom the Danes had chased through the land, his noble mind forgot the cakes, and they were burnt. "What!" said the cowherd's wife ..."you will be ready enough to eat them by-and-by, and yet you cannot watch them, idle dog?"' A fugitive king, lost among his own people, is a universal tale that recurs in the Old Testament (King David in the Book of Samuel) and in the *Ramayana* (where Lord Rama goes into forest exile). But the legend of Alfred's travails has a special significance: it symbolizes the moment at which it was suddenly possible that England and Englishness might be wiped out altogether. With no English-speaking kingdoms left, the country would gradually speak Norse. Instead, the turning point came later that same year, 878. Alfred raised a fresh army from Somerset, Wiltshire and Hampshire and overwhelmed the Danes at the battle of Edington, a victory commemorated by a white horse carved on the hillside overlooking the battlefield.

Alfred's story benefits from the fusion of three powerful elements. First, Alfred has the luck of good spin, historically speaking. As well as a near-contemporary biography written by Asser, one of his bishops, there is the Anglo-Saxon Chronicle, a unique document of current events commissioned by the king, together with the bounty of many other records: Alfred's will, a peace treaty, several royal charters and one or two letters. Secondly, thanks to Bishop Asser's biography, Alfred comes down to us as a great man but also a complex one, subtle, wise and all too human (apparently he was a martyr to piles). The third and clinching element of his greatness lies in one, indisputable quality: he was not merely victorious at the crucial battle of Edington, he also brought the Danes to heel with the peace treaty of Wedmore and set about Anglicizing his kingdom.

Alfred understood that his power-base in the south was insufficient to guarantee that peace with the Danes would hold, or that Englishmen living outside Wessex in, for example, Mercia (roughly, the present-day Midlands) would not be gradually drawn back into the Danish empire. As king of Wessex, Alfred ruled only over people who lived in the counties of the south-west, around the ancient capital city of Winchester. He had no power over people who lived further afield, in Oxfordshire for example. Yet his survival against the Vikings depended on men and money from the kingdoms outside Wessex. He had to retain political control of territory that was not his by appealing to a shared sense of Englishness, expressed in the language. Alfred consciously used the 'soft power' of English to create a sense of national identity.

Without Alfred, the history of England would have been quite different, and certainly less nationalistic. Decisively for the progress of the vernacular, it was his inspiration to use English, not Latin, as the basis for the education of his people. At the age of nearly forty, amid what he called the 'various and manifold cares of his kingdom', he learned Latin so that he could oversee the translation of various key texts, notably Bede's *History of the English Church and People*. Alfred described this campaign to win minds and hearts through cultural propaganda in his famous preface to Gregory's *Pastoral Care*. 'South of the Thames', he writes, there is literally no one who can translate 'a letter from Latin into English'. He goes on to argue the urgent need to 'translate certain books which are most necessary for all men to know, into the language that we can all understand', so that, as he puts it, 'all the youth of free men now among the English people . . . are able to read English writing as well'. The champion of the English language, he was also the founder of English historical prose, in the Anglo-Saxon Chronicle.

This remarkable document is the key to Alfred's afterlife as 'The Great'. Possibly it was in Winston Churchill's mind when he set out to write his own history of the Second World War. ('Remember,' he teased Stalin during a dispute about their mutual interpretation of the recent past, 'if I live long enough I may be one of the historians.') In fact, when Alfred died at the age of fifty in 899, not even the

Chronicle, the house journal of his short reign, identified him as the figure he would become. Over the succeeding centuries his 'greatness' grew and flourished as subsequent generations found different kinds of inspiration in his story. By the eighteenth century Alfred had become the hero-king of conservative fantasy: Sir Richard Blackmore's twelve-volume verse epic *Alfred* (1723). Most influential of all is *Alfred: A Masque* (1740) by James Thomson and David Mallet, written and performed for Frederick, Prince of Wales, the son of George II. This pageant celebrates Britain's imperial destiny, and closes with a chorus ('Rule, Britannia!') that quickly became an unofficial national anthem. To men of the late eighteenth century, Alfred was not just a proto-imperialist, he was even understood by some American revolutionaries to be a symbol of liberty, a man fighting tyranny on behalf of his people, and winning against the odds. One of the newly founded US Navy's first battleships, seized from the British, was renamed *Alfred*, became the flagship and was commanded by John Paul Jones. Later, to the Victorians Alfred was an almost devotional figure. The radical Chartists liked to equate 'the Code of Alfred' with the freedoms promised in the People's Charter. The publication in 1852 of *The Whole Works of King Alfred* was part of a revival that included G. F. Watts's massive oil painting *Alfred Inciting the Saxons to Prevent the Landing of the Danes by Encountering Them at Sea*, and culminated in 1901 (wrongly thought to be the millennial anniversary of his death) with a bizarre ceremony at Winchester. Thereafter, the Alfred who burned the cakes became part of England's national myth. In a popular television poll conducted by the BBC in 2001, he was ineradicably a 'great Briton'.

6

Alfred's role in fostering national consciousness was vital, but history is not written by kings alone. For most people, there was the everyday business of raising families and putting food on the table. On the ground, Anglo-Saxon and Dane lived peacefully alongside each other for several generations. The similarity of Norse and Old English meant that both sides could communicate, in a rough-and-ready fashion that accelerated a linguistic merger: the word endings of an inflected language like Old English were slowly eliminated; Norse words like *skirt*, *skin* and *sky* were borrowed, adding another dimension, more light and shade, to the variety of the language. By AD 900 English had developed many of the characteristics for which it is known today. In the traffic between Dane and Saxon, it had become simplified. It was practical, direct and rich in synonyms: you can *rear* (English) or *raise* (Norse) a child. Soon it would develop the flexibility in which verbs could become nouns, and new foreign words became co-opted into everyday usage.

The fusion of Saxon and Norse traditions is epitomized in *Beowulf*, the undisputed masterpiece of Old English literature, and recently reimagined as a popular animation. This 3,000-line poem, a tale of the Geatish hero who fights dragons and monsters from the sea, was the first to be written down in a European vernacular language. *Beowulf* reveals a reflective mind, obsessed with the transience of life, and with the keeping of dignity in the face of defeat. Darker still is the predicament of Beowulf's famous monster. Grendel never speaks. Deprived of language, he can utter only desperate cries of inarticulate rage. He becomes the personification of darkness. Like some kind of evil figure from *The Lord of the Rings*, he is described as a 'hellish fiend' and a 'grim spirit'. And so, from *Beowulf* comes the first expression of a creative dialogue within the English literary tradition.

J. R. R. Tolkien, whose works also helped to inspire a new generation of make-believe in the Harry Potter series, first visited Middle-earth in the aftermath of military service during the Great War. Demobilized and unemployed, he was given a job working on the definition of 'W' words like *waggle*, *wake-wort* and *wampum* for the still unfinished *Oxford English Dictionary*. Something in Old English spoke to Tolkien. He once described the consequences of his encounter with a single word – *Earendel* – as 'a curious thrill...as if something had stirred in me, half wakened from sleep. There was something very remote and strange and beautiful behind those words, if I could grasp it, far beyond Ancient English.' Tolkien's Middle-earth is a nostalgic fantasy, but it derives some of its inspiration from the historical reality of ninth- and tenth-century Anglo-Saxon England. After centuries of fighting this had evolved into a sophisticated society. The 'shires', idealized by Tolkien in *The Hobbit*, were further subdivided into 'hundreds', with their own courts of justice. The government of the regions and a still-primitive central government were linked by the shire-reeve, or *sherriff*. This, as virtually every historian has noted, was the most thoroughly organized and administered government in early medieval Europe. It had a vigorous economy, a strong coinage, a sophisticated culture, and a prose dedicated to law and administration. From the middle of the tenth century a steady flow of charters, diplomas and writs, expressed not in Latin but in the common tongue, made Old English the premier vernacular of the western world, the precociously advanced medium of an independent-minded society isolated from, but trading with, the wider world, Globish in embryo.

7

The stability achieved by Alfred was short-lived. By the end of the first millennium England's population was settled but still vulnerable. In 994 the Danes renewed their attacks and, led by King Cnut (the wave-resistant Canute of legend), transformed England into a Danish colony. Although Cnut reigned for nineteen years, in 1042 the *witan* that chose a new king, Edward the Confessor, was dominated by fiercely independent Anglo-Saxons, led by Godwin, earl of Wessex. So Edward was never his own man. Within seven years the court was divided between the English (led by Earl Godwin) and the French (led by the bishop of London). Edward strengthened his ties with Normandy, and possibly promised his throne to the duke in a secret arrangement. He struggled on for a further eleven years, but died on 5 January 1066. Harold Godwinson, who had been Edward's right-hand man, was crowned king the next day. In April 1066 came a terrifying omen: Halley's comet, a celestial portent with a fiery tail, appeared in the heavens, presaging catastrophe. Perhaps news of Norman invasion plans had already filtered back to the court. Across the Channel, as spring moved into summer, William of Normandy began to assemble the largest invasion force since the emperor Claudius in AD 43. The history-minded English people might place this threat in the context of a thousand years of foreign assault and enemy occupation, but they would have been wrong. This was not just another invasion, or even a new cultural revolution, though it would be both those things. In the pre-history of the world's English, this was 'The Conquest'. Ten sixty-six was a unique European event, different from all previous invasions. In the first place, this cross-Channel assault was a bold military challenge to a mature and vigorous rival, an independent society that was quite the equal of Norman France. In consequence, secondly, the stakes were much higher. Duke William, marshalling his army at the mouth of the Somme, was risking total victory, or utter annihilation. It was a huge gamble, finally, whose outcome would inspire centuries of complex Anglo-French relations, and many competing stories in prose and poetry, from Henry V and the archers of Agincourt to the siege of Orléans and the martyrdom of Jeanne d'Arc. That was in the future. As it turned out, the Norman Conquest was a close-run thing, and Harold might even have won.

The last English king marched into Kent to confront the invader on 14 October 1066. According to the Anglo-Saxon Chronicle, Harold 'came against him [William] at the hoary apple tree' which stood at the junction of the roads leading out of Hastings towards London. Fighting on the field of Senlac, the English had the home advantage. The Saxon shield-wall was dug in at the top of a ridge, and the French had to attack uphill. As the Bayeux Tapestry indicates, it was a brutal battle, one of the longest in medieval history. The fortunes of war swayed backwards and forwards, as each side struggled for the decisive breakthrough. Finally, after hours of bloody attrition, Harold was killed, together with both his brothers, 'and many good men'. Darkness fell, and, in the sombre words of the Chronicle, 'the French remained masters of the field'.

In the tradition of previous invasions, the surviving Saxon earls, and the archbishop of Canterbury, immediately proclaimed a new English king – Edgar the Atheling – on the assumption that this latest upset would follow time-honoured custom: the triumphant Normans would simply take over the machinery of government, rule through Anglo-Saxon surrogates and go home. Under that scenario, the influence of France would have been confined to some diplomatic niceties and a few French feasts. But William could not go along with this tradition, even if he had wanted to. The *raison d'être* of his army was that, if it were victorious, his commanders and their followers should enjoy the spoils of war – treasure, estates and titles of nobility. No sooner was the battle of Hastings won than the Normans marched through the heartlands of Anglo-Saxon England, terrorizing its people into submission. It was the end of *Englaland*; and it should have been the end of *Englisc*. Certainly, the omens were not good.

On Christmas Day 1066 William I was crowned at Westminster, in a chaotic ceremony that mixed Saxon and Norman rites. This gave legitimacy to the new regime, but it did not guarantee its future tranquillity. William the Conqueror understood this only too well. After Christmas he gave orders for the construction of the castle that would become the Tower of London to begin. An imposing chain of Norman forts became the enduring symbol of William's conquest. Saxon architecture, based on timber, brick and straw, always suggested a harmonious community among all classes. Norman stone was much more imposing, designed to convey the power of the state and the inflexible will of its alien king, as the new Norman lexicon of *fortress*, *siege*, *assault* and *prison* suggests. From now on the governors and the governed would live in separate worlds. And English became the mother tongue of an oppressed people, their sole means of self-expression.

2. Defeat into Victory

The DNA of Self-Expression

'I see somebody now!' she exclaimed at last. 'But he's coming very slowly – and what curious attitudes he goes into!'

'Not at all', said the king. 'He's an Anglo-Saxon Messenger – and those are Anglo-Saxon attitudes. He only does them when he's happy.'

Lewis Carroll, *Through the Looking-Glass*

1

England's bleak annihilation by the Normans has become softened with time; history has pastoralized the French oppression into the 'Norman Yoke'. But *war* is a Norman word: the Conquest was cruel and comprehensive. One clue to its severity comes about nine hundred years later, on the outbreak of the Second World War: this military victory followed by a military occupation was especially admired by the Nazis. In particular, Heinrich Himmler, head of the SS, developed a fascination with the Bayeux Tapestry, an obsession monitored in some disbelief by Station X, Bletchley Park.

Soon after the fall of France in 1940, the Bayeux *Propagandastaffel* (propaganda office) asked to see the famous relic. There were many angles to Nazi interest, aside from art history: the tantalizing example of the Norman fleet's successful Channel crossing; history's message that England could, after all, be subjugated by disciplined military might. Finally, madder and more chilling, the Bayeux Tapestry, probably the work of Anglo-Saxon weavers, was seen by Himmler and his *Ahnenerbe*, 'the Ancestral Heritage' unit, as an example of Aryan art by Germanic craftspeople at its finest. In 1941, with the war going Germany's way, Goebbels arranged for Lord Haw-Haw to broadcast an account of the role the Tapestry might play in the run-up to a successful Nazi invasion of England. This provocation inspired a patriotic leader in *The Times* pointing out that 'most English boast of their Norman heritage'. The profound national assimilation of an enemy culture is the remarkable lesson of the Norman Conquest. In a pattern that would be repeated, on a smaller scale, in dozens of subsequent cultural, legal and political transactions, defeat was turned into victory, and conquest to consanguinity. Harold, the free and independent English king and his army, might have been killed at Hastings, but his people – the men who had not fought; the women-folk and their children at home – survived to endure and subtly to transform, a wholesale foreign occupation.

How the English language weathered the occupation – and why William could not wholly conquer – will always be a matter for debate, but some things are indisputable. Most obviously, the pre-Conquest Old English vernacular, both written and spoken, was too well established, too vigorous and, thanks to its fusion with the languages of Scandinavia, too sturdy to be obliterated. Its strength was its adaptability and its usefulness; in a dire social emergency, it would become the focus of an English survival instinct. Something else was going on, too, a subtle cultural accommodation to an alien power, a mixture of aggressive covert resistance and ingenious collaboration. There's a famous poem, *The Owl and the Nightingale*, that celebrates English cunning in the face of Norman might: 'With only a little strength, but through ingenuity, one may conquer castle and town. One may bring down walls with deceit and throw bold knights off their horses.' Through word of mouth, a process that was contagious, adaptable, populist and subversive, during two hundred years (the equivalent of the Napoleonic Wars to the present day) Norman and Anglo-Saxon experience became merged into a single, polyphonic harmony. But it came at a price.

2

At first, like the Nazis in occupied Europe, William moved swiftly to take control of his new kingdom. Having seized London and organized his coronation, he confiscated the lands of those who had fought and died at Hastings; purged the English Church; and began install-ing loyal followers at strategic points throughout the kingdom. He had to face the fact that, away from the south, almost all the kingdom was opposed to the Normans. But it was not a wholly mindless oppos-ition, devoid of principle. Anglo-Saxon England had celebrated the rule of law. Its island people had developed an innate sense of their rights as individuals, which they expressed, with subtlety and deter-mination, in the prose and poetry of Old English. The drumbeat of all the earliest English writing musters the individual against the nameless threats of the outside world – dragons, armies and invading kings. By 1066 the DNA of self-expression had become encrypted into the Anglo-Saxon way of life, and William found himself up against it at every level of society. As early as 1068 he was marching against rebellions in York, Durham and the north, crushing his ene-mies with unprecedented severity.

In a paradox typical of English, the national trauma of the Conquest strengthened its European roots. About 10,000 words were absorbed from French, of which some 75 per cent survive to the present day, for instance, *allegiance*, *serf* and *banquet*. Occupation by a foreign power was hardly new for the English (in many ways, they had known little else for a thousand years), but never had their subjugation been so comprehensive. One important witness to the invasion and its after-math is the Anglo-French monk Orderic Vitalis, who, barely two generations after the Norman landing, compiled a record of life under the French. It is a grim picture. 'Foreigners grew wealthy with the spoils of England,' writes Vitalis, 'while her sons were either shamefully slain or driven as exiles to wander hopelessly through for-eign kingdoms.' The irony of this testimony is that Orderic Vitalis embodied the outcome of all such occupations: the son of a Norman father and English mother, he had mixed blood.

Life for the first Normans in England was a choice between mar-riage or massacre. Across the country, Anglo-Saxon men and women were making new family alliances, possibly in defiance of local hos-tility, or taking revenge against the hated invader. The record of the English courts tells the most vivid tale: the *murdrum* law opens a window onto the reality of Anglo-French relations in the shires.

Coexistence was heavily policed. The *murdrum* law simply stated that, in the event of an unsolved killing, the local 'hundred' had to pay a fine, unless it could prove that the victim was English. Dead bodies do not speak: this was a law designed to safeguard the lives of French settlers living among a hostile English population.

The continued strength of English national consciousness is illustrated by another document that is sometimes taken as a symbol of Norman administrative efficiency: the Domesday Book, 'the book of the day of assessment', which emerged from the king's council in 1085. William's belief that he could quantify what he had just conquered through statistics is really a backhanded French compliment to English national identity. The Domesday Book was intended to be a complete record of the entire kingdom, down to the last acre. Commissioners were sent out across the land, and sworn evidence of ownership and domestic inventory was collected – a nice Anglo-Saxon touch, this – from juries composed of Norman and English. In the end, it was not a complete survey – that proved to be impossible – but it was the most advanced of its kind in Europe at the time.

The statistics of the Doomsday Book tell one story, but they scarcely articulate the two most remarkable aspects of the Norman Conquest in the longer term: the pragmatic coexistence of Anglo-Saxon and Norman, and, as a result, the evolution of English speech. Against all the odds, English culture – contagious, adaptable, populist and subversive – was not just surviving, but flourishing. Barely a hundred years after the Conquest, one chronicler wrote that 'the two nations have become so mixed that it is impossible today, speaking of free men, to tell who is English and who is of Norman race'. This is not surprising. A Norman knight married to an English wife, living in his manor house deep in the English countryside, would find himself surrounded by English peasants, served at table by English maids, his estates managed by an English steward. If he had children, they would speak French to their parents, but would play with English children and quickly become bilingual. Such a knight who wanted to prosper in England would have to pick up some English with which to conduct his business and to overcome the natural resentment of his feudal subjects.

A twelfth-century miracle story expresses the intricacies of the Anglo-Norman cultural maze. A friend of St Wulfric of Haselbury, a certain Brother William, laid hands on a dumb man who had been brought before him. At once, the story goes, the man became miraculously bilingual, speaking both English and French. The local parish priest, a man named Brichtric, complained that this was unfair. He had served the Church faithfully for many years and yet Brother William had made it possible for a total stranger to speak two languages while he, Brichtric, had to remain dumb in the presence of his bishop. Even though he was a priest, Brichtric knew little or no Latin, and no French.

These Anglo-Norman cross-currents are vital. Now, in the passing of successive French and English generations, the complexity of Old English became simplified, coming closer to the sound and rhythm of everyday speech. Slowly, the inflections and diphthongs of Old English died out and its irregular prepositional structures became standardized. Over at least two centuries the basic syntax of the world's English – subject, verb, object – became established, flourishing in a variety of dialects, some of which still survive. In this way, Old English became Middle English, exposed to the influence of French, as new Anglo-Norman words like *mercy*, *bailiff*, *fruit* and *grace* indicate. Sir Walter Scott was the first to notice that Norman vocabulary illustrates a new sophistication in the kitchen, with terms such as *beef*, *mutton* and *veal*. There were modifications to grammar and syntax, too. English idiom began to pattern itself after French expressions. 'To hold dear' follows the Old French *tenir chier*. 'Do battle', 'have mercy', 'make peace' and 'take pains' also have Old French sources.

Many of these crucial innovations were happening below the literary radar, and would not appear on paper until the end of the thirteenth century. In 1154, indeed, about a hundred years after the destruction of the English court, the English monks who wrote the Anglo-Saxon Chronicle abandoned their work for ever. 'Doomsday' continues to resound through the faltering record of Old English under foreign rule in a faint and melancholy echo. The last poem composed in a now marginalized literary language was a celebration of Durham by an anonymous poet. To Saxons, Durham Cathedral was numinous; it was the home of Bede and St Cuthbert, and in the poem's closing line the saint is said to be waiting for 'doomsday', perhaps like the civilization of England itself. A great silence appears to descend on English prose.

Off the page, however, the oral culture, now in noisy high spirits, became the focus of popular self-expression. English, the native tongue – informal, demotic, vigorous and profane – survived as a spoken language for which literacy would be a late development. In court, Church and government circles, French was established as the smart and Latin the professional language. Old English was invariably direct, earthy and plain (*fire, work, love, strong, heart*). French words were courtly, formal and remote (*glory, cordial, fortune, guile* and *sacred*). Eventually these interwoven threads would yield a wealth of synonyms. Triptychs of words like *go–depart–exit*; *rise–mount–ascend*; and *time–age–epoch*, illustrate how the capacity to express fine distinctions comes directly from the Conquest. With three languages in play, the majority of English people experienced the humiliations of a linguistic apartheid: religion, law, science and court literature were all conducted in languages other than English. The elites, who operated in government, became hopelessly isolated from everyday life. This separation had a long aftermath. There is a telling moment in Shakespeare's *The Winter's Tale* when Autolycus meets a simple shepherd in the company of a clown:

SHEPHERD   My business, sir, is to the king.

AUTOLYCUS   What advocate hast thou to him?

SHEPHERD   I know not, an't like you.

CLOWN   (*aside to the shepherd*) Advocate's the court-word for a phea-
             sant. Say you have none.

SHEPHERD   None, sir. I have no pheasant, cock nor hen.

AUTOLYCUS   (*aside*) How blessed are we that are not simple men!

Consider, for instance, the story of Bishop William of Ely, chancellor of England during the reign of Richard the Lionheart (*Cœur de Lion*). Disgraced politically, the bishop tried to escape from England disguised as a woman and carrying under his arm some cloth for sale. He reached Dover but was discovered when asked by someone what he would charge for an ell of cloth. The chancellor could not respond, and was exposed, because he knew no English. The ordinary people did not abandon their mother tongue. Among Saxons, *in extremis* even educated French- and Latin-speakers would switch to the vernacular. In another contemporary account, on the life and death of Thomas Becket, written in Latin, the chronicler reverts to English to narrate a warning-shout to one of the murderers: '*Hugh de Morevile, ware! Ware! Ware! Lithulf heth his swerde adrege!*' ('Look out! Lithulf has drawn his sword!') A mild linguistic schizophrenia touched all classes in different ways.

The collision of Anglo-Saxon identity with Norman French repression had one profound and unintended consequence: a popular culture of intensely free expression. English under the Normans became the default position for subversive and contrarian ideas, a profound and instinctive antipathy to foreign rule. When William I died in 1087 the chronicler observes with grim satisfaction that worldly wealth and power are 'deceitful and transitory'. Human frailty notwithstanding, the Norman settlement survived, though the twelfth century was often marred by civil war, starvation and widespread misery. Traditionally, English fortunes reach their nadir with the reign of King John at the start of the thirteenth century. As the English people suffered, the fragments of their poetry that survive become rich in elegiac expressions of longing for the lost world of the Anglo-Saxons. Then as now, the English were good at locating a golden age in the recent past. The present, writes the chronicler, is full of 'horror'. The landscape, once free, is dominated by 'castles', 'prison' and 'taxation'. The people are 'wretched', 'cursed' and 'forlorn'. One contemporary poem, from the early thirteenth century, 'The Grave', compares an Englishman's home to the confines of a tomb.

3

The worse the experience of the Norman settlement, the more attractive the myths of old Britain. For the Saxon, the misty past offered the consolation of nostalgia. For the Anglo-Norman, there was the appeal of ancient heroes untainted by Saxon ways. Around 1136 or 1138 (accounts vary) an Oxford cleric, styling himself Geoffrey of Monmouth, completed a chronicle entitled *The History of the Kings of Britain* (*Historia Regum Britanniae*) derived from Geoffrey's conversations with the librarian of Malmesbury Abbey. This immensely popular, wonderfully fanciful, epic narrative of pre-Saxon British history was said to have been based on 'an ancient book in the British language', though no one has ever tracked down such a volume. Geoffrey of Monmouth had already compiled *The Prophecies of Merlin* (*Prophetiae Merlini*), so it was predictable that the most influential parts of his *History* should be devoted to the fabulous exploits of the British hero prophesied by the Welsh wizard Merlin.

Folk tales about King Arthur, the once and future king, had been circulating within the oral culture for centuries. Geoffrey of Monmouth gave them a new, literary impetus for a new audience of Anglo-Norman nobility, priests and courtiers. By implication, he also supplied a romantic model of kingly government to which all patriots could subscribe. Geoffrey's *History* also repeated some other potent national myths that will recur in the evolution of the English language: the story of King Lear and his three daughters; the tale of Cymbeline, king of Britain, and his daughter Imogen; the legend of Merlin; and the transport of Stonehenge from Ireland to Salisbury Plain. As many have noticed, Geoffrey brings to these essentially Celtic and British stories a profoundly English sensibility. It is as though Norman rule, far from eradicating English culture, had actually strengthened and intensified its expression. In this way, the story of Arthur's reign became attached to what Peter Ackroyd has called 'the national linguistic enterprise'.

Arthur's name and fortunes have long since passed into legend. This was powerfully assisted by the appearance of an early bestseller, composed in the fifteenth century by a wayward knight named Sir Thomas Malory, an epic whose full title is 'The Birth, Life and Acts of King Arthur, of his noble Knights of the Round Table, their marvellous Enquests and Adventures; th'Achieving of the Sangreal, and in the end the dolorous Death and Departing out of the World of them All'. Malory's publisher, William Caxton, named this volume of some 800–1,000 pages *Le Morte d'Arthur*, a romantic title by which it has been known and admired ever since. Malory's book was an immediate hit. Henry VII would christen his first-born Arthur; Henry VIII's Field of the Cloth of Gold was inspired by Camelot; poets as far apart as Spenser, Milton and Tennyson looked back to Malory, and it is said that T. E. Lawrence kept a copy of *Morte d'Arthur* in his saddlebag during the Arab Revolt. In popular culture, Chandler's Philip Marlowe was originally called Philip Malory; meanwhile, Walt Disney turned part of it into an animation, *The Sword in the Stone*, based on T. H. White's novel of the same name, itself an unacknowledged inspiration for J. K. Rowling.

Next to *Morte d'Arthur*, there is the urtext of the British libertarian tradition, Magna Carta. The loss of Normandy in 1204, the worst crisis of King John's unhappy reign, had accelerated the growth of an English identity. French would survive at court, but it would become steadily marginalized as the language of the governing elite. There is a suggestion that some high-flown English words modelled on French, such as *gauntlet* and *hamlet*, became the vogue among social climbing nouveaux riches. As troubles piled up at home, King John's adventures overseas culminated in an annihilating defeat at the battle of Bouvines. From then on there would be no chance of indefinitely postponing a showdown with his barons at home. The moment of truth came in June 1215 when, after weeks of disorder in London, the king met an aristocratic delegation of his discontented subjects in a field at Runnymede, a short ride from Windsor Castle.

This extraordinary occasion was convened to debate a document, whose literal meaning, 'the big charter', signalled how much longer it was than any previous statement of grievances. For that, in the first instance, was the true nature of Magna Carta, a sequence of some sixty-three clauses, originally entitled 'A Charter of Liberties'. There were promises to banish foreign mercenaries. There were prohibitions of the capricious exercise of the royal will (for example, the sovereign's power to force a baronial widow to remarry so that the crown could collect an often ruinous remarriage fee). There were clarifications of tenants' rights, and so on. Broadly, the king promised to restore the government by law as it had stood in the reign of his father, Henry II. Subsequently Magna Carta has been revered as the lawyerly preamble to a free society; William Pitt the Elder called it 'the Bible of the English Constitution', a myth especially dear to the United States. In 1956 the celebrated English judge Lord Denning described Magna Carta as 'the greatest constitutional document of all times – the foundation of the freedom of the individual against the arbitrary authority of the despot'. Really it was no such thing: hardly a people's charter, and certainly not a constitution. At the same time, it did contain language which would later become a touchstone of individual liberties: 'No free man shall be arrested or outlawed or exiled or in any way ruined, nor will we go or send against him, except by the lawful judgement of his peers or by the law of the land. To no one will we sell, to no one will we deny, or delay, right or justice.' The principle of habeas corpus, which has a resonance to this day, was one of the individual freedoms established in this argument between a feudal king and his court. When, in December 2006, the law lords of the House of Lords came to rule on the use of torture their landmark ruling used language that deliberately harked back to this moment in the history of English freedoms.

4

The century after Magna Carta was one of English mastery. After the upheavals of the previous hundred years, there were just three reigns, Henry III (1216–72), his son Edward I (1272–1307), followed by his son Edward II (1307–27). The Anglo-Norman kingdom now consolidated its authority, while Europe-wide prosperity increased the English population to about 3.5 million, for whom the English language became the universal expression of an emerging English patriotism. At the start of the thirteenth century a dispassionate observer could plausibly have described the British Isles as a region that was potentially British, French or English. By the beginning of the fourteenth century an English king indisputably sat on an English throne ruling essentially English subjects for whom English was the common tongue. The surviving French in government were now often denounced as 'foreigners'. One English bishop, Robert Grosseteste, obviously of

Norman blood, attacked the French at court as 'not merely foreigners; they are the worst enemies of England. They strive to tear the fleece and do not even know the faces of the sheep; they do not understand the English tongue...'

King and barons remained at odds, but their disputes were expressed in the vernacular. When the latest dramatic reductions in the autocratic powers of the king, the 'Provisions of Oxford', were finalized (1258), the documents were written up not just in Latin and French (as usual), but also in (Middle) English, the mother tongue of the people whose liberties were being championed by the rebellious barons. Magna Carta, by contrast, had been written exclusively in Latin, for an elite audience of peers and clergy. Later, this Oxford meeting would become known as 'the Mad Parliament'. What followed was a moment of popular madness that was not exactly civil war but certainly anti-monarchical, against Henry III. Rebel forces led by Simon de Montfort took the king's son hostage in 1265, though his life was never threatened. This, observes the historian Simon Schama, was 'the closest that England came to being a republic before the seventeenth century'. When Henry III died seven years later, his successor, Edward I, had not forgotten the lesson of his father's reign. The new king was acutely conscious of his national identity. On one occasion he whipped up patriotic feeling against the king of France, declaring that it was 'his detestable purpose, which God forbid, to wipe out the English tongue'. Edward I would accommodate Magna Carta and the Provisions of Oxford while at the same time commanding the loyalty of all his people, in Wales, Scotland and Ireland as much as in the English shires.

Edward's reign was dominated by costly military campaigns, first in Wales and then in Scotland. As nationalism flourished on its borders, at home in England ordinary people now became increasingly conscious of their identity as Englishmen and women. In *Parliament* – this formerly French term was now in general use – the lords temporal and spiritual (the bishops) were joined by the chosen representatives of the county courts and boroughs known as 'the Commons'. By 1295 and the so-called Model Parliament, a tentative sketch of English democracy in an age of European feudal monarchy was on the drawing board. After another period of chaos, tyranny and disorder during the reign of Edward II, his heir succeeded his father in 1327. Tellingly, the new king at once declared that 'the affairs that concern him and the estate of his realm shall be directed by the common counsel of his realm, and in no other wise'. Edward III reigned for fifty years. In the words of one historian, he 'was the only sovereign between Canute and George III who was never troubled by rebellion, or treason, or plot'. The main explanation for this happy outcome is the obvious one: England and its people were absorbed in the satisfying business of fighting France.

5

The Hundred Years War, conventionally dated 1328–1453, had many unintended consequences but none was more crucial to the renewal of English than the transformation of an Anglo-Norman province into *l'Albion perfide*, the home of 'the British'. By the fourteenth century this had become a hybrid race, uniquely committed to waging war, on land and sea, against 'the French', a people whose arrogance, vanity, strange habits and stranger cooking never failed to arouse suspicion and hostility. The making of a national identity became focused on the Church, on the battlefield, and on the vague but comforting sense of superiority embodied in the British tradition. Later this historic conflict between France and Britain, fought on a global scale, would have worldwide economic, political and cultural consequences. Initially at least, a hundred years of intermittent fighting across the Channel contributed to England's sense of its identity. The growing power and spread of the vernacular was expressed by a contemporary poet who wrote:

> Common men know no French
> Among a hundred scarcely one.

A new note of nationalistic pride in English is sounded in the introduction to a long biblical poem, *Cursor Mundi*. 'This book', writes the anonymous poet, 'is translated into English for the love of the English people, English people of England, and more the common man to understand...' If being a native of this island involved following deeply coded instincts of self-expression and the assertion of the rights of an 'Englishman', it also involved feeling anti-French, a mood that can be traced back to the Conquest.

In prosecuting the war with France, Edward III drew on all his kingdom's most potent myths to mobilize national opinion behind the Cross of St George, the English flag. This was also the inspiration for that supreme chivalric English club, the Order of the Garter, dedicated to God, the Virgin Mary and Edward the Confessor. The king's court revelled in the ritual of this quasi-Arthurian fellowship. During Pentecost in 1344 the king and queen went so far as to recreate the Round Table at Windsor Castle, presiding over a sumptuous occasion in fur-trimmed gowns before making their way to the chapel in a procession of knights and barons. Edward's queen, Philippa, was a remarkable woman, compared by the chronicler Froissart to Guinevere. When she died, in 1369, the court was touched by months of mourning that, for once, echoed the recent experiences of the common man. Next to the war with the king of France, the second great enemy of Edward's reign was King Death.

6

Plague, like warfare, is an engine of change. The Black Death purged English culture and society without regard for accent, class or rank. In 1347, among tens of thousands, the plague carried off both the archbishop of Canterbury and Edward III's daughter Joan. In some towns, Bristol for example, as many as half the population perished; in Leicester 700 inhabitants died in just three days. 'The pestilence grew so strong', wrote one Yorkshire monk, 'that men and women dropped dead in the streets.' When the plague hit London, 300 were dying every day within the square mile of the City. One Irish Franciscan, 'waiting among the dead for death to come', wrote that he was leaving 'parchment...in case anyone should be alive in the future'. At this point in the manuscript, a second pen adds, 'Here, it seems, the author died.'

The direct result of this inexplicable horror was the near annihilation of the French language in England. In the grammar schools, English became the vernacular of education. A decade after King Death the symbol of this sudden shift is the wide circulation and popularity of *Piers Plowman*, a long English poem written in 1362 (revised in 1377) by a provincial poet named William ('Long Will') Langland. A celebration of English individualism, *Piers Plowman* is an allegorical narrative, composed in unrhymed alliterative verse, an English occasionally disparaged by contemporaries as a 'barbarous' form of the language. *Piers Plowman* opens in the Malvern Hills. A man named Will falls asleep and has a vision of a tower on a hill and a fortress (*donjon*) in a deep valley. Between these symbols of heaven and hell there is a 'fair feeld ful of folk', representing mankind. At the beginning of the poem, the humble ploughman Piers offers himself as the narrator's guide to Truth. The subsequent quest is expressed through a series of dream-visions and an examination into the lives of three allegorical characters, Do-Well, Do-Better and Do-Best.

Langland was an outsider who came from the West Midlands, where old English ideals had survived most strongly, but he had spent a life of poverty in London, serving as a humble chantry clerk, striding the streets in a long ragged coat. Shaven-headed and emaciated, he was as strange, prophetic and eccentric as William Blake, for whom *Piers Plowman* would later become an inspiration. Langland's vision was of a world out of joint, where 'Mede' (corruption) was rife at court, in the law and in the Church. His vision spared no one: friars were ignorant of Scripture and concerned only with their stomachs; pilgrims pursued prostitutes; feudal lords kept riotous retainers. Langland's predictions were as dire as his denunciation. The Church, 'a dunghill covered in snow', would not survive. The king would be overthrown. Famine would force the idle into employment. 'Common labourers' might storm heaven while the wise and witty fried in hell.

Here was a decisive moment. After centuries of repression, the recognition of 'Everyman' and the 'true commons' was finally becoming a universal English theme, expressed in the simple English words that hold good still. It is part of the enduring appeal of the world's English that its origins are associated with the history of the many, not the few, and with the street, not the court or cloister. At first, mixed with xenophobia, this new mood was confined to the upper echelons. When the 'Good Parliament' met in 1376 it elected a speaker who arbitrated a full-blown debate in which the Commons launched attack after attack on King Edward III's councillors, and demanded the immediate expulsion of 'foreign' merchants. Then, in June 1381, scarcely five years into the reign of the young king Richard II, came the riotous sequence of popular protest known as the Peasants' Revolt, which was a vivid demonstration of the ideas that had been fermenting in the country at large. In truth, these few days of violent dissent were not led by peasants, and were, at least in the early stages, less a 'revolt' than a rolling tide of rowdy rustic revelry converging on London from Essex and Kent. The tipping point was a new poll tax, imposed on a resurgent agricultural community whose determination to take charge of their communities, in the aftermath of the Black Death, gave them little patience with central government. The 'true commons' (squires, reeves, publicans, and so on) took to the highway to appeal to the king against the iniquities of the system. Symptomatic of the confused popular aspirations, some of the marchers swore an oath to defend King Richard.

When the men of Kent emerged with a leader, Wat Tyler, much of the rhetoric was anti-clerical, urged on by a maverick itinerant preacher, John Ball, who denounced the clergy for their greed and worldliness, in the spirit of Langland and *Piers Plowman*. In the end, the fury of the mob was directed against the archbishop of Canterbury, not the crown. With remarkable courage, the king actually rode out to Mile End to meet the protesters and listen to their confused grievances, tactfully speaking to them in plain English. Wat Tyler is said to have addressed him with 'Brother, be of good comfort', but the other rebels, according to the *Anonimalle* chronicler, began with 'Welcome to our lord king Richard, if it please you, and we will not have any other king than you.' In a manner characteristic of English social protest ever since, the atmosphere was a mixture of riotous assembly and Cup Final, in which celebrations of a 'world turned upside down' were combined with rough declarations of loyalty to the crown.

Symbolically, however, these riotous June days established in the English popular imagination the importance of the king's justice (that is, the law) as the supreme arbiter of civil society. As the chronicler Thomas of Walsingham noted scornfully, the protesters 'considered that no name was more honourable than that of community, nor, according to their stupid estimation, were there to be any lords in the future, but only the King and Commons'. In immediate practical terms, this flowering of English individualism expressed itself in the closing decades of the fourteenth century and throughout the fifteenth in the drive for an English translation of the Bible, a movement led by John Wyclif and his Lollards, a word meaning 'mutterers' or 'mumblers'.

Wyclif, a Yorkshireman, was a fellow of Balliol College, Oxford, but less a scholar than an English intellectual. He was a former diplomat who had wrestled with the authority of Church and State, their respective roles and the secular exercise of Church power. What, Wyclif asked, were bishops and archbishops doing as the king's servants? Why were members of the clergy exempt from some taxation? Why was Scripture ignored in the everyday conduct of a would-be Christian society? Wyclif's message was deeply subversive: everyone was equal before God. No priest, prince or pauper, no one in a state of mortal sin, could rightfully assert dominion over anything, or anyone. Most Lollards were artisans, but Wyclif's ideas also caught on in the upper reaches of London society. From time to time, Lollardism would express itself in violent episodes like Sir John Oldcastle's abortive uprising in 1415. From the cultural point of view, the importance of the Lollard community was its intention to meet for readings of the vernacular Bible. In 1388, another milestone, this was finally possible when Wyclif became the first man to translate the Bible into English.

Enthusiasm for English now touched all classes of society. In 1356 the mayor and aldermen of London ordered that court proceedings should be heard in English; in 1362 the chancellor opened Parliament in English; and King Richard II, steeped as he was in French culture, always spoke to his subjects in English, whatever he might use at court.

In a fitting climax, Geoffrey Chaucer's decision to write about English commoners, from the Miller and the Prioress to the Pardoner and the Wife of Bath, is another symbolic moment in the tumultuous last years of the fourteenth century. It was one thing for religious zealots to appropriate English to an evangelical purpose, but it was something else for a great poet to make English, not Latin, his muse. Once again, the marketplace and self-expression were intimately related. In *The Canterbury Tales*, Chaucer expresses his bawdy vision of English life in his mother tongue because that was what his audience wanted to hear. In the words of the chronicler William of Nassyngton, 'Simple or learned, old or young, All understand the English tongue.'

7

Geoffrey Chaucer's French first name and half-French surname (from the Old French *chaustier*, shoemaker), marks him out as of Norman descent. His career reflects the dynamic upward mobility of the English bourgeoisie. Born in 1340 of a provincial middle-class family in the wine trade, he was educated as a squire in a noble household, later joining the king's retinue. Everything about his upbringing pointed to a professional career dominated by French and Latin, but Chaucer was an English original, and an individualist. 'Ech man for him-self,' he writes in *The Knight's Tale*, 'ther is non other.' In his writing life, first as a translator and imitator, he began to explore the joys of the vernacular. Some of his mature work offers clues to the life of the poet. In *The Parlement of Foules*, for instance, he reports how he reads in bed at night because he cannot sleep. From 1370 to 1391 he was active on the king's business at home and abroad. Like any European civil servant, he negotiated trade in Geneva, and later made a diplomatic mission to Milan, where he indulged a taste for the Italian poetry of his contemporaries, Petrarch and Boccaccio. During his time as the king's servant he completed much of his best work, *The House of Fame* and *Troilus and Criseyde*, and translated *The Consolation of Philosophy* by Boethius.

Around 1387 he began work on his masterpiece, *The Canterbury*

Tales, poems in English he would either have read aloud in the traditional manner or, as was becoming the custom, passed around among
friends and patrons. A famous illustration to an illuminated manuscript depicts him reading to the court at Windsor. 'He must have
been a man', observed Dryden, writing in the seventeenth century of
the debt English culture owes to its first great poet, 'of a most wonderful comprehensive Nature' because he expressed 'the various Manners and Humours...of the whole *English* Nation'. Chaucer himself
seems to have been unsure of exactly what he had achieved. Towards
the end of his life he published a book for younger readers, *A Treatise
on the Astrolabe*, in which he expresses doubt whether his 'lighte Englisshe' (easy English) could be substantial or complex enough to
describe such a weighty subject as astronomy. His successors were in
no doubt of his pioneering importance. To the poet Spenser, he was
quite simply 'the well of English undefiled', and elsewhere, 'the pure
well head of Poesie'. Chaucer's vernacular aesthetic was fresh and contemporary, but the poet is modern in another way, too. He was acutely
conscious of literary influence and always emphasized that his work
was based on a classical and European tradition, on 'books' for which,
in a strikingly modern way, there was now a fierce public appetite.
The word 'boke' appears in a variety of knowing contexts throughout
his writing. Chaucer, notes the critic Peter Ackroyd, 'relies upon borrowings and adaptations in order to forge an English sensibility'.

By the turn of the fifteenth century the power and influence of
books was central to the everyday life of the new, moneyed class
which Chaucer represented. At the same time, the liberating use of
the vernacular could be dangerous. One expression of the state's
anxiety was the declaration, in the Constitutions (1407 and 1409) of
Thomas Arundel, archbishop of Canterbury, which made the vernacular illegal. 'No one', decreed the archbishop, 'should hencefor-
ward translate any text of holy scripture into the English tongue.' In
this climate, books in English could quite easily stray into the potentially fatal territory of heresy and dissent. In the coming century
English translations of the Bible would become the new frontier in a
ceaseless quest for freedom and originality.

3. 'Lighte Englisshe'

Medieval Mass Communications

> Big Brother and the Party and the Thought Police could all be swept into nothingness by a single splendid movement of the arm. That too was a gesture belonging to the ancient time. Winston woke up with the word 'Shakespeare' on his lips.
>
> George Orwell, *Nineteen Eighty-Four*

1

The making of the world's English, which owes so much to historical forces such as industrialization and the expansion of empire, gets virtually no help from the nature of the language itself. As many have observed, English contains one serious design flaw: its apparently irrational spelling conventions. Homonyms like 'bare' and 'bear' are all very well, but why should a word that sounds like 'nite' appear in print as 'night', or 'threw' as 'through'? It's a problem that turns out to have medieval antecedents.

One day in fifteenth-century London a well-known translator and literary man was sitting in his study. Idly, he began to browse a book that had recently been translated from Latin into French, a paraphrase of Virgil's *Aeneid*, and then, he says, he took up pen and ink and 'wrote a page or two' in English. In the new cultural economy, books and libraries had become fashionable among the rich and powerful. But when he came to read over his work later, he was dismayed to encounter so many 'strange terms' and was afraid he would be accused of translating in a way that 'could not be understood by common people'. So now our English literary pioneer, fired up with the need to communicate, describes consulting 'an old book' in his quest for a workable literary vernacular. But he got no help there, either; the English therein, he writes, was 'so rude and broad I could not well understand it'. The more he drilled down into the roots of the language, the worse his predicament: it was 'more like to Dutch than English'. As if that was not bad enough for the would-be translator, there was the problem of regional variation: 'Common English that is spoken in one shire', he observes, 'varies from another.'

These are the words of William Caxton, who was not only Chaucer's near contemporary, but also the first to print an edition of *The Canterbury Tales*. Both men are intensely modern and innovative figures. They could never have met – Chaucer died in 1400, perhaps ten years before Caxton was born – but author and publisher are well matched. Both had a fierce desire to be read, and understood, by the common reader. Only in retrospect does their profound originality seem either obvious or natural. Indeed, Caxton's recollection of his spelling troubles suggests that a typically English mix of trial and error, spurred on by market forces, was the driving inspiration for modernizing the vernacular.

Once again, the printer has an instructive tale, drawn from his career as a merchant, to illustrate what he was up against in the struggle to tame the mad vigour of a language born, as he puts it, 'under the domination of the moon'. Caxton describes how a trader named Sheffield, becalmed in the Thames, en route to the Continent, rowed ashore for a meal, asking for 'mete and specially egges': what we know today as 'the full English'. Even close to London, this request for a simple breakfast was so misunderstood that the 'good wife' of the inn to whom Sheffield addressed himself declared that she did not speak French. To which the hungry merchant crossly replied that he did not speak French, either, but that 'he would have egges'. Again: more blank incomprehension. Then another diner helpfully chipped in, speaking of 'eyren', not 'egges'. Aha, so you meant 'eyren'? replied the good wife. 'Eyren? Egges?' It was all the same to Sheffield, but at least the matter was resolved. Now 'the good wife said that she understood him well'. At this point in his story, like a man holding forth in the pub, Caxton exclaims, 'Lo, what should a man write these days "egges" or "eyren"?' It was, he concluded, hard to please every man because of 'diversity and change' in the language. But if anyone had the stamina for modernization it was surely Caxton.

The genius of Chaucer had already made the disdained vernacular – 'lighte Englisshe' – at once lyrical, literary and fashionable. Now Caxton would make it intelligible. Chaucer is impossible without his printer-publisher; it is Caxton's edition that will iron out some of the wrinkles and clarify the obscurities. He is the first in a long line of great editors. At the same time, Caxton is unthinkable without Chaucer's 'lighte Englisshe', and he was always the first to concede that point. Chaucer, he wrote in the 'Prologue' to his edition of the poet's work, in the prototype of the publisher's blurb, was 'first foundeur and embellissher of our English'. But the modernization of 'our English' was not just a literary affair. Kings continued to play a role, too.

In the last years of Chaucer's life, the tragic reign of Richard II, at first so promising, and with such a strong interest in the arts, deteriorated swiftly into turmoil, and humiliation. Parliament was now the focus of opposition. By the 1390s, when Richard briefly recovered his royal authority, London had become the centre of extraordinary popular energy in which ambitious, worldly men with an appetite for politics and business began to play a crucial role in the fortunes of the crown. These were the Londoners who had rallied to the crown during the Peasants' Revolt in 1381. What would they do now, and where would their loyalties lie? For the moment, Richard's marriage to Isabella of France was part of an elaborate Anglo-French rapprochement in which England would play a European role. When this noble vision failed, England became isolated and the king was doomed. It was a turning point in the fortunes of 'lighte Englisshe'.

Richard II never commanded his people as much as he should have done to ensure the survival of the Plantagenet dynasty. Large parts of England were in the hands of some half-dozen barons, any one of whom had the means to challenge the crown. When in 1399 Richard's cousin Henry Bolingbroke, who had been in exile, landed at Ravenspur in Yorkshire, conducting the first effective invasion of England since 1066, with troops thoughtfully supplied by the king of France, aristocratic rebellion turned into a popular uprising, and finally expressed itself as a parliamentary 'trial'. Brought to Westminster, amid extraordinary scenes, the king was charged by the English peers and commons, with mismanagement and 'perversity'. After his 'Renunciation' had been read to Parliament in September 1399, and Henry Bolingbroke approved as King Henry IV to cries of 'Yes, Yes, Yes', Richard was banished to Pontefract Castle, where he died, aged thirty-two, allegedly of starvation. In *Richard the Second*, Shakespeare asks the essential question, 'What subject can give sentence on his king?' In 1399 the answer was: an aristocratic English subject, supported by the mass of the English people.

The new king, a usurper, was never free from the constraints of a strong council or a vigilant Parliament. Strangely, for one propelled into power by popular discontent, Henry IV was never reconciled to his subjects. Although he surrounded himself with 'new men', and told his first Parliament that his aim was 'common profit', it was left to his son Henry V to fulfil every Englishman's dream, and declare war on France.

2

War might shape events; propaganda would influence perception. Now, with a growing print culture, 'public opinion' was emerging as a political and cultural force. Henry V consciously used English as part of an aggressive nationalism, like Alfred the Great so many centuries before. Henry understood the rallying power of his language, as Shakespeare acknowledged in his portrait of the king.

> Then shall our names,
> Familiar in his mouth as household words,
> Harry the king, Bedford and Exeter...

Henry V was the first English monarch since the Conquest to use the vernacular in official documents, including his will. Appealing to a shared sense of Englishness, he united the country behind him. His first campaign in France (1413) was brutal and inconclusive, but it gave a clear indication of the new king's priorities: he would take the war to his foes. Now he set about mobilizing all the forces of Church and State to conduct a successful campaign across the English Channel. Perhaps he was learning from Edward III: war was the quickest way to unify a fractious people. France would define his reign. Normandy would be where 'King Harry' would express a resurgent cultural and military self-confidence.

In August 1415 Henry sailed from Portsmouth, but his expedition did not prosper. The English army was racked with disease. The French were well armed, defending their territory along the river Somme. Henry's strategy was to lure the enemy into battle, but the English grew steadily weaker with disease. When, finally, the two sides met, a French army of 30,000 faced an English force of scarcely 5,000. But then the unthinkable happened: the village of Azincourt would be the scene of a defining moment in post-Norman Englishness, a test, a victory and a legendary vindication. The annihilation of French chivalry by England's yeoman archers has often been told. Henry V may or may not have been a great general, but he was a brilliant propagandist. He made sure that his people at home knew about his astonishing success. Shakespeare's play *Henry the Fifth* is based on *The Famous Victories of Henry the Fifth: containing the Honourable Battell of Agin-court*. Nearly 200 years after the event, Shakespeare's version gave rhetorical and literary impetus to a national myth that was already well grounded.

The king's dispatches from France were written in English. As a result, the home front was so inspired with patriotic fervour that his triumphant and joyous return to London, via Canterbury and Blackheath, became a quasi-Roman triumph. A chorus of 'beautiful girls dressed in virgin white, rejoicing as if to a David at the fall of Goliath', sang 'Welcome Henry the Fifth, King of England and of France'. Triumphal arches along the route through Cheapside gave thanks to the Almighty, St George and the Plantagenet king. This was the moment at which the Hundred Years War (which still had thirty – at times, humiliating – years to run) became something to celebrate and remember. An anonymous chronicler noted that the king, dressed in a purple robe, passed through the ecstatic crowds, 'not with a haughty look and a pompous train but with a serious countenance and a reverend pace'.

As subsequent English leaders from Elizabeth I to Margaret Thatcher have discovered, nothing sustains their reputation like a military victory abroad. Henry V will always be Shakespeare's King Harry, popular for his close identification with the sentiments of the common man. In 1422, the year of the king's premature death from dysentery, the London Company of Brewers noted with approval that 'the most excellent lord king Henry the Fifth hath procured the common idiom to be commended by the exercise of writing ... [and] the greater part of the lords and trusty commons have begun to make their matters [to be] noted down in our mother tongue'. The child king, Henry VI, who followed his charismatic father, would reign through several decades of suffering and disorder. When he was declared mentally unstable in 1453 the country plunged into the chaos of the Wars of the Roses, but the Englishness celebrated by Henry V grew ever stronger, reinforced by a booming economy and the flowering of English town life. The 1430s were a decade marked by a new sophistication in the arts. Europeans who had once despised the English as provincial barbarians were now forced to concede that English letters were not only vigorous but distinctive.

3

Popular discontent and the modernization of the English language continued to go together. In Jack Cade's rebellion, which broke out in the summer of 1450, the rebels were very different from the knights and burgesses who had risen up in the Peasants' Revolt. Fiercely patriotic, they expressed their grievances in a manifesto infused with strong ideas of popular justice, 'The complaint of the commons of Kent'. The rebels, a mass of disgruntled gentry, peasants and yeomen from the Home Counties, directed much of their immediate anger against the 'traitors' at court who were responsible for recent failures in France, and for the humiliation of English pride. As a result, they declared, the king had been diminished. 'His lands are lost, his merchandise is lost, his commons destroyed, the sea lost, France is lost, himself so poor that he may not pay for his meat or drink; he oweth more than ever did king in England.' The object of this strange fealty, Henry VI, conducted himself with rather less distinction than Richard II in 1381, but had no great difficulty in containing the rebellion. There was some looting, mob violence and a few gruesome beheadings, but by mid-July it was all over, a tumult that was, paradoxically, a conservative protest, more about the 'lack of governance' than a desire to overthrow the king. 'These faults amended,' said the men of Kent, 'we will go home.'

In *Henry the Sixth, Part Two*, one of his earliest plays, Shakespeare explores the troubling confusion felt by 'the commons' here. It should be 'a felony to drink small beer'; state records should be burned, literacy abolished and prisoners set free. 'The first thing we do', exclaims one rebel in a famous line, 'let's kill all the lawyers.' An unhappy clerk is seized by the mob. 'Away with him,' says Cade, 'hang him with his pen and inkhorn about his neck.' Shakespeare dug deep into the disturbing transformation in human status and consciousness achieved by medieval mass communications. With brilliant insight, he shows Jack Cade accusing an enemy of his revolt with corrupting 'the youth of the realm' through the wicked agency of 'a grammar school': 'whereas before, our forefathers had no other books but the score and the tally [the stick on which small debts were calculated], thou hast caused printing to be used and, contrary to the King, his crown and dignity, thou hast built a paper-mill.' The 'men about thee', Cade concludes, damningly, 'usually talk of a noun and a verb and such abominable words as no Christian ear can endure to hear'.

Throughout the fifteenth and subsequent centuries a sustained clarification of spoken and written English puts Shakespeare and his contemporaries into the antechamber of the modern world. Chaucer is at best semi-intelligible to the twenty-first-century reader. From the 1600s almost everything in English is comprehensible to modern eyes and ears. By the 1700s a writer like Alexander Pope is completely accessible. (For example, Michel Gondry's film *The Eternal Sunshine of the Spotless Mind* (2004) finds its title in a direct quotation from Pope's poem 'Eloisa to Abelard'.)

Confronted by the fathomless mysteries of linguistic change, experts have been occasionally reduced to something close to academic voo-doo. Otto Jespersen, the great Danish linguist, is perhaps the most famous of these. In 1909, to explain how the long, stressed mono-thongs, syllables both throaty and low, of Middle English were moved from the back of the mouth towards the lips and teeth, becoming lighter, higher and shorter in articulation, Jespersen coined the term 'Great Vowel Shift'. Every subsequent history of the English language has paid lip-service to this jargon, but no one has – or ever can have – a definitive explanation for this change in the sound system of English. All we can say with any certainty is that, approximately from the 1450s, increased social mobility and economic prosperity were encourag-ing a new literacy among new classes throughout the kingdom, and a matching change in articulation.

Townspeople and country gentry alike could see that a mastery of reading and writing was the way to better yourself. Just as the inter-net has sponsored an explosion of global literary communication through emails and blogging, so in the fifteenth century there was a boom in letter-writing, typified by the Paston letters. The corres-pondence of an obscure Norfolk family, who translated themselves from ambitious peasants to knights of the shire in two generations, reveals determined provincials proud of their Englishness. The lan-guage of these new letter-writers was, to use an old English word, 'naked', that is, fresh, unedited and direct. English-speaking people, still confined to England, wanted to express their experience of schol-arship, business, trade, fashion, politics and law in a standardized ver-nacular that worked as well in conversation as on the page. Their language flourished alongside their upward social mobility. A simpler rendering of the spoken English vowel, like the Great Vowel Shift, would slowly become reflected in a new clarity in the written word.

In any culture, it is impossible to quantify the tides of influence between the written and the spoken word but, comparable to the impact of the World Wide Web in the 1990s, the spread of printing in the late fifteenth century was a milestone of incalculable consequence. Printing introduces a crucial modern separation between spoken and written mass communications. In the digital twenty-first century you will not always find ink and paper, but you cannot escape the printed word; it defines our civilization. Printing has been described as 'the third revolution' in human communications, after the invention of writing and the alphabet. It began in the 1450s with Johannes Gutenberg, a German businessman from Mainz.

4

Before Gutenberg, books were costly, rare and handmade. The composition of a single volume was a laborious business, closer to an art than a craft. A single copy might take a month or two to produce (one 1,272-page commentary on the Bible took two scribes five years, 1453–8, to complete). The technology of such manuscript volumes derived from nature. Scribal ink was manufactured either from lamp-black (carbon soot), mixed with water and gum, or from gall, which was extracted from oak galls. These were formed when gall wasps stung oak twigs to lay their eggs, creating a tiny, apple-like berry. Caustic gall would actually etch the parchment to which it was applied, but increasingly paper was taking parchment's place. Paper, designed to receive the marks of the quill or the brush, was made from rags and had the hard unyielding texture of parchment. At first neither ink nor paper was appropriate for newfangled movable type. Gutenberg's career was a frustrating story of bankruptcy, opportunism and disaster cut short by untimely death. But his invention was fundamental to the European Renaissance. In 1455, writes the historian John Man, 'all Europe's printed books could have been carried in a single wagon'. By the turn of the sixteenth century, there were more than 10,000 printed titles in circulation, and millions of individual copies.

In the fifteenth century the turning point came abroad, and in the most surprising way. The man who brought the new technology to London was neither a scholar nor an artist (though he was partly both of these), but that engaging hustler William Caxton, a former diplomat and cloth merchant from the Home Counties. In 1462, now in his early forties, Caxton found himself in Bruges, looking after the British colony there as part-ambassador and part-governor. Before his term of office ended in 1470 he started work on a translation of some Troy legends, compiled by a French monk, and dedicated to the duke of Burgundy. Possibly because he could see no market for his efforts in England, which was then mired in civil war, Caxton abandoned his task and laid it aside. Then chance took a hand. When Caxton's governorship ended, he was invited to the court of Burgundy, whose duchess was Margaret of York, sister of the new king, Edward IV. She had been married to Charles the Bold of Burgundy as part of Burgundy's anti-French alliance with England. During Caxton's audience the conversation turned to books. Margaret asked to see his work-in-progress and, having ticked him off – he reports that she 'found a fault in mine English' – eventually commissioned him to complete the translation. Then Caxton moved to Cologne and began the wearisome work all over again.

It was in Cologne – another chance encounter – that he met Ulrich Zel, a member of Gutenberg's printing circle, who had recently set up shop there. Caxton was finding the rigours of penmanship exhausting. He was suffering eyestrain and writer's cramp. Moreover, there was quite a demand for his work building up among 'diverse gentlemen and my friends'. Printing seemed to offer a blessed release from the servitude of scribing, and a way of satisfying the market. So, fretting about his overheads, a 'great charge and dispense', he hired one of Zel's assistants, Johann Veldener, to instruct him in the mysteries of movable type. Like someone who has just discovered the joys of word processing, Caxton – a man in his fifties, whose adult life had been dominated by parchment, ink and quills – found printing a revelation. In no time at all he had acquired a press, some type and his own assistant, another German named Wynkyn de Worde, who would play a vital part in what followed. The first printed book in English, *The Recuyell* [summary] *of the Historyes of Troye*, appeared not in London but in Bruges, in 1475.

In his own words, Caxton had been 'born and learned mine English in Kent'. As soon as he could, he came home to England, a retired businessman of literary inclinations with a new hobby that quickly became an obsession. In the autumn of 1476 he set up his press in the precincts of Westminster Abbey, right on the path leading from the king's palace of Westminster (where the Houses of Parliament now stand) to the great Abbey church itself. Caxton's relocation to the seat of English Church and government was a decisive move. Passing his printing shop, every day, on this supreme thoroughfare were courtiers, lawyers, priests, peers, burgesses and the human flotsam and jetsam attracted to the place that is still referred to as 'the Westminster village'. Typically, it was not just a shrewd business head that inspired this move. Caxton had family reasons for choosing Westminster: several other Caxtons were living thereabouts.

Caxton is an attractive, original and thoroughly English character: a man of gusto and good humour, of business acumen and pronounced political loyalties. In retirement from the world of European courts and business, he must have thought his future was behind him. Never was a man less likely to put on airs and graces. He always affected an appealing English modesty, referring to himself, ironically, as 'the symple person William Caxton'. When it came to rendering in print his spoken English, 'as broad and rude as in any place of England', he was full of apologies that it lacked the refinements of Latin or French. 'Pardon me', he wrote in the dedication to the *Recuyell*, 'of this rude and comyn Englisshe, for I confesse me not learned ne [nor] knowing the art of rethoryk [rhetoric] ne of such gaye terms as now be said in these dayes.' Once established, however, there was no stopping him. He became the first editor-publisher, printing the works of Chaucer, and other poets like Gower and Lydgate, and Thomas Malory's *Morte d'Arthur*. He also translated bestsellers from France and Burgundy, and became rich. And his decision to reproduce, in printed form, the English of London and the South-East had a decisive impact on the making of modern English. Perhaps, in his secret heart, he saw himself as an agent of linguistic stability in a rapidly changing cultural landscape. 'Certainly our language', he once wrote, 'now used varyeth ferre [far] from that which was used and spoken when I was borne.'

Confronted by the unruly nature of late-fifteenth-century English, Caxton achieved the essential simplification in a manner that was both practical and pragmatic. He writes that he would print 'the common terms that are used every day' because they were easier to understand 'than old and ancient English'. He goes on, with a credo that any publisher can understand, saying that his work is for readers who 'feel and understand in feats of arms, in love and in noble chivalry'. In other words, he wants a mass audience. English, says Caxton, is for the many not the few. 'Lighte', or easy, the English of William Caxton is a self-confident means of expression with international, even global, potential.

Like Chaucer, Caxton was a man of his time, speaking London English, and situated in the heart of the political establishment. His rendering of the vernacular echoes the sound of the words he would have heard around his office in Westminster. So his spelling of 'right' reflects the fifteenth-century pronunciation *richt* (*ch* pronounced as in *loch*), and he also preserved some residual Chaucerian features: 'knight' sounded closer to *ker-nicht*, from the German 'Knecht', than to the *nite* we use today. Elsewhere, the new clarity and directness of the written word derives from a bureaucratic house style developed at court for administrative purposes known as Chancery English. This, too, was transformed by Caxton into a new *literary* standard. In other words, he fixed the language on the printed page before its writers and teachers had fully reconciled the divergences between the written and the spoken. Hence the baffling inheritance of English spelling conventions.

The chaotic and exasperating spelling of contemporary English continues to evolve. In its present guise, it derives from this moment in the late fifteenth century, *c.* 1470–1500, a tribute to Caxton's importance. The printer-publisher himself would probably be horrified to find that his spelling conventions had become an orthodoxy. He himself recognized that English language and culture were always in flux. For Caxton, the best you could do was to make the written version of your thoughts as clear and as precise as possible. This is a strand of English prose that runs directly to George Orwell, for whom 'good prose' should be 'like a window pane'. Latin and French might be the prestige languages for the elite but, for 'the commons', anything and everything could be expressed in English.

4. Eating Paper, Drinking Ink

Shakespeare & Co.

Our English tongue, which hath been the most harsh, uneven and broken language of the world...is now continually refined, every writer striving in himself to add a new flourish unto it; so that in process, from the most rude and unpolished tongue, it is grown to a most perfect and composed language.

Thomas Heywood, *Apology for Actors* (1612)

1

The parallels between the 1470s and the first decade of the third millennium are a reminder of the many continuities in the evolution of the world's English. Caxton was hardly alone in his fascination with the new technology. Print and printing liberated new energies and sponsored new professions. The stationers of London became a city guild, like the skinners and the fishmongers, setting up workshops for book production in and around Paternoster Row, the centre of English publishing, until it was destroyed during the Blitz. It is not difficult to understand the impact of printing on fifteenth-century Europe: there is a precise analogy with the global IT revolution. Cherished crafts and time-honoured practices were swept into oblivion. Caxton and his contemporaries discovered, as we have done, that technological time seems to move faster than chronological time.

From 1470 to 1520 the pace of change was relentless. As the new technology caught on, the books that most commonly appeared in print were prayer books and catechisms. The Sarum liturgy, for example, went through twenty-nine printings between 1475 and 1500. Then, as now, books were a middle-class phenomenon, depending on education and a growing literacy. The bestsellers of the time, for example, Caxton's *The Game and Playe of the Chesse*, were aimed at the lucrative gentry market. Newly founded schools made a big investment in books, and England's numerous churches were eager to acquire well-printed editions of the Bible. But what sort of Bible? And who should have access to it?

To the inhabitants of England in the Middle Ages, the Church was a clerical aristocracy, a university, a security system and a legal authority. It controlled society, belief, ideas and many aspects of everyday life. The churches were also the scene of theatre, fund-raising, gossip and concerts. At the centre of this universe was the interpretation of God's word. In Latin, it remained exclusive and mysterious, the property of priests. In the 'rude' English of the 'true commons', the Bible could inspire free thought, sponsor debate and provoke the congregation to lively self-assertion. At the flashpoint of faith, technology and the dynamic vernacular, the Holy Bible in English became the battleground for a century of religious and political controversy. During the fifteenth and sixteenth centuries translating and publishing the Bible in the language of the common people became as revolutionary an act as, in the eighteenth century, advancing the proposition that states should be ruled by democratic institutions, not kings.

When the ruling elites began to understand the power of books and reading to challenge the status quo, the Church moved to protect its monopoly of thought. The Constitutions of Thomas Arundel had already declared translations of Scripture into English to be illegal. In 1416 another edict had established a procedure for annual examinations to identify 'those believing in errors or heresies, owners of suspicious books in the English tongue'. The main objection to Wyclif and the Lollards was that, through translation into English, the word of God could be misrepresented, especially (as sometimes occurred) if women preachers distorted the divine message. One such Wyclif disciple was reported as teaching that Mary did not remain a virgin after the birth of Jesus and, even more shocking, that the Bible did not support such a belief. Possessing Wyclifite texts was dangerous: Thomas Denys was burned for his beliefs in 1513; his disciples were forced to watch his martyrdom, and to throw their books into the fire with him.

Now the booming economy played its part. The more English, not Latin or French, expressed the hopes and dreams of a newly confident English nation led by English-speaking kings, the greater the market for English books. By the mid-fifteenth century there were even bishops, notably Reginald Pecocke, who were risking their lives to argue for the right to conduct religious debate in English. Increasingly, the vernacular was moving into intellectual territory previously dominated by Latin and French. English became the language in which the latest generation of reformers inveighed against priestly power. Richard Hunne, a wealthy Londoner, who was martyred for his opposition to the clergy, wrote in the prologue to his translation of the Bible that 'poor men and idiots have the truth of Holy scriptures, more than a thousand prelates'. Soon the new technology of printing would be put to the service of religious reform.

Cultural change flourished in chaotic times. The years in which Caxton and his press became established at Westminster were years of widespread social and economic uncertainty, a generation of political turmoil. The Wars of the Roses, a phrase actually coined by Sir Walter Scott, hardly touched the lives of the common people, but were fought with bitter cruelty between the opposing armies of the Yorkists and the Lancastrians. After three decades of murderous civil war the two sides were united by Henry Tudor, who was crowned king as Henry VII.

At court, the new dynasty could impose a new discipline on the warring aristocratic families of England, but it could do little to curb the people's appetite for access to education, power and influence. From the 1500s London was a city where ideas as much as goods were being traded at a pace that frightened the authorities, triggering waves of book-burning and repression. Now the vernacular Bible became the symbol of a liberated print culture, and then, intriguingly, of a liberated king. Once again, the breakthrough came across the Channel, in Europe. William Tyndale's ruling passion was to render the defining texts of the culture in a version that even 'the boy that driveth the plough' could grasp. His lifelong ambition, which eventually would lead to his death at the stake, was to place the Scriptures before the laity 'in their mother tongue'. Tyndale saw that the

Lollards' English manuscript Bibles were all very well. A printed Bible in English would be something else. When Tyndale was prevented from raising money in England to fund his venture, he went abroad, backed by a wealthy patron. In 1526 some 3,000 copies of Tyndale's *New Testament* were printed in the German city of Worms, and smuggled back to England. From that moment on, the Bible in English became the text that would dominate the reign of Henry VIII, politically, culturally and domestically.

The new reign began with high hopes, but by the 1520s Henry's obsession with siring a male heir inspired a desperate remedy. In 1527, supported by Cardinal Wolsey, he took the first steps towards divorcing his queen, Catherine. When this seemed to risk a confrontation with the Holy Roman Emperor, he drew back temporarily. Besides, he was distracted from divorce by his infatuation with Anne Boleyn.

2

Up to the moment at which Henry was first introduced to this daughter of an ambitious Kent courtier, Thomas Boleyn, the king had showed scant interest in the Reformation that had been sweeping Europe since 1519, the year of Luther's 'ninety-five theses'. When Anne Boleyn became a maid of honour to Queen Catherine, the vivacious, self-confident, nineteen-year-old brunette with the goggling, almond eyes and the flirtatious manner quickly attracted the king's attention. Sexual intrigue was soon braided with radical religion. By the summer of 1526 Henry's courting of Anne was obsessive. He confessed to her in his letters that he had been 'one whole year struck with the dart of love'. Anne was certainly a singular woman. Among her many original qualities was an interest in, and a commitment to, the vernacular Bible and evangelical reform. At some risk, she spoke up in the infatuated king's presence for Tyndale's *New Testament* and even pleaded for mercy to be shown to some persecuted reformers. Almost as decisively, in 1528 she gave Henry a banned copy of William Tyndale's *On the Obedience of a Christian Man and How Christian Rulers ought to Govern*. To the Church, this challenge to its authority was anathema; to the king, trapped in a barren marriage, Tyndale's polemic seemed to suggest a way out of an impossible situation.

Once Henry could convince himself that the 'bishop of Rome' exercised a power that was illegitimate, the way forward was clear. As head of the English Church, the king could follow his heart's desire and award himself a divorce from Catherine. Anne Boleyn bolstered her lover's confidence in this act of national defiance by assembling a team of pliable divines, who were charged with digging out comforting historical precedents for Henry's behaviour. The *Collectanea satis copiosa* (sufficiently copious collection) duly proved that, in the early days of the Church, the spiritual jurisdiction of England had been separate from Rome and, moreover, that princes (*vide* Henry) should be accountable to the Almighty, not to his vicar-on-earth. Implicit in these dusty arguments was a virile sense of nationhood, expressed in Latin but deeply English in spirit and intention. The overthrow of the pope was not an issue of principle, but the practical solution to a temporary problem. Inadvertently, but with profound consequences for the growth of a dynamic society and its language, Henry laid the foundations for a plural cultural and religious environment in which a new attitude towards dogma could flourish. 'There was never anything by men so well devised, or so surely established,' wrote Archbishop Cranmer, 'which in age and continuance of time hath not been corrupted.' After the Reformation, the English-speaking world would always tolerate, even welcome, conflicts, tensions and uncertainty. Its language would do the same.

As soon as Henry began to flex his royal muscles as the supreme head of Church and State, all kinds of unintended consequences flowed from this act of defiance. The king now found himself showing a new interest in lecturing his clergy. He told one astonished church assembly that he was even minded to take a hand in an English translation of the Bible. By 1530 notions of royal supremacy had become so advanced that he could declare that he was the chief of all 'spiritual men' in the kingdom. This aggressive superiority was echoed in the repeated assertion of England as more than a 'realm', in fact as an 'empire'. The new buzzword in the king's discourse became 'imperial'. There were plenty of European empires it was inadvisable to fight, but from this 'imperial' position it was a short step to launching an assault on a rival local empire, the English Church. This was an organization so unfeasibly rich, worldly and all-powerful through its place in Christendom that a strong-willed king like Henry could easily pick a fight with it.

Some men, notably Thomas More and Bishop John Fisher, held out against the king's Act of Supremacy, and paid with their lives, but in May 1532 the majority of the Church capitulated and 'the Church of England' became established by law. This vital step in the development of a more crusading English identity marked the beginning of the English Reformation, but it was not yet a Protestant revolution. The monasteries were still intact, mass was still celebrated, and – never mind those Lollard translations – passages from the Bible were still intoned in Latin. When Henry's new queen Anne was crowned in Westminster Abbey by the new archbishop of Canterbury Thomas Cranmer, the ritual was conducted in Latin, though the instincts of the men involved, Henry, Cranmer and the new chancellor Thomas Cromwell, were all for a radical assertion of Englishness. The emblem of this instinct was the so-called Great Bible 'in Englyssh', commissioned by Cromwell, and eventually published in 1539. The preface to the second edition of this landmark volume clearly stated its democratic intention. It was expressly 'for all manner of persons, men, women, young, old, rich, poor . . . and all manner of persons of whatever estate and condition'.

3

The Great Bible marked the coda to five tumultuous years in the making of England. At first, driven forward by the wily Cromwell, Henry had embarked on a crusade against the forces of conservatism in the legislative and pagan frenzy known as the Dissolution of the Monasteries, following an Act of 1536 to this effect. The assault on these cloistered communities was motivated by the need to finance England's conflict with Roman Catholic Europe and the pope: church coffers were groaning with centuries of accumulated wealth. In the process, some 15,000 monks and nuns and an entire way of life, based on Latin, were swept away, to the great advantage of the vernacular.

In the north of the country there was widespread resistance, culminating in the Pilgrimage of Grace, led by Robert Aske under the banner of the Five Wounds. By great good fortune, the king never had to fight his people, or even meet the rebels, as Richard II had done. In the end, they turned out to be loyal to the old Church *and* the old king. While popular upheavals threatened the king's composure in the provinces, in London and at court, the annihilation of the queen's party and the queen herself was remorselessly driven forward by Cromwell, who, in May 1536, secured her execution.

During these tumultuous years, the stuff of English legend, Thomas Cromwell also masterminded a campaign to make the English Bible central to everyday English life. Patriotism and Scripture were thus fused together and Rome became xenophobically demonized as the home of the enemy. In 1538, another radical injunction, outlawing the veneration of holy relics as a mark of popery, ordered an English Bible to be placed in every English parish church. But the more the evangelicals pressed forward to purge the state of Roman influence, the more they divided among themselves. Cromwell fell (and was executed) in 1540. Already a counter-attack had begun, the beginning of a century-long feud between Protestant (English) and Catholic (European) expressions of the faith.

Once the king had given his approval, English bibles became an accepted mode of radical self-expression. The word of God was not yet literature (that would come with the King James Bible, the Authorized Version), but it was now linked to libertarian assertions of social renewal. The year after the Dissolution of the Monasteries, Tyndale's disciple Coverdale published his vernacular translation of the Bible. From 1535 to 1568 no fewer than five major new versions were published – Matthew's, Taverner's, Cranmer's (the Great Bible), the Geneva and the Bishop's Bible – and became the most widely read texts of the sixteenth century, with a huge influence on the dissemination of English. These resounding popular texts created a new imaginative world in which the deepest things of human existence were put into everyday English speech, a liberation of mind as much as of language. In the words of the scholar Stephen Greenblatt, 'Without the great English translation of the New Testament and the sonorous, deeply resonant Book of Common Prayer, it is difficult to imagine William Shakespeare.'

4

There are some great conjunctions of place and personality – Athens in the fifth century BC, Philadelphia in the 1770s, St Petersburg in 1917 – that defy analysis, and leave us awestruck. London in the 1590s has long been recognized as one of these. Elizabeth I, daughter of Anne Boleyn, had finally succeeded to the throne in 1558, reigning for nearly half a century as 'the Virgin Queen'. About one hundred and fifty years after her death, Samuel Johnson was one of the first to rhapsodize about the creative glories of the reign. 'From the authors which rose in the time of Elizabeth,' he wrote, 'a speech might be formed adequate to all purposes of use and elegance.' Then, having listed the translation of the Bible, the works of Francis Bacon, Sir Walter Ralegh, Edmund Spenser and Sir Philip Sidney, and finally 'the diction of common life from Shakespeare', Johnson concluded that 'few ideas would be lost to mankind, for want of English words in which they might be expressed'. Some 500 years after the Norman Conquest, all the threads of a polymorphous culture had become woven together into a new tapestry of unequalled artistic splendour and one, moreover, that was largely confined to London, a world capital that has always projected a strange kind of intimacy.

This sense of rare cultural community was intensified by the revolution in grammar school education and book production achieved under the Tudors. Shakespeare's was an age in which, among the privileged, the book was now a familiar item of everyday use. Between 1558 and 1579, there were 3,850 new books published in London. This increased dramatically to 7,430 between 1580 and 1603, the years of Shakespeare's debut. John Guy has calculated that, in a population of about 4 million, there were perhaps two books per head of population in the course of a generation. It was part of Shakespeare's good fortune to be writing for an audience that was insatiably hungry for the printed word.

In 1599, the *annus mirabilis* in which Shakespeare, aged thirty-five, completed *Henry the Fifth*, wrote *As You Like It* and *Julius Caesar* back to back, revised twenty Sonnets and began a first draft of *Hamlet*, London had a population of about 500,000. Here, as much as a third of the adult population expressed their appetite for new ideas and new language by going to the theatre approximately once a month. Perhaps it is no wonder that the playhouses attracted such a galaxy of literary talent, young meteors who blazed across the creative firmament in a decade of astonishing achievement. Writers will always gravitate towards the good money and the new audience. 'At some moment in the late 1580s,' Greenblatt writes in his biography, *Will in the World*, 'Shakespeare walked into a room – most likely in an inn in Shoreditch, Southwark, or the Bankside – and quite possibly found many of the leading writers drinking and eating together: Christopher Marlowe, Thomas Watson, Thomas Lodge, George Peele, Thomas Nashe, and Robert Greene.' This extraordinarily gifted group, writes Greenblatt, 'shared a combination of extreme marginality and arrogant snobbishness'.

At that moment, much the same could have been said of England and its language. Shakespeare's 'sceptred isle' was still a small nation, but one just beginning to find its international voice. Sir Philip Sidney, a true Elizabethan, at once a poet, courtier and soldier, observed: 'But for the uttering sweetly and properly the conceite of the minde ... which is the ende of thought ... English hath it equally with any other tongue in the world.' This was by no means a universal opinion. Francis Bacon, like many of his educated contemporaries, preferred to express his finest thoughts in Latin, and considered that English would 'play the bankrupts with the books'. To confer respectability on their upstart language, writers like Bacon and Thomas More ransacked the classical past to create new words: *habitual*, *catastrophe* and *thermometer*. More himself is said to have coined *absurdity*, *contradictory*, *exaggerate*, *indifference*, *monopoly* and *paradox*. Fierce cultural nationalists disparaged such neologisms as 'inkhorn terms', championed 'plainnesse' and attacked writers who 'serche out of some rotten Pamphlet four or fyve disused woords of antiquitee, therewith to darken the sence unto the reader'. Shakespeare himself wittily alludes to this debate in *Love's Labour's Lost* when Berowne finally declares his love for Rosaline, announcing that he will shun 'taffeta phrases, silken terms precise'. Instead, he says,

> My wooing mind shall be express'd
> In russet yeas and honest kersey noes.

In Shakespeare, then, the fusion of Latin, French and English is completed in a canon of plays and poems that puts the vernacular to work: 'Grace me no grace', protests the Duke of York in *Richard the Second*, 'and uncle me no uncle.' In plays like *King Lear* and *Cymbeline*, for example, Shakespeare takes the stories of Albion and reworks them into universal dramas. Luck and genius often go together: Shakespeare was born into an age that, in the words of the curate Nathaniel in *Love's Labour's Lost*, seemed to eat paper and drink ink. Just seven years after his death, a volume of Shakespeare's complete works – the First Folio – was published by two players, John Heminges and Henry Condell, who had known and acted with him since the 1590s. The Shakespeare legend begins with their preface: 'His mind and hand went together ... wee have scarse received from him a blot in his paper.' Recent scholarship has shown that Shakespeare was actually an inveterate reviser, but his story often gets repeated with hints of the miraculous. 'Others abide our question,' wrote Matthew Arnold, the Victorian poet, 'thou art free ... Out-topping knowledge.' Leaving aside some of the later bardolatry, the life of England's greatest writer still embodies a kind of quintessential Englishness.

5

Shakespeare was born and raised a provincial and an outsider, in Stratford-upon-Avon, the heart of old England, but far from the court or the university cloister. He never completely forgot his origins. Warwickshire words are scattered through his lines, like poppies in a wheatfield: *ballow*, a north Midlands word for a cudgel; *batlet*, a local term, used into the twentieth century, for the bat used to beat clothes in the wash; *gallow*, meaning to frighten; *geck*, a word for a fool; *mobled* for muffled; and *vails*, a Midlands term for perks or tips. When, in *Macbeth*, Banquo is described as 'blood bolter'd' (having his hair matted with blood), it is not difficult to imagine Shakespeare remembering that in Warwickshire snow is sometimes said to *balter* on horses' feet.

His mother, Mary, was an Arden, one of Warwickshire's most distinguished families, with ancestry stretching back to the Domesday Book. His father, John, who had married well, was in the leather goods and wool trade, and a prominent figure in the town, though often on the wrong side of Church and civil law. Imagery drawn from the leather business and from the countryside is found in all Shakespeare's plays, sometimes with a literary topspin. 'Is not parchment made of sheepskins?' asks Hamlet. 'Ay, my lord,' answers Horatio, 'and of calf skins too.' In *Twelfth Night*, Feste signals the treacheries of everyday speech, joking that 'A sentence is but a cheverel glove to a good wit, how quickly the wrong side may be turned outward.' When, in *A Midsummer Night's Dream*, Puck reports to Oberon on the 'translation' of Bottom the weaver into an ass, Shakespeare draws on his countryside experience:

> As wild geese that the creeping fowler eye,
> Or russet-pated choughs, many in sort,
> Rising and cawing at the gun's report,
> Sever themselves, and madly sweep the sky;

Like the English language in which he revelled, Shakespeare was a literary magpie, and, to borrow his own description of Autolycus in *The Winter's Tale*, a 'snapper-up of unconsidered trifles'. Not everyone admired the young poet's astounding ability to invest borrowed literary material with dazzling new meaning. To his bitterly envious contemporary Robert Greene, on his deathbed, he was 'an upstart Crow, beautified with our feathers...in his own conceit the only

Shake-scene in the country'. At the turn of the seventeenth century, the English language was similarly 'beautified' with the 'feathers' of almost every European cultural tradition, as well as its own. It was, as George Steiner has written, one of those moments in western history when it was possible 'to enclose in poetic speech a total view of human action, a *summa mundi*'. Also at work in the equation is Shakespeare's genius, his gift for language. 'To Shakespeare,' writes Steiner, 'more than any other poet, the individual word was a nucleus surrounded by a field of complex energies.'

Shakespeare was a master of artistic synthesis. He never found any difficulty in combining his experience with an extraordinary range of European literary material. In the alchemy of his imagination, Stratford, the home of his youth and retirement, lurks behind the façades of his Verona, Syracuse or Padua, just as the 'citizens' of his Vienna, Rome or Athens seem to have stepped straight out of Cheapside or Southwark. It was in London, during the last decade of the sixteenth century and the first decade of the seventeenth, that the actor-playwright from the sticks secured his national reputation as a writer who could do what he wanted with English, marrying Anglo-Saxon, Anglo-Norman and classical traditions in a weave of poetry and storytelling that thrilled and entranced the audience at the Globe. *Macbeth*, written in 1605–6 at the height of his powers, is a showcase of Shakespeare's mastery, and some striking new words, notably *assassination*. Macbeth's lament after the murder of Duncan is a brilliant distillation of several centuries' culture:

> Will all great Neptune's ocean wash this blood
> Clean from my hand? No; this my hand will rather
> The multitudinous seas incarnadine,
> Making the green one red.

This famous speech is the work of a writer with an eye for an audience that is simultaneously after both high and low culture. Having flattered the classically educated men of substance sitting at the side of the stage, or in the twopenny seats, with a scintillating Latinate phrase ('The multitudinous seas incarnadine'), Shakespeare repeats it

in good, plain old English ('Making the green one red') for the benefit of the groundlings crammed into the pit. 'Multitudinous' will also
be a reminder to his readers that he's a magician of language with one
of the largest vocabularies – some 30,000 words – of any English
writer. Associated with innovation, he also coined several common-
or-garden words in everyday use: *amazement*, *gloomy* and *equivocal*, for
instance. Additionally, *antipathy*, *critical*, *demonstrate*, *emphasis*, *horrid*,
modest, *prodigious* and *vast* are all new to English in the sixteenth century, and they all make an early appearance in Shakespeare's work.

Some of his best lines continue to inspire extraordinary devotion.
In *I Married a Communist*, Philip Roth has a memorable riff on the
clown Feste's bitter comment to Malvolio, 'thus the whirligig of
time brings in his revenges':

Those cryptogrammic *g*'s, the subtlety of their deintensification – those
hard *g*'s in 'whirligig' followed by the nasalized *g* of 'brings' followed by the
soft *g* of 'revenges'. The hissing surprise of the plural noun 'revenges'.
Guhh. Juhh. Zuhh. Consonants sticking into me like needles. And the pul-
sating vowels, the rising tide of their pitch ... The low-pitched vowels giving way to the high-pitched vowels ... The assertive lengthening of the
vowel *i* just before the rhythm shifts from iambic to trochaic and the prose
pounds round the turn for the stretch. Short *i*, short *i*, long *i*. Short *i*, short *i*,
short *i*, boom ! Revenges...

Words and phrases from Shakespeare's plays have become seeded into
the titles of countless novels and films from *Brave New World* (Aldous
Huxley) and *The Sound and the Fury* (William Faulkner) to *The
Glimpses of the Moon* (Edith Wharton) and *The Dogs of War* (Frederick
Forsyth). His plots inspire adaptations and spin-offs, and his unforgettable phrase-making recurs on the lips of millions who do not
realize they are quoting Shakespeare: 'a fool's paradise'; 'the game is
up'; 'dead as a doornail'; 'more in sorrow than anger'; and 'cruel,
only to be kind', for example. His plays have been an inspiration to
composers, painters, sculptors, poets, novelists and film-makers. It's
nice to note that the motto of Shakespeare's theatre, the Globe, was
'Totus mundus agit histrionem' ('The whole world is a playhouse'),

while Hamlet, Macbeth, Lear, Shylock, Portia, Romeo and Juliet are universal figures. The plays from which they spring, many rooted in ancient English myths, have become archetypal stories. More than Dante for the Italians, Goethe for the Germans or Pushkin for Russia, Shakespeare remains an icon for English-speaking peoples throughout the world and, as Marjorie Gerber argues in *Shakespeare and Modern Culture*, remorselessly influential.

Shakespeare and his work often crops up in the New World, but never so memorably as in Mark Twain's *Adventures of Huckleberry Finn*. The scene in which 'the King of France' and 'the rightful duke of Bridgewater', impostors both, rehearse their 'Shakespeare Revival' is one of Twain's finest, beginning with a discussion of *Hamlet*, initiated by the 'duke':

'Oh, I've got it – you can do Hamlet's soliloquy.'

'Hamlet's which?'

'Hamlet's soliloquy, you know; the most celebrated thing in Shakespeare. Ah, it's sublime, sublime! Always fetches the house. I haven't got it in the book – I've only got one volume – but I reckon I can piece it out from memory. I'll just walk up and down a minute, and see if I can call it back from recollection's vaults.'

Eventually, having struck 'a most noble attitude' and 'frowning horrible every now and then', the 'duke' performs it in a way, relates Huck, that 'just knocked the spots out of any acting I ever see before.' Twain has tremendous fun with the material, beginning the 'duke's' speech from *Hamlet* as follows: 'To be or not to be; that is the bare bodkin . . .'

6

In the world's English, only the King James Bible is as universal and as influential as Shakespeare. It is, indeed, impossible to imagine the English-speaking world without the glittering majesty of its most sonorous passages, the austere beauty of its prose, and the endlessly quoted phrases and sentences that have become braided into the texture of contemporary reference. Amazingly, this 'Authorized Version' of 1611, the year Shakespeare completed *The Winter's Tale*, was written by a committee.

Early in his reign, the Hampton Court Conference (1604), chaired by Elizabeth's successor, King James I, decided that the increasingly bitter doctrinal friction between Anglicans and Puritans should be soothed by 'one uniforme translation'. In an act of entrepreneurial collaboration typical of the age, six translating teams were instructed to base their 'Authorized' versions upon previous English editions, translating afresh, but also comparing their work with the other vernacular Bibles, from Tyndale to Parker. In the final stages of its work, this committee would go through the drafts of the translation, reworking it so that it would not only read better, but sound better, the quality for which it is world famous. The translators relished this instruction. In their preface 'to the Reader' they remarked, 'Why should we be in bondage to them [words and syllables] if we may be free, use one precisely when we may use another no less fit, as commodiously?' Such was the versatility of English society and its language at the beginning of the seventeenth century that the majesty of the 'Authorized Version' could spring from the quills not of a single writer, a Marlowe or a Shakespeare, but a team. In some famous passages, these humble translators were touched with genius:

In the beginning was the Word, and the Word was with God, and the Word was God. The same was in the beginning with God. All things were made by him; and without him was not any thing made that was made. In him was life; and the life was the light of men. And the light shineth in darkness; and the darkness comprehended it not.

Again, equally memorable:

To every thing there is a season, and a time to every purpose under the heaven: a time to be born, and a time to die; a time to plant, and a time to pluck up that which is planted; a time to kill, and a time to heal; a time to break down, and a time to build up...

The King James Bible was, as Adam Nicolson has written, 'England's equivalent of the great baroque cathedral it never built, an enormous and magnificent verbal artifice, its huge structures embracing all four million Englishmen, its orderliness and richness a kind of national shrine built only of words'. Some of these words have proved more durable than many fashions. For instance, this famous passage from the twelfth chapter of Ecclesiastes:

Or ever the silver cord be loosed, or the golden bowl be broken, or the pitcher be broken at the fountain, or the wheel broken at the cistern: then shall the dust return to the earth as it was: and the spirit shall return unto God who gave it. Vanity of vanities, saith the preacher; all is vanity.

The afterlife of this landmark publication is nowhere stranger than in the 'new-found-land' of America. The first New England settlements always championed the use of the Geneva Bible, a text that appealed particularly to Nonconformist and separatist congregations. By a remarkable paradox, as Nicolson observes, 'by the end of the seventeenth century, the King James Bible came to be treasured as much by Americans as by the British'. Perhaps this is hardly surprising: America would be a country constructed out of words, almost all of them English.

The one hundred and fifty years that preceded the Revolutionary War of the 1770s would see the transplanting of a language and its culture to a new, and often hostile, environment in which, against the odds, it would develop and flourish in accordance with the wholly new circumstances of the New World. Crucially for the future, this unique process would dramatically increase its global range and influence. This was the moment at which the English founders of the language gave way to the American pioneers.

PART TWO

Pioneers

5. 'A Whole Country of English'

Reinventing Freedom and Originality

If you want to live intelligently beyond the blackmail of the slogans and the unexamined rules, you have only to find your own . . . The Declaration of Independence. The Bill of Rights. The Gettysburg Address. The Emancipation Proclamation. The Fourteenth Amendment.

Philip Roth, *The Dying Animal*

1

Years after the American Revolution had passed into history, one of its principals, John Adams, a chubby Boston lawyer who later became the second President of the United States, recalled the rising tide of pre-revolutionary sentiment in the thirteen colonies. In a letter to Benjamin Rush, his friend and co-revolutionary, Adams described how, in 1774, during the run-up to the break with Britain, he stopped one winter's night in a roadside tavern some 40 miles from Boston. Adams's story offers a paradigm.

As I was cold and wet, [writes Adams] I sat down at a good fire to dry my greatcoat and saddlebags. There presently came in half a score substantial yeomen of the neighborhood who began a lively conversation upon politics. One said, 'The people of Boston are distracted.' Another answered, 'No wonder the people of Boston are distracted; oppression makes wise men mad.' A third said, 'What would you say, if a fellow should come to your house and tell you he was come to take a list of your cattle that Parliament might tax you for them?' 'What would I say?', replied the first, 'I would knock him on the head.' After much more reasoning in this style, [another] who had as yet been silent, broke out, 'Well, it is high time for us to rebel. We must rebel sometime or other: and we had better rebel now than at any time to come . . .'

In microcosm, this example of the world's English in its infancy contains three elements of great future significance. First, and most obvious, all the participants are conducting their debate, some 3,000 miles from London, in American English, a common language of which they are inordinately proud, as we shall see. Secondly, their frame of political reference is exclusively English, linking oppression, taxation and Parliament. When these elements are fused they will make a third, instinctually eloquent, anti-authoritarian and demo-cratic. But that is not the whole story. Although the conversation that Adams overheard contains a set of allusions to the dissenting origins of the thirteen colonies, in the beginning there was more than just dissent involved, though that provided some of the intellectual gristle. There was trade and exploration at stake, too. To put it another way: there was adventure, glory and the quest for fabulous new riches, possibly the sort that grows on trees.

2

Long before the Revolution, during the momentous decade 1600–1610, and the transition from Elizabethan to Jacobean England, London was buzzing with stories about the opportunities in the New World. One of John Donne's most celebrated poems compares the explor-ation of his mistress's body to an American voyage:

> And sailing towards her India, in that way
> Shall at her fair Atlantick Navell stay . . .

'O my America!' exclaims the poet, 'my new-found-land'. American dreams filled the imaginations of many ambitious young men; the young Donne applied unsuccessfully for a secretarial job in Virginia.

Everyone was looking across the Atlantic. In 1605 Ben Jonson col-laborated on a play, *Eastward Ho!*, in which Seagull, a sea captain, tantalizes a would-be emigrant, Spendall, with news from Virginia: 'A whole country of English is there, man. I tell thee, gold is more plentiful than copper is with us . . . they have married with the Indians who are so in love with them that all the treasure they have lay at their feet . . . Why man, all their dripping pans and their chamber pots are pure gold, and for rubies and diamonds, they go forth on holidays and gather 'em by the sea shore . . .' Finally, says Seagull, echoing Jack Cade: 'You shall live freely there, without sergeants, or courtiers, or lawyers.' That same year, inspired by similarly tempting promotions, three ships crossed the Atlantic, cruised in the West Indies and then headed up the east coast, intending to settle somewhere north of the Spanish in Florida, and south of the French in Canada.

In April 1607 these pioneers sailed into Chesapeake Bay. After about a month they reached the James river, where they moored in six fathoms off a wooded island which they named after the new king: Jamestown. Possibly thanks to the leadership and determination of Captain John Smith, who pronounced the stark but simple truth, 'He who will not work neither shall he eat', the men of Jamestown survived, by the skin of their teeth, where previous expeditions had perished. In this way, the English established a bridgehead on the eastern seaboard; their language and culture would never be the same again.

Just before his death at the age of fifty-one, Captain Smith published *The True Travels, Adventures, and Observations of John Smith in Europe, Asia, Affrica* [sic] *and America*, a farrago of tall tales so egregious they inspired an immediate lampoon, 'The Legend of Captaine Jones', by a Welsh clergyman. Smith himself died broke, solitary and despised, back in London. His final essay, 'Advertisements for the unexperienced [*sic*] Planters of New England or any where', was full of advice about colonizing techniques: bring your wives; don't forget to plant corn, etc. Yet, in his quixotic way, Smith helped to sustain the romantic ideal of an American exile.

Two years after the Jamestown landing, another ship, the *Sea Venture*, sailing to supply these first Virginians, was wrecked on an island 500 miles due east of Charleston, South Carolina. This was the spot known to Shakespeare – who was inspired by the incident to write *The Tempest* – as 'the vex'd Bermoothes'. In 1612 this became Bermuda, the second English colony in the New World. Shortly after these perilous episodes of freebooting adventurism there was another emigration, further north, the settlement of New England in the Massachusetts Bay Colony.

The men and women who embarked for the New World on board the *Mayflower* in 1620 were a mixed bunch, driven by a tangle of idealistic, colonizing, self-interested and religious ambitions. The Pilgrim Fathers, a minority, went to America to escape, in Andrew Marvell's words, 'the prelate's rage'. They hoped to find an austere wilderness in which they could establish a kingdom of God on the Geneva model. Other puritans, men like John Winthrop, were prompted by the more commercial considerations that had galvanized the first Virginians. The literary critic Philip Rahv has wittily characterized the Virginians and Bostonians, respectively, as 'redskins' and 'palefaces'. Whatever their motivation – profit or redemption – both groups were inspired by the appeal of exploring a new frontier, and the dream of a fresh start. In the long term, America would massively extend the range and expression of English; in the short term, the New World gave it a shot in the arm. To the north, French traders and fur-trappers contributed to the linguistic rainbow that would culminate in modern Canada, one of the most culturally innovative societies in the world and, potentially, a key player in the development of Globish.

Words have always been the key to North America. In the United States, Barack Obama was propelled into the presidency as much by the power of his rhetoric as by his programme; and word of mouth passed on his message. America remains a society which continues to find its identity in language, and which now projects itself, globally, through the world's English. Obama's campaign slogan 'Change We Can Believe In' was a phrase that resonated with a global audience. By chance, the Pilgrim Fathers included a prose writer of rare talent, who could capture the American adventure in a style that could be passed down through the generations. William Bradford, the historian of the *Mayflower*, was also the first governor of the Plymouth colony. Bradford translated his experiences into the first great document of American English, *The Historie of Plimouth Plantation*, in which he described the settlers' situation that first winter on Cape Cod: 'Being thus passed the vast ocean, and a sea of troubles, they had now no friends to welcome them, nor inns to entertain or refresh their weatherbeaten bodies; it was muttered by some that if they got not a place in time, they would turn them and their goods ashore...' To this outbreak of defeatism, the stoic Bradford utters a resonant challenge. 'But may not and ought not the children of these fathers rightly say – Our Fathers were Englishmen...'

Astonishingly, some of the native Americans encountered by Bradford and his fellows in this bleak landfall were not perhaps as foreign as might have been anticipated. Some, indeed, were already speaking 'broken English'. An explanation for this linguistic miracle, later repeated in English colonies across the world, was soon forthcoming. 'At length,' Bradford continues, 'they understood by discourse with [one native], that he was not of these parts, but belonged to the eastern parts where some English ships came to fish, with whom he was acquainted and amongst whom he had got his language.' Next to conquest, the explanation for the precocious spread of English, Spanish and French in North America lies in trade. Merchant ships plying the eastern seaboard between tiny English settlements like Jamestown (and Charleston), together with the traffic of the first black slaves (who actually arrived the year before the *Mayflower*), helped to scatter seeds of English, Spanish and French among the native American tribes.

Appropriately, the first recording of English in New England was pidgin, which the settlers rendered as follows: 'Umh, umh, me no strawmere fight Engis mon. Engis mon got two hed... If me cut off one hed, he got nodon...' Some of the first American colonists, for example William Penn, founder of Pennsylvania, had a great admiration for the tribal languages they encountered. 'I know not a language,' wrote Penn, 'spoken in Europe, that hath words of more sweetness and greatness, in *Accent* and *Emphasis*, than theirs.' Everyday English vocabulary became enriched with so-called 'wigwam' words: for instance, *pow wow*, *totem*, *papoose*, *moccasin*, *squaw* and *tomahawk*. These borrowings were inspired by the novelty of inventing an American way of life. 'New circumstances', Thomas Jefferson would write later, 'call for new words, new phrases, and the transfer of old words to new objects.' From a twenty-first-century perspective, the novelty of American English is also mixed with a distinctly archaic flavour, derived from its seventeenth-century beginnings. Among many language fossils, Americans use *mad* for 'angry', as Shakespeare did; *platter* for 'dish'; and *fall* for 'autumn'. The typically American use of 'I guess' goes further back, to Chaucer. If you can hardly construct the simplest sentence without words of Anglo-Saxon origin: 'is', 'I', 'man', 'drink' or 'house', equally you can hardly convey the force and direction of such a sentence without 'okay', 'yeah', or 'get' and 'go'.

3

The English settlement of North America, which began with advertising and ended with a written constitution, was part of a much wider global movement that witnessed the expansion of the first British empire. In this new theatre, the old European rivalries persisted, often as violently as before. It was trade and conflict with Spanish, French, Dutch and even German settlers that contributed to the unique flavour of American English, words like *stampede*, *crevasse*, *spook*, *yankee* and *hoodlum*. Competition with the French stimulated the opening up of two great rivers, the St Lawrence to the north and the Mississippi in the Midwest. Conflict on these redneck frontiers would eventually boil over into almost continuous warfare throughout the eighteenth century. For the English, the east coast was the prize possession. Immigration to New England boomed: some 20,000 colonists between 1620 and 1643. Between the easygoing capitalism of Virginia and the pasty-faced austerity of puritan Massachusetts, there was a chain of middle colonies – New York, Rhode Island, Pennsylvania, Maryland, Delaware and North Carolina – which quickly developed flexible egalitarian communities where ordinary men and women, new Americans, could go about their everyday life untroubled by bishop or king.

America's reinvention of freedom still had its paradoxes. In Maryland, for example, it was actually the first Lord Baltimore who established an English colony with religious toleration. This new society put into practice some of the ideas that English libertarians had been debating for centuries: the abolition of primogeniture, the custom of electing, not appointing, state officials, and the practice of debating local issues in 'town meetings'. For these people the English Civil War (1642–9) and the subsequent Commonwealth (1649–60) were a double blessing: the overthrow of King Charles and the Royalists held up the example of a society free from rank and class, and also gave currency to radical ideas.

In the Putney Debates of 1647, for example, one of the most extraordinary political discussions in English history took place. This forum for the discussion of fundamental democratic principles threw up an exchange of ideas about freedom and equality that inspired centuries of libertarian discussion. At first, when two puritans discussed the idea of universal suffrage, their language reflected the received wisdom of the people's struggle as it had been expressed since Norman times:

Cowling: Since the Conquest, the greatest part of the kingdom was in vassalage.

Petty: We judge that all inhabitants that have not lost their birthright should have an equal voice in elections.

To this, a man named Rainborowe responded with a famous opinion:

For really I think that the poorest he that is in England hath a life to live, as the greatest he; and therefore truly, sir, I think it's clear that every man that is to live under a government ought first by his own consent put himself under that government.

The influence of the Levellers who met in Putney continues to reverberate through English political theory and these debates remain a touchstone of libertarian discussion.

As well as reinforcing the honourable tradition of political dissent, establishing the Commonwealth also distracted the English government from colonial interference. By the time Cromwell was dead and the monarchy had been restored, the American colonies had begun to outgrow the society from which they had sprung, and to develop ideas about the just society that reached back to Wat Tyler and beyond. After 1660 it was the law that would become central to

American life, and it was the law to which Americans would turn to regulate their society. By one of the many ironies in this story, the best wisdom on constitutional reform came, not from the thirteen colonies, but from London, in the work of a government official employed in colonial affairs, the English philosopher John Locke. Not the least of America's appeal to such a would-be social engineer was its status as a tabula rasa, a blank canvas on which the enquiring mind could project bold, new and experimental ideas.

Locke, a man of retiring disposition and profoundly influential opinions, was born to a West Country puritan family in 1632. After studying medicine at Oxford, he became secretary to the Board of Trade and Plantations thanks to Anthony Ashley Cooper, the first earl of Shaftesbury, his powerful patron. English, culture as much as language, is full of contradictions. The liberal pioneer of 'consciousness and the self' who invested in the slave trade is also the author of *Two Treatises on Civil Government* (1689) and *An Essay Concerning Human Understanding* (1690) and the 'philosopher of freedom' who first argued for 'the separation of powers'. Locke believed that man is, by nature, both reasonable and tolerant. Crucially, he was an English thinker who taught both that the purpose of government was the preservation of liberty and property and also that, in some circumstances, revolution against an absolute ruler is at once a right *and* an obligation.

On Locke's death in 1704 a colonial rejection of crown authority was still unthinkable, and the strongest link between Britain and America, after language, was the inheritance of English common law. However, with the passage of time the settlers' experience of the New World was making America separate, distinctive and proud. Symbolic of this mood was a new breed of American patriot for whom the imperious Britannia of James Thomson's masque *Alfred* seemed increasingly dictatorial, oppressive and at odds with their core beliefs and values. A single decade from the mid-1730s saw the birth of many men who would be the main players in the forthcoming Revolution: George Washington (1732), John Adams (1735), Patrick 'Give me liberty or give me death' Henry (1736), John Hancock (1737), Samuel Chase (1741), John Penn (1741) and, finally, Thomas Jefferson (1743).

The vigour and originality of this generation was an American phenomenon. But this thriving new society was also symptomatic of Britain's global ambitions, by land and sea. Eventually, this would collide with American nationalism, but in the short term, as British possessions, the thirteen colonies would be swept up in the century-long struggle with France that culminated in the Seven Years War (1756–63). Britain's victories in the most brutal war of the eighteenth century not only enlarged its empire but also invigorated the colonial economy and strengthened American nationalism. Thus, when it seemed logical to the government in Westminster to meet the cost of empire by raising additional revenue and passing the Stamp Act (1765) the American colonists protested vehemently. Appropriately for a society that had always defined itself through words, the crisis that had been brewing for so long began with a furious argument about a tax on documents.

James Otis of Massachusetts, coining a new expression, declared that 'taxation without representation is tyranny'. Nine colonies drew up a Declaration of Rights and Grievances (1765), which sponsored a succession of anti-British agitations. In 1768 the state of Massachusetts compiled a new list of 'grievances' against the British government, to which Westminster responded by dispatching two infantry regiments to Boston. The following year Virginia formally rejected Britain's right to tax the colonies. The revolutionary 1770s began with the 'Boston Massacre' and the 'battle of Golden Hill' in New York, a riot provoked by the attempts of the local British militia to remove a 'liberty pole'. In 1773 another riot, against the importation of cheap tea, became the 'Boston Tea Party'. Britain was now at war throughout New England. With many misgivings, all the colonies rallied in support of Massachusetts. The next year, 1774, the first American Congress met in Philadelphia. American nationalism was building from a mood of sullen opposition to colonial rule towards a convulsion of revolutionary fury.

If there was to be a storm, there first had to be a lightning strike. This necessary explosion was ignited by a little book, attributed to an unnamed 'Englishman', and published by Robert Bell from a print shop on Third Street, Philadelphia, on 9 January 1776. The book was

Common Sense, the bestselling American pamphlet of the eighteenth century. In no time at all there were more than 120,000 copies in circulation, some twenty-five editions in 1776 alone, and its ideas were the talk of the eastern seaboard. 'Who is the author of *Common Sense*?' asked the *Philadelphia Evening Post*. 'He deserves a statue in gold.'

Thomas Paine, soon unmasked as the author of this sensational pamphlet, is one of the founding fathers of the world's English, a man of libertarian rhetoric and mercenary polemical instincts. Paine made his name by out-Englishing the English: exaggerating the most distinctive of English traits, and selling it as a basis for revolt. When he had first landed in Philadelphia, in 1775, more dead than alive from a transatlantic crossing, Paine was a down-on-his-luck English immigrant, a former maker of ladies' corsets, with nothing in his pocket besides a letter of introduction from Benjamin Franklin. Hunger concentrates a man's mind. He had written *Common Sense* (the title came from another revolutionary, Benjamin Rush) in a few hectic weeks. Rarely has a single volume achieved such an instantaneous effect, possibly because it was published on the same day George III pledged in Parliament to put 'a speedy End to these disorders'.

Common Sense is a model of popular journalistic brio, written to be understood by all readers, high and low. George III was singled out as the 'royal brute' responsible for all the ills of America. Nailing his colours, Paine then took the logical step of calling for war, and calling for independence. 'Why is it that we hesitate?' he asked. 'The sun never shined on a cause of greater worth... For God's sake, let us come to a final separation... The blood of the slain, the weeping voice of nature cries, "'TIS TIME TO PART"'... The birthday of a new world is at hand.' Not for the last time in this story, a few well-turned phrases and an eye for vivid expression transformed a previously leaden debate into pure gold.

By the spring of 1776 the delegates to the Congress began to gather in Philadelphia with only one burning question on their minds: to separate, or not to separate? At the start of May their revolutionary deliberations were interrupted by the sound of cannon fire from the Delaware river: two British ships trying to break through the blockade and attack the city. War, which had already touched the people of Boston and New York, had finally come to the city of brotherly love. With a fine sense of timing, the next day, 10 May, John Adams proposed a resolution that the individual colonies should assume the powers of government, 'to secure the happiness and safety of their constituents'. It passed unanimously. The way to full independence was clear.

Adams told Jefferson: 'You can write ten times better than I can.' So Jefferson would draft the declaration, a monument to English in the Age of Reason, and an advertisement for America's grand ambitions as an independent world power: 'We hold these truths to be self-evident: that all men are created equal; that they are endowed by their Creator with certain unalienable rights, that among these are life, liberty and the pursuit of happiness...' Jefferson, another founding father of the world's English, intended his words, he wrote later, to be 'an expression of the American mind'. His intention was simple: to place his people, the Americans, 'among the Powers of the Earth'. In fact, he achieved his goal in a quite unexpected way: after 1776 his words would give revolutionary movements from Paris to Havana an English-language blueprint for populist revolt. Signed on 2 (not 4) July, the Declaration was celebrated as soon as the news came through. In New York, it was read out to Washington's troops, who went on the rampage; that same night a large crowd toppled an equestrian statue of George III. Back in London, the American news was greeted with panic, consternation and dismay. Jefferson understood that political independence not only reflected more profound differences between Britain and America but would also inspire new forms of self-expression. 'Judicious neology', he wrote, 'can alone give strength and copiousness to language, and enable it to be the vehicle of new ideas.'

After the victory of ideas, there came the almost unthinkable spectacle of victory in the field. On the morning of 17 October 1781 a single British officer, following a ragged boy and waving a white handkerchief, stepped out from the smoke of battle, amid the roar of American cannon, to sue for peace. When the negotiations with General Washington were complete so was Britain's national humiliation. The 7,000 men of the British army became prisoners of war, marching into captivity with furled regimental colours between the silent columns of their threadbare revolutionary enemy, who lined the road out of Yorktown. The British general, Lord Cornwallis, could not face such a shameful scene and skulked behind in his shattered headquarters. His men, many of them drunk on cheap rum, marched into oblivion behind Negro drummers beating a slow march. Some of the defeated British officers wept. The band played a melancholy traditional air, 'The World Turned Upside Down'. It was the end of the first British empire.

Finally, there was the United States Constitution, ratified on 17 September 1787. Tom Paine had already galvanized American imaginations with *Common Sense* and *The Rights of Man*. 'We have it within our power', he wrote, 'to start the world over again.' The Constitution reinvented the idea of popular liberty, but it was less a radically original document, more a triumph of synthesis expressed in American English. It was not the first national document to guarantee the rights of citizens, and it also drew on British legal and political theory, French Enlightenment ideas and the western intellectual tradition from ancient Greece to eighteenth-century Poland. It did not tackle slavery, denied women the vote and could not prevent civil war. Despite this, the Constitution, rooted in the power of 'the people', not a king, was a text that founded a modern democratic republic and transformed world history. With its twenty-seven Amendments (to date), the Constitution of 1787 remains the everyday basis of American government, and the guarantee of the American citizen's expectation of 'life, liberty and the pursuit of happiness'. Next to Magna Carta, but far more explicitly than that fuzzy parchment, it remains the supreme national mission statement.

4

For Adams, Jefferson, Franklin and the other leaders of the American Revolution, American English was the proud badge of independence, a language with a future. In the tradition of Alfred the Great, Henry V and Elizabeth I, they understood the role of words, written and spoken, in shaping popular consciousness. 'English is destined', wrote Adams in 1780, 'to be in the next and succeeding centuries more generally the language of the world than Latin was in the last or French is in the present age.' The new Constitution inspired a new name. Appropriately, it was the brilliant propagandist Tom Paine who coined 'the United States of America', a name that stuck. This self-confidence inspired the Congress to resolve in 1778 that when the French foreign minister visited the new republic and its legislature all 'replies and answers' to him should be put 'in the language of the United States'.

America was already a polyglot society, but English was unavoidably the mother tongue. In 1790, when the first census was taken, 4 million Americans were counted, and 90 per cent were descendants of British colonists. But what kind of English? Hardly the English of the oppressor, 'the turgid style of Johnson, the purple glare of Gibbon', as Benjamin Rush put it. English should be 'improved and perfected', a familiar refrain. But how? In urgent consideration of this question, John Adams believed that a new kind of English could be exploited to advance the cause of America. During the coming century, he predicted in a prescient burst of patriotic pride, the 'American population will produce a greater number of peoples who will speak English than any other language'. The result of a United States Academy to promote American English as a public institution would be national glory. 'England will never have any more honor,' he wrote, 'excepting now and then imitating the Americans.' Others went further. Some zealous Americans proposed the introduction of Hebrew (the language of the Bible), or possibly Greek. This last suggestion was rejected on the grounds that 'it would be more convenient for us to keep the language as it was, and make the English speak Greek'.

The degree to which English in America had become a political issue is illustrated by a curious procession that took place through the streets of New York on 23 July 1788. The occasion was the ratification of the new Constitution. The demonstrators included all classes, professional men and labourers. In the procession, a group of young men, calling themselves the Philological Society, carried through the streets a book inscribed *Federal Language*. The coat of arms they carried emphasized the strong desire of many Americans to break with British English and its Augustan traditions: 'Argent three tongues, gules, in chief; emblematic of *language*, the improvement of which is the object of the institution. An *eye*, emblematic of *discernment*, over a pyramid, sculptured with Gothic, Hebrew and Greek letters. The Gothic on the *light* side, indicating the *obvious* origin of the American language from the Gothic...' The words are Noah Webster's.

The most famous of all America's dictionary-makers and a lifelong, even obsessive, champion of American English, Noah Webster is as influential in the making of the world's English as William Caxton. From his *Dissertations on the English Language* of 1789 to his great monument of 1828, *An American Dictionary of the English Language*, universally known simply as *Webster's*, his work is a landmark. The future lexicographer was born in Hartford, Connecticut, and trained as a lawyer. Like many American revolutionaries, he turned from law to teaching as a means of making his living in hard times. It was an inspired career change. When Britain was at war with her colonies, America's schoolbooks, imported from London, were in short supply. So, in the gung-ho spirit of the New World, he set about filling the gap in the market. Between 1783 and 1785, still in his twenties, Webster published three elementary books on English – a speller, a grammar and a reader – to which he attached the grandiose title *A Grammatical Institute of the English Language*.

But it was the 'blue-backed' *American Speller* that turned out to be the runaway bestseller, 80 million copies in Webster's lifetime, second only to the Bible, with which it was often sold. The *American Speller* became central to the education of the rising generation. In the early days it was standard teaching practice to assemble all the pupils in class and have them read columns of the speller aloud in unison. 'The master gave the signal to begin, and all united to read, letter by letter,' one pupil recalled, 'pronouncing each syllable by itself, and adding to the preceding one till the word was complete. Thus a-d *ad*, m-i *mi*, *admi*, r-a *ra*, *admira*, t-i-o-n shun, *admiration*.' This inculcation of Standard American English was an early consequence of independence, and culturally for the American people every bit as important.

5

Noah Webster's was just one practical response to the challenge of independence. Throughout American society the idea of radical innovation was expressed in all manner of ways, both homespun and highflown. The mood of can-do enthusiasm reached up even as far as the great American critic, the 'Transcendentalist' Ralph Waldo Emerson, who, in his Phi Beta Kappa address of 1837 at Harvard University, defined the American way as a ceaseless quest for originality as well as for a liberation from the burden of the past, especially in its European manifestations. The American scholar, Emerson declared, 'plies the slow, unhonored, and unpaid task of observation...He is one who raises himself from private considerations, and breathes and lives on public and illustrious thoughts. He is the world's eye. He is the world's heart.' In a striking new rendering of that ancient English belief in self-expression, Emerson celebrated what he dubbed this new 'self-trust' in ringing periods: 'The people delight in it; the better part of every man feels, This is my music, this is myself. In self-trust, all the virtues are comprehended. Free should the scholar be – free and brave.'

Next to frontiers of the mind explored by adventurous intellectuals, there was the practical challenge of the West. If there was one place where men and women could articulate their quest for originality in their day-to-day lives it was on the ever-expanding American frontier. In the seventeenth century the West had begun just down the road. 'I did greatly fear for Abigail's safety,' wrote one Massachusetts father, having sent his daughter 15 miles to visit some relatives in another settlement, 'as she is gone into Duxbury. It is her first journey into the West, and I shall pray mightily for her early return.' In those early days the phrase 'gone west' was used to refer to the frontiersmen who went into Pennsylvania, Ohio and Illinois and disappeared. Before the Revolution, the West reached deep into the Appalachians. The way thither, scouted by an English doctor, one Thomas Walker, was a break in the hills that came to be known as the Cumberland Gap. Thousands of new Americans (many from Ulster and the Western Isles of Scotland) trekked along this Wilderness

Road, in the footsteps of pioneering legend Daniel Boone, and then, beyond those rolling hills, to the teeming north–south frontier of America's great rivers. By the time of the Revolution, the French were trading vigorously up and down these natural highways, selling fur, grain, molasses and whisky. Once the Revolutionary War was over, the traffic of the Missouri, the Illinois, the Wabash and the Ohio flooded into the mighty Mississippi, creating a mobile society whose energetic quest for originality moved the engine room of the United States from the east coast to the Midwest.

'Going west' became the latest expression for making a new start. It was only a matter of time before the white man (fur-trappers, houseless war veterans, cattle-rustlers and all the urban flotsam of the East with a taste for adventure) would encounter the native Americans. When in 1803 President Jefferson (as he had become) secretly contrived to acquire the vast state of Louisiana (recently ceded to Napoleon by the Spanish) in exchange for $16 million (the money needed by the emperor for his campaigns), the territory of the new United States increased by 140 per cent at the stroke of a pen. Never did Jefferson, an inveterate shopper, make a better bargain. The Mississippi, the river frontier of the New World, was about to enter its golden age. Typically, for a man with an enquiring mind, Jefferson had no sooner concluded the Louisiana Purchase than he commissioned an inventory of his latest acquisition, in an expedition that would become part of the American myth.

Meriwether Lewis, who had been Jefferson's private secretary, and his partner William Clark were both US officers in what was known as the Corps of Discovery. In 1804 they set out from St Louis. By the time they reached the shining waters of the Pacific in November 1805, after a gruelling trek, they had opened up the West and claimed it for the republic, setting the United States on a collision course with the native Americans, the Sioux, the Creeks and the Cheyennes. The eventual genocide was not inevitable: those first western explorers had considerable respect for North American Indians, giving them sincere assurances about their inalienable land rights and sacred tribal customs. The generation of men who followed Lewis and Clark was not so scrupulous. But, as Calvin Coolidge put it, the business of

America is business, and the Indians seemed to stand in the way of profit. In 1830 the cotton states of Mississippi, Alabama and Georgia banished the tribal kingdoms, and President Andrew Jackson, a life-long enemy of the American Indian, enacted a Bill that would drive all native American tribes west of the Mississippi. The Cherokee appealed to the Supreme Court, and were supported by the Chief Justice, but Jackson ordered in the army and the tribes fled west, beyond Oklahoma, with terrible losses.

Meanwhile, even more remote, in the far West, across the territory we know as Arizona, Nevada, Utah and California, decades of scrappy skirmishing between pioneering American traders and the Mexican army erupted into full-scale war in 1846. This vicious sideshow might have dragged on for some years, but in 1848 there was a new distraction, thought by some to be a 'Yankee invention' to reconcile west-erners to the creation of the state of California from land previously held by Mexico: the discovery of gold in the hills of northern California. This, finally, was the fulfilment of Captain Seagull's promises to the gullible Spendall. In the course of the next two generations, a succession of curious Britons, from Charles Dickens to Oscar Wilde, would head out west to see for themselves exactly what it might amount to. The Irishman drank the silver miners of Leadville under the table before formulating a Wildean paradox: 'We really have everything in common with America nowadays,' he declared, 'except, of course, language.'

6. 'Common Hopes and Common Dreams'

Lighting Out for the Territory

You must know I have undertaken to prophesy that English will be the most respectable language in the world and the most universally read and spoken in the next century.

John Adams, 1780

1

From the British surrender at Yorktown in 1781 to the end of the American Civil War in 1865 official relations between the two countries oscillated from the chilly to the arctic: there was no love lost between the wounded imperial power and its feisty former colony, and often a lot of mutual suspicion which occasionally erupted into bouts of open hostility. Symbolic of the changing role of the New World in global affairs, the proclamation in 1823 by President James Monroe of his eponymous 'Doctrine' established that the western hemisphere was now a US 'sphere of influence', and no longer available to recolonization by any European power. Monroe also renounced all US interest in the affairs of Continental Europe, focusing his people's attention on developing their interests in the unexplored parts of North and Central America. This era of Manifest Destiny saw the United States expand ever westward, breathing new life and energy into the English-speaking world, enlarging it dramatically and shifting its centre of gravity from the British Isles to the New World.

The path of reconciliation between the shattered parts of the first British empire was smoothed, in the mixing of a shared culture and language, by some curious transatlantic exchanges. At first, British visitors to the United States felt as if they were landing on the moon.

'It is an absorbing thing to watch the process of world-making,' wrote Harriet Martineau in 1837, after a visit to the new republic. 'When I look back upon it now, it seems as if I had been in another planet.' British arrogance, not unknown even today, encouraged an instinctive defensiveness in the American visitor to London. From as early as 1735 there had been attacks on the 'barbarous English' of the colonists and jokes about 'Americanisms' such as *antagonize*, *belittle* and *placate*. Dr Johnson had written trenchantly about 'the American dialect, a tract of corruption to which every language, widely diffused, must always be exposed'. Nathaniel Hawthorne, the acclaimed author of *The Scarlet Letter*, described being 'continually thrown upon his national antagonism by some acrid quality in the moral atmosphere of England'. After a stay of four years (1853–7), as Liverpool consul, Hawthorne wrote that 'These people think so loftily of themselves, and so contemptuously of anybody else, that it requires more generosity than I possess to keep always in perfectly good humor with them'. These antagonisms inspired a new genre, in which each side tried to make sense of the other. In three classic examples, the work of Fanny Trollope, Charles Dickens and Mark Twain contributed to an enhanced sense of Anglo-American consciousness.

Domestic Manners of the Americans, by Fanny Trollope, mother of the novelist Anthony Trollope, is still in print, acute and highly entertaining. Mrs Trollope narrated her travels through the South with a winning brio and a rather scandalized irreverence. If America's 'domestic manners' were bad enough, the accents of its language were something else, she noted, redolent 'less of freedom than of onions and whisky'. *Domestic Manners* was an early word-of-mouth Anglo-American publishing sensation. 'In every stage coach and in all societies', wrote one Englishman in New York, 'the first question was "Have you read Mrs Trollope?"' Her success identified a potentially important new readership.

Perhaps there is no inspiration quite like the prospect of the bestseller list. For Dickens, America became a new literary market to conquer; he crossed the Atlantic with high hopes. 'No stranger', he wrote, 'could have set foot upon those shores with a feeling of livelier interest in the country, and stronger faith in it.' Sadly, the excesses of America's literary and newspaper class quickly soured his enthusiasm. When the author of *Pickwick Papers* denounced American publishers' pirating of his work, he fell foul of the American press, which behaved with its habitual delight in celebrity, cheerfully printing stories that Dickens considered to be lies. The upshot of this unhappy visit was *American Notes* (1842) and then *Martin Chuzzlewit* (1843–4), neither of which did much to improve Anglo-American relations. Mrs Gamp's 'All the wickedness of the world is print to him' might reflect Dickens's disenchantment with American letters, but he also contrived to have some fun with east coast literary pretension in his merciless skewering of two American literary ladies: ' "Mind and matter", said the lady in the wig, "glide swift into the vortex of immensity. Howls the sublime and softly sleeps the calm Ideal in the whispering chambers of Imagination. To hear it, sweet it is." '

And yet, after all these conflicts, 'these bloody wars and vindictive animosities', confessed Nathaniel Hawthorne, 'we still have an unspeakable yearning towards England'. (Even George Washington always had his carriage made to the most fashionable British specifications.) No one's yearning was more 'unspeakable' or entertaining than Mark Twain's. 'I would like to stay here about fifteen or seventy-five years,' he wrote during his first visit to England. The fruit of this love affair, *A Connecticut Yankee in King Arthur's Court* (1889), contributes an unusual footnote to the world's English, the exploitation of an ancient British myth to satirize modern technology and social theory. *A Connecticut Yankee* takes place in an imaginary sixth century, and contrasts the experience of an American 'born in a wholesome free atmosphere' with the 'pitiful' slavishness of Britons who were, Twain declared, 'nothing but rabbits'. Here, once again, is the authentic rasp of the pioneering Midwest, America's heartland. The constant expansion westward throughout the nineteenth century would redefine the expression of American English, sustaining its reputation for simplicity and directness. This process was already well under way when along came the new discovery – gold – that would give the world's English a Pacific as well as an Atlantic frontier.

2

The Gold Rush of 1849 was one of the most extraordinary crazes ever to sweep the United States, and it united the country from east to west in a fever of shared acquisitiveness. In the words of the *New York Herald*, 'All classes of our citizens seem to be under the influence of this extraordinary mania...Poets, philosophers, lawyers, brokers, bankers, merchants, farmers, clergymen – all are feeling the impulse and are preparing to go and dig for gold and swell the numbers of adventurers to the new El Dorado.' This was the impact of the Gold Rush: it inspired city-dwelling easterners who knew nothing of the land, and even less about transcontinental travel, to go out west, and perhaps get rich quick, coming home 'with a pocket full of rocks'. In the first year alone, 1849, an estimated 100,000 of them, mainly young men in their twenties, headed for California, and were as stunned by the experience as if they had been caught up in a full-scale war.

They had a phrase for it, now forgotten. They used to say that they had 'seen the elephant' which came to mean experiencing a catastrophe, or being matured by reality. The phrase cropped up during the US presidential campaign of 2008 in a discussion of how best to present Governor Sarah Palin to the American people as a potential Vice-President. One Republican consultant commented that, 'I think they [the Republican Party] ought to toss her into the deep from the outset; let her get it over quickly. Everything else after that is: "You've seen the elephant."' In the Gold Rush, many for whom 'seeing the elephant' was a regular experience found it difficult to express what they were going through. One doctor wrote to his wife that it was impossible to describe his journey to the West, 'but when I have an opportunity I will give you enough to satisfy you that 1849 will ever be a memorable epoch in the history of our country. Neither the Crusades nor Alexander's expedition to India can ever equal this emigration to California.'

Astonished by the adventure, separated from their loved ones, alone in a vast and hostile wilderness, the Forty-niners responded like city people: they wrote about it, in American English. They published books by the hundred, kept diaries by the thousand, and scribbled uncountable numbers of letters home. They were the first – and the last – frontiersmen to have the education and the inclination to describe what they saw and heard. What is more, once they arrived in the Sierra goldfields, they had the leisure to write: very few returned home within the year as they had planned. Shipped east by letter and newspaper, the idiom of the West, its phrases and vocabulary, passed swiftly into universal currency. Ever after, the American West would be the place where a man could 'luck out' and 'strike it rich': if things 'panned out', after he had 'staked a claim', there was the prospect of *pay dirt*, even a *bonanza*. This was as true of the Californian madness in '49 as of the dot.com boom of the 1990s.

The Gold Rush was a freak, a story of rags-to-riches (or rags) that ran counter to the regular pioneer experience. The majority of new Americans, consolidating the Revolution in day-to-day life on the land, were tough, dour people, battling against adversity and the elements in hopes of making a better life for their families. One such quintessential midwesterner, farming in Kentucky, married an illegitimate Virginian girl, 'a bold, reckless, daredevil kind of a woman, stepping to the very edge of propriety', and had a son. When nothing went right, the father and his family upped sticks to Indiana, where things went from bad to worse. The wife died and the farm never prospered. The boy's childhood was a succession of disappointments and setbacks. By the time he was twenty-three, he was living in New Salem, Illinois, managing a small store, having just failed to get elected to the local legislature, a young man apparently without any serious prospects or great expectations. But in 1834, this classic no-hoper began to teach himself law, and to make his way in the world. His name was Abraham Lincoln, and his first campaign speech for the Illinois state legislature gave a taste of the pleasures to come. 'My politics', he said, 'is short and sweet, like an old woman's dance. I am in favor of a national bank, a high and protective tariff, and the internal improvement system. If elected, I will be thankful. If beaten, I can do as I have been doing, work for a living.' Later, when William Dean Howells came to write his *Life of Abraham Lincoln* he effortlessly mythologized his hero's study of the great English jurist William

Blackstone, describing how Lincoln 'threw himself under a wide-spreading oak, and expansively made a reading desk of the hillside. Here he would pore over Blackstone day after day ... utterly unconscious of everything but the principles of common law.'

3

Abraham Lincoln's early career offers the wonderful parable of the outsider in American politics. In 2007–8, not coincidentally, it became a touchstone for the presidential campaign of the junior senator from Illinois, Barack Obama, who launched his run for the White House with a speech 'in the shadow of the Old State Capitol'. Here, 'where Lincoln once called on a divided house to stand together', the candidate placed himself self-consciously at the service of 'common hopes and common dreams'. There were other historical echoes. In 1858, as in 2008, America was in trouble. When Lincoln was elected to the presidency in 1860, the American republic, not yet a century old, was divided and directionless. The root of the problem confronting the nation was the one issue on which the Founding Fathers had been silent: slavery.

Jefferson, in old age, had considered the impending conflict between the slave-holding states of the South and the free states of the North and, in a famous letter, had written that 'This momentous question, like a firebell in the night, awakened and filled me with terror.' In Jefferson's time, the threatened conflagration was in the future. Eventually, the issue, like all great issues in the United States, came before the Supreme Court, which, after months of controversy, ruled that a slave was not a citizen. The court said that Congress was powerless to exclude slavery from a free state. This satisfied no one. By the end of 1860 South Carolina, Mississippi, Florida, Alabama, Georgia, Louisiana and finally Texas had seceded from the Union and proclaimed 'the Confederate States of America'. This was the challenge that confronted the newly elected President in the New Year of 1861. Lincoln did not waste time. He declared the secession void and vowed to 'hold, occupy and possess' all government property. In April he ordered the fleet to relieve the beleaguered Union forces defending Fort Sumter at the mouth of Charleston Harbor in South Carolina. The American Civil War had begun.

From the outset, Lincoln was clear in his own mind what was at stake. Two years before, he had said, in a memorable statement, 'I believe this government cannot endure permanently half slave and half free. I do not expect the Union to be dissolved; I do not expect the house to fall; but I do expect it will cease to be divided. It will become all one thing, or all the other.' From the opening salvos at Fort Sumter, the war between the states was an unequal contest. The Union in the North had all the advantages: more men, more money and more *matériel*. Yet for four years the South not only refused to surrender to superior force, it also inflicted grievous wounds on the armies of the North. There were several battles – Vicksburg, Shiloh, Bull Run, Manassas, Antietam – all of them inconclusive. What sustained and united the South was not its defence of the indefensible (slavery), but its ancestral passion for a way of life, a homeland and a habit of being. The South was, and remains, quite different from the rest of the continental United States, and the southern armies, led by Robert E. Lee, a figure of tragic dimensions, fought to retain that integrity in a way the North never could. It was a poignant struggle between an old and a new way of life whose scars can still be found on the American body politic.

Lincoln, echoing the Declaration of Independence, had already expressed the principle for which the South was fighting. 'Any people,' said Lincoln in 1847, following Locke, 'anywhere, being inclined and having the power, have the right to rise up and shake off the existing government and form a new one that suits them better.' The question, of course, was: who are 'the people'? This – and their right to self-expression and self-determination – is a recurring theme. It was to the proper loyalties of 'the people' that Lincoln returned, in the aftermath of one of the bloodiest and finally most decisive encounters of the Civil War, the battle of Gettysburg. His speech still stands out as one of the high points in American prose, a brilliantly succinct redefinition of national purpose, uttered in language the people could understand and constitutional lawyers could debate ever after.

4

The doomed heroism of the Confederate armies on the rolling harvest fields of Pennsylvania in July 1863 has often been described: Lee's foolhardy gallantry; Pickett's Charge, and so forth. At the end of it, the South was defeated, the Confederacy smashed and the Union saved, but at a terrible cost in death, destruction and national division. The slaves were free (Lincoln had signed the emancipation order in 1863), but where did the end of hostilities leave 'the people'? By one of those remarkable, chance inspirations, Lincoln knew what he had to say on this subject, and when the moment presented itself, he seized his opportunity with the instinctive touch of political genius. But it was not, on the face of it, an auspicious moment.

In the aftermath of battle, the fields of Gettysburg were littered with thousands of bodies (both men and horses) rotting in the summer sun. Even when Confederate prisoners and press-ganged civilians had buried some 8,000 corpses in shallow graves, the atmosphere of Gettysburg was still hellish. There were relatives looking for their dead, hogs rooting out and eating half-buried bodies, and dazed local inhabitants trying to conduct everyday life in a neighbourhood that had become transformed into a swampy cemetery, stinking of death. All in all, it was an apt metaphor for the impact of civil war upon the states.

The Pennsylvania authorities, led by the governor, were anxious to tidy up the battlefield, rebury the bodies so hastily interred and consecrate a fitting memorial. Once work had begun on the 17-acre site, the governor's agent, a man named Wills, asked the country's principal poets – Longfellow, Whittier and Bryant – for a funeral address, but each refused. So, on 23 September, barely two months after the battle, Wills approached the nation's champion orator, Edward Everett, a man who could be relied upon to hold his audience spellbound for hours at a stretch. Surprisingly, at this stage no one had thought to approach President Lincoln. Eventually, as part of a general summons to the Federal Cabinet, he and some assorted celebrities were asked to participate in the formal burial of the Union's dead. When it came, the President's invitation was combined, almost casually, with a request for 'a few appropriate remarks'. Lincoln saw his opportunity, and rearranged his schedule so that he would arrive in Gettysburg the evening before the ceremony with ... what? Notes scribbled on the back of an envelope? Words pencilled on a piece of cardboard as his train chugged through the autumn countryside of Pennsylvania? The myth of Gettysburg obscures the truth of what actually took place there, but one thing is certain: Lincoln knew exactly what he was doing, and he was a man who, in Garry Wills's words, 'composed his speeches thoughtfully. It is impossible to imagine him leaving his speech at Gettysburg to the last moment.'

On the day of the ceremony, Lincoln, who was wearing long white gloves, rode out through the mud on horseback for about a mile to a raised platform which had become surrounded by a crowd of at least 20,000. Everett, the star attraction, was already in place, his text before him, composing himself for his speech, which he proceeded to deliver, during more than two and a half hours, to general satisfaction. This was what the people had come to hear, and this was 'the oration' that was widely and approvingly reported in the national press next day. When Lincoln spoke, in his high, midwestern tenor, reading from one or two pages of text, it was all over in about three minutes. Lincoln began:

Four score and seven years ago our fathers brought forth on this continent a new nation, conceived in liberty and dedicated to the proposition that all men are created equal. Now we are engaged in a great civil war, testing whether that nation, or any nation so conceived and so dedicated, can long endure. We are met on a great battlefield of that war. We have come to dedicate a portion of that field.

So much for preamble. Now he had to move onto a higher plane in his second paragraph:

But, in a larger sense, we cannot dedicate – we cannot consecrate – we cannot hallow this ground. The brave men, living and dead, who struggled here, have consecrated it, far above our poor power to add or detract. The world will little note, nor long remember, what we say here, but it cannot forget what they did here. It is for us the living, rather, to be dedicated here to the unfinished work which they who fought here have thus far so nobly advanced.

At the time, Lincoln exclaimed 'that speech won't *scour*'. But it did, and it would eventually do far more than disinfect the poisonous atmosphere of the battlefield. As Garry Wills puts it, 'the nightmare realities have been etherealized in the crucible of his language. Lincoln did for the Civil War what he accomplished for the single battlefield. Slavery is not mentioned, any more than Gettysburg is. The discussion is driven back and back, beyond the historical particulars, to great ideals that are made to grapple naked in an airy battle of the mind.' With a brilliant, and benign, sleight of hand, Lincoln had substituted a new constitution for America in the minds of his listeners, as more than one contemporary newspaper noted. The mourners of Gettysburg walked away from the cemetery on the hillside, writes Wills, 'under a changed sky, into a different America. Lincoln had revolutionized the Revolution, giving people a new past to live with that would change their future indefinitely'. Lincoln's Gettysburg Address, the work of a man steeped in the rhythms of the Bible and well versed in the mysteries of Shakespeare, is one of the high points in the making of the English-speaking world, a marriage of the booming newspaper business, the oral tradition and word of mouth in an integrated (but not yet united) society. And he had done it in just 266 words.

5

Lincoln united the country with ten carefully crafted sentences in November 1863. Two years later, another midwesterner, a young man also raised on the frontier, who shared its ethos, its beliefs, even its humour – democratic, individualistic, egalitarian – would give it the voice by which it would become known to the wider world. This next founding father of the world's English was born Samuel Clemens in 1835, the year Halley's comet appeared in the pre-Victorian skies. When, as Mark Twain, he died in 1910 the comet was once again cutting a fiery track through the heavens, and he was now more famous than any American writer has ever been. It is difficult to resist interpreting the life of Clemens/Twain as a mixture of meteor and portent. As his biographer Ron Powers puts it, 'his way of seeing and hearing things changed America's way of seeing and hearing things... he was the Lincoln of American literature'. In his prime, one hundred years after the Declaration of Independence, Twain was a great Yankee original who rendered the vocabulary and tone of the American vernacular (previously despised) in a way that was neither parody nor caricature but literature. Twain gave us Huckleberry Finn, but he also gives us *The Simpsons*.

Like Lincoln, Clemens was the product of the booming Midwest, a man of the dawning age of mass communications. As a young man, he got his pilot's licence to navigate riverboats up and down to New Orleans. When the Civil War put an end to riverboat gambling, the riotous society of hustlers, quack doctors, itinerant preachers and highfalutin midwesterners, young Clemens – scarcely eighteen – left the river and set off west into a kind of lifelong exile. He would return to the place that had shaped him only in the pages of his three masterpieces, *The Adventures of Tom Sawyer*, *Life on the Mississippi* and *Adventures of Huckleberry Finn*. Silver and gold drew him out west, but his luck was so bad that the first time he turned up, offering to write for a newspaper, he looked more like a hobo than a hack. As he found his journalistic voice, Samuel Clemens became Mark Twain, taking his pseudonym from the language of the river he loved. 'Mark twain' – mark two, a depth of twelve feet, safe water – was the leadsman's cry, and it has inspired no end of psychobabble about the significance of the alter ego, 'the most recognised alias in the history of aliases'. Twain himself had no truck with that, either. At the height of his fame, he told a fan, 'I have been an author for twenty years, and an ass for fifty-five.'

Twain's break as a writer came in a way that is now nearly incomprehensible, with the publication of a humorous story. In December 1865, almost a year after Lincoln's second inaugural, the New York *Saturday Press* published a story (in the form of a letter to another humorist, Artemus Ward) entitled 'John Smiley and his Jumping Frog' (later 'The Celebrated Jumping Frog of Calaveras County'). Read today, it will scarcely raise a smile; in 1865 it made its author a national sensation. Overnight Twain became a literary rock star, launched, in the words of his biographer, 'into the vapour of national fame'. He toured the country, dazzling packed houses with humorous lectures. Next, like the good journalist he was, he signed up to join a celebrity cruise to the Holy Land, sponsored by the brother of Harriet Beecher Stowe. 'Send me $1200,' he cabled his editors, with the peremptory chutzpah that never left him, 'I want to go Abroad.' Twain's voyage was the making of him. On board, the passengers were 'convulsed with laughter at his drolleries and quaint original manner', and entranced by his drawling profane speech. At home, the readers of his dispatches were equally convulsed.

Long before the 'Wild Humorist' returned to the States and reworked his pieces into *The Innocents Abroad*, he had become permanently and universally famous. The white suits, author photographs and cigars followed soon after. Then, like any young man who has made his fortune and wants to settle down, he fell in love. Olivia (Livy) Langdon's parents were dismayed, but there is no seduction like laughter and fame; Twain's languorous bad-boy routine was outselling Fanny Kemble. Marriage coincided with publication of his first bestseller, *The Innocents Abroad*. The newly-weds lived at a headlong pace. Twain said he was 'the busiest white man in America'. Then, in the first of fate's hammer blows, his firstborn son died of a fever, a death that seems to have sent Twain back to his own boyhood. By 1876, partly thanks to the invention of the typewriter, he had delivered the first draft of *Tom Sawyer*, recognized at once as a classic of children's literature. Fame and success resumed their assault. Twain certainly pioneered the life of the American literary celebrity. More globetrotting followed and some disastrous investments in speculative enterprises. Throughout these years of wandering and extravagance, he was incubating his masterpiece.

6

At first Twain returned to his roots without the benefit of a fictional disguise. In hindsight, *Life on the Mississippi* is just the curtain-raiser to *Huckleberry Finn*. Then he turned to storytelling, 'a kind of companion to Tom Sawyer'. The first chapters, written in the aftermath of *Tom Sawyer*, continued the mood with the sharp ironic humour of its famous opening line: 'You don't know about me, without you have read a book...made by Mr Mark Twain, and he told the truth, mainly.' But when, after a troubled hiatus, he returned to the manuscript in 1882/3 what had begun as a celebration and a reminiscence became a darker elegy. Now he was appalled by the trend of modern American life in the dying century. For Mark Twain the surest bulwark against the sterilizing tide of progress became his pen.

With Huck Finn, he could remember life on America's great river as a permanent thing, a place of menacing sunsets, starlit nights and strange dawns, of the confessions of dying men, hints of buried treasure, murderous family feuds, overheard shoptalk, the distant thunder of the Civil War and two American exiles, Huck the orphan and Jim the runaway slave, floating down the immensity of the great Mississippi. Huck's is a journey that profoundly transforms both characters, but in the end, Huck, like his creator, breaks free from bourgeois inhibition, from those who would 'adopt' and 'sivilize' him. 'I can't stand it,' he says. 'I been there before.'

Another American from St Louis, T. S. Eliot, addressing the genius of Twain, once wrote that he was 'one of those writers, of whom there are not a great many in any literature, who have discovered a new way of writing, valid not only for themselves but for others'. Hemingway put it more succinctly. 'All modern American literature comes from one book by Mark Twain called *Huckleberry Finn*. It's the best book we've had. All American writing comes from that. There was nothing before. There has been nothing as good since.' The voice of a new America comes through loud and clear from the first page to the last. *Huckleberry Finn* is a book that celebrates the lost world of childhood, the space and mystery of the Midwest. Above all, it mythologizes the issue – race – that had tormented the Union for so so many decades. Huck Finn floats down the great river that flows through the heart of America, and on this adventure he is accompanied by the magnificent figure of Jim, who is also making his bid for freedom.

7. 'The Audacity Of Hope'

From Slavery to Redemption

Abused and scorned though we may be, our destiny is tied up with
the destiny of America. Before the Pilgrims landed at Plymouth, we
were here. Before the pen of Jefferson scratched across the pages of
history the majestic words of the Declaration of Independence, we
were here...

Martin Luther King, 'Letter from Birmingham Jail', August 1963

1

V. S. Naipaul is among the greatest novelists at work in the English
language today. The author of *Guerrillas* and *A Bend in the River* has
made the world's English his own with the sure touch of genius. His
story says a lot about the way in which, from the seventeenth century
onwards, English came to be scattered to some of the most remote
parts of the world, often in the worst possible circumstances. But –
contagious, adaptable, populist and subversive – it flourished, through
word of mouth, to the point where it became art and literature as
much as a necessary communication.

Naipaul was born in 1932, and was raised in Trinidad in the Caribbean, an outpost of an empire whose literary masters were Wordsworth, Dickens and D. H. Lawrence. Naipaul has described the
confusions of this inheritance. 'I couldn't have the assumptions of
[English] writers,' he reports, 'I didn't see my world reflected in
theirs.' Wordsworth's daffodil was 'a pretty little flower, no doubt;
but we had never seen it.' Foreign books made the most sense when
they could be adapted to local conditions. In *Bleak House*, Dickens's
rain had to become a tropical downpour. But the English of Trinidad
was Naipaul's mother tongue. There was no other. Slowly, painfully,

he had to remake it for his own purposes. This he proceeded to do through a lifelong process of trial and error typical of the world's English.

No one dwelling in comfort on the higher ground of Anglo-American society should ever forget that a brutal trade in human lives was a motor of the British and American economies throughout the eighteenth and part of the nineteenth century. But, as Naipaul's story shows, out of this horrifying traffic comes the music of African, Caribbean and the 'Black English' of the United States of America. Of all the cultural odysseys described here, none is so poignant or disturbing. Naipaul's story involves the transmigration of Indians, via Africa, to the Caribbean. But the slave trade left its mark all over the domestic English landscape. On the outskirts of Bristol, one of England's oldest ports, the departure point for many fabulous journeys, including *Treasure Island*, lies the village of Henbury. There, in the country graveyard of St Mary's Church, is the tomb of Scipio Africanus, a black slave. The epitaph to the young man who died here at the age of eighteen is a poignant memorial to the mingling of English and African culture:

> I who was Born a Pagan and a Slave
> Now sweetly Sleep a Christian in my Grave
> What tho my Hue was dark my Saviour's sight
> Shall change this darkness into radiant light.

The grave of Scipio Africanus is a sombre reminder that Bristol, still a monument to Regency riches, was for 150 years the apex of the most ruthless trading set-up in the history of capitalism. Ironically, in the making of the world's English, the fruits of this shocking exchange have been a source of constant enrichment, from Harriet Beecher Stowe to Martin Luther King. The legacy of the African experience, over many centuries, includes *safari* (derived from Swahili), *mumbo-jumbo* (from Mandingo), *homeboy* (from Xhosa), and even *honkie*, Black English slang for whites, which comes from *honq*, the Wolof word for 'pink'. Such lexical fossils are eloquent of much darker times.

2

'Humanity', wrote Aristotle in his *Politics*, 'is divided into two: the masters and the slaves.' The first Englishman to explore the Atlantic triangle (Europe–Africa–New World–Europe) during the mid-sixteenth century was William Hawkins, from Devon, who sailed to Guinea in West Africa in 1532 and brought back a local chieftain as a souvenir. During Elizabeth I's reign there would be several more voyages to Guinea, in which the use of English became an important by-product. Slaves, insisted one trader, 'were in England well used, and were kept there till they could speake the language, and then they should be brought againe to be a helpe to Englishmen in this Countrey...' In 1562, John Hawkins, son of William, made the journey from which historians date the beginning of the slave trade. Hawkins enjoyed the approval of the queen, who hoped that the Africans would not be transported without their free consent, something which, she declared, 'would be detestable and call down the vengeance of Heaven'. Hawkins, who was not troubled by the vengeance of heaven, cruised into the Sierra Leone river, captured some 300 Africans and sailed across the North Atlantic to Hispaniola, where he exchanged his cargo for hides, ginger, sugar and a fabulous consignment of pearls.

These early voyages contributed to the making of a new kind of English. On board the slave ships, the English spoken would already have been highly idiosyncratic. *Palaver*, transmitted into pidgin from the Portuguese *palavra*, meaning 'talk', always suggested difficulty. (Conversation with Portuguese sailors was troublesome and argumentative.) Even if the captain and his vessel were from England, many of his crew would have been foreign. Sailors who worked for many ships and many captains would have known the Mediterranean seafaring lingua franca, Sabir, a creole with strong Iberian connections dating to the Crusades. The influence of Sabir is found in two famous African English words, *pickaninny* and *savvy*, both of which have Mediterranean origins. *Pequino* is Portuguese for 'small'; *savez-vous?*, French for 'do you know?' *Wishy-washy* also comes via this route. By the end of the sixteenth century slave English was sufficiently established for Christopher Marlowe to give a kind of pidgin English to Barabas in *The Jew of Malta*. 'Very mush', says Barabas, 'Monsieur, you no be his man?' Out of the dreadful trade in human lives came the music of African or Black English, something strange and wonderful that Shakespeare seems intuitively to have grasped. Caliban, the demonic slave in *The Tempest*, celebrates a fleeting moment of freedom in an exuberant, primitive rap song:

> 'Ban, 'Ban, Ca-Caliban,
> Has a new master – Get a new man.

Caliban also denounces Prospero's mastery of his brutal existence:

> You taught me language; and my profit on't
> Is, I know how to curse. The red plague rid you
> For learning me your language!

Word of mouth – the acquisition of language – among Africans could be a matter of life and death. The pidgin English of the slave ships was an essential means of communication among the captives. To eliminate the risk of mutiny and rebellion, the slaves who spoke the same languages (Wolof, Temne or Mandingo) would be separated for the so-called 'Middle Passage'. The mixing of slaves was deliberate. As William Smith wrote in *A New Voyage to Guinea* in 1744, 'by having some of every Sort on board, there will be no more likelihood of their succeeding in a Plot, than of finishing the Tower of Babel'.

3

Slowly, Black English evolved, at first in the oral tradition, but eventually in prose. While there was Scipio Africanus and his fellows in Bristol, and numerous Calibans in the Caribbean, there were also many individual slaves scattered across North America, developing a new kind of English. About 5,000 slaves were transported each year across the Atlantic. In addition to Bristol, many English West Country ports, like Falmouth and Plymouth, dabbled in the trade, sending one or two ships apiece to join the slave fleets off west Africa. Occasionally, there were disasters. The *Luxborough* caught fire on the return journey from Jamaica. Captain Kellaway and his crew escaped the blazing wreck in the ship's dinghy, surviving on the flesh of their dead companions and drinking their own urine. Despite such catastrophes there was a steady influx of Africans throughout the colonies. In New England, one French refugee reported in 1687 that 'there is not a house in Boston, however small may be its means, that has not one or two slaves. There are those that have five or six.' In Britain, the latest European war, finally resolved by the Treaty of Utrecht (1713), yielded a sought-after prize, the Asiento, that is, the contract to export slaves and other goods to the Spanish Indies. The rise and fall of the South Sea Company has often been presented as symbolic of the excesses of early eighteenth-century capitalism. For the English-speaking world, however, its significance is rather different. From 1717 to 1731 the South Sea Company sold no fewer than 64,000 slaves in North America, and the list of its investors reads like a roll-call of British society under George I: the Speaker of the House, more than half the lords and commons, the lord chancellor and the entire royal family. From the artistic community, John Gay, Alexander Pope and John Vanbrugh were all investors. Their involvement speaks of a deep national association with slavery that touched all classes. When the crash came Sir Isaac Newton lost £20,000 and was said to have been unreconciled, to the end of his life, to the fateful words 'south sea'.

Even the shabby, contrarian figure of the journalist Daniel Defoe was caught up in the fever of slave capitalism. In his time, Defoe had been imprisoned for debt and pilloried for his satire, but for the launch of the South Sea Company he composed a pamphlet puffing its potential, and declaring that he could not recall 'an undertaking of such consequence'. The association of slavery and literature was renewed, in fiction, with the appearance in 1719 of *Robinson Crusoe*. The enigmatic companion of Crusoe (a name derived from the corruption of the Dutch 'Kreutznaer'), Man Friday, is not an African, but 'Friday' is a direct translation of the West African 'day name'

Globish

Cuffy or Cuffee, which suggests that Defoe was familiar with the conventions of pidgin and creole. The success of Defoe's remarkable first novel, composed when its author was in his fifty-ninth year, speaks of a deep British fascination with seafaring adventure, irrespective of its moral dimensions (before his shipwreck, after all, Crusoe was a would-be slaver).

4

Slavery raised in an acute form the issues of individual liberty that English radicals had been grappling with for centuries. In England, it was writers more than politicians who first articulated the ethical arguments against slavery. James Thomson (the author of 'Rule, Britannia!'), Richard Savage and even Alexander Pope all came out against slavery. Pope asked the essential question:

> Why must I Afric's sable Children see
> Vended for Slaves, though form'd by Nature free...?

Afra Behn's *Oroonoko, or the History of the Royal Slave* was one popular rendering of anti-slavery opinion. In the words of the historian Hugh Thomas, the importance of Behn's 'contribution to the preparation for the abolitionist movement can scarcely be exaggerated. She helped prepare literary people's minds for a change on humanitarian grounds.' In London, the book trade responded with a new genre of slavery reportage, notably John Atkins's *Voyage to Guinea, Brasil, and the West Indies* (1735), which described the reality of the trade in horrifying detail. The victims of slavery had their say, too, braiding the black experience into the texture of English life. Elizabeth Marsh's *The Female Captive* told an extraordinary story of a half-Jamaican woman's adventures in Morocco, and was part of a strangely modern trend that enabled all kinds of reader to 'compass the earth and seas, visit all countries, and converse with all nations ... without stirring a foot'. Such volumes gave ammunition to the English anti-slavery movement.

The issue was never straightforward. There were, for instance, good men like Captain John Newton, author of the hymn 'How Sweet the Name of Jesus Sounds', who used to read prayers twice a day to his slave crews, and claimed to have put down an onboard slave rebellion 'with the Divine Assistance'. The tortured interaction of African slavery and English literary life continued throughout the eighteenth century, through the strangest of connections. In 1752, a Gold Coast prince, usually referred to as William Ansah Sessaracoa, became the latest dark-skinned captive to excite the English imagination. The prince, who had been sent to England for an education in 'manners' by his royal father, was taken up by the king and became, in Horace Walpole's words, fashionable at 'all the assemblies'.

The nation's institutions had been painfully forged to allow the expression of individual freedoms and, in a limited way, the rights of man. Thoughtful people now began to ask how, with its history, England could also be Europe's biggest slaving nation. Between 1765 and 1769 the celebrated Oxford professor of law William Blackstone's landmark volumes, *Commentaries on the Laws of England*, established the case against slavery more comprehensively than any previous jurist had done. The wisdom of Blackstone's analysis trickled down into the immensely successful play *The Padlock* (1768) by Isaac Bickerstaffe and also into Walpole's satirical *Account of Giants Lately Discovered* (1766).

These anti-slavery opinions, in turn, began to find their way across the Atlantic. But before the outbreak of the American Revolution, the history both of the slave trade and of the institution of slavery in England reached a turning point in 1771–2 with the prosecution of the Somerset case, an English cause célèbre: the trial of a runaway slave kidnapped by his erstwhile master near Covent Garden, in defiance of habeas corpus. In June 1772, after years of legal wrangling, Lord Chief Justice Mansfield freed James Somerset, but made it plain that his judgement had no bearing on the general legality of slavery in England. Still, there was now a recognition that the days of slavery were numbered. On the evening of 22 June Dr Johnson's black servant Francis Barber organized an impromptu celebration at his master's house as well as a 'frolick' for about 200 people at a London tavern. Slaves and their Black English might be oppressed, but they were inescapably a familiar element of metropolitan life in London, Liverpool and Bristol.

By the late eighteenth century perhaps as many as a quarter of the ships in Liverpool were engaged in the African trade. Pidgins and creoles were part of its cultural inheritance; and in 1783 one of its slaving masters, Captain Collingwood, became the centre of the most iconic case to excite libertarian opinion on both sides of the Atlantic, the terrible story of the *Zong*. This slave ship had sailed with some 400 slaves from the port of São Tomé, lost its way in the Caribbean and run short of water. Captain Collingwood summoned his officers and pointed out that slaves who died of natural causes would be a loss to the owners, but that if they were thrown alive into the sea (on safety grounds), they would only be 'a loss to the underwriters'. Despite the crew's protests, 133 sick slaves were eventually jettisoned in this way; a further ten jumped of their own volition. When the underwriters refused to pay up, the *Zong* case came to court. The failure of the action eventually inspired J. M. W. Turner to paint his anti-slavery masterpiece *The Slave Ship* (*Slavers Throwing Overboard the Dead and Dying, Typhoon Coming on*). Until 1807, when the slave trade was abolished, the issue continued to reverberate through British and American public life.

5

Across the Atlantic, in the West Indies and in the southern states of America, slavery was beginning to yield more strange fruit in the beginnings of Afro-Caribbean and Afro-American culture. In his *Information for Those Who Would Remove to America*, Benjamin Franklin attempted a version of plantation creole, another measure of its recognition in everyday American life: 'Boccarorra [a form of 'buckra', meaning a 'white man'] make de Black Man workee, make de Horse workee, make de Ox workee, make ebery thing workee; only de Hog. He, de Hog, no workee; he eat, he drink, he walk about, he go to sleep when he please, he libb a gentleman.' This is, of course, just a crude caricature. There were many levels of competence and expression. Slaves recently shipped from Africa would depend on pidgin. Those who had been transported from the West Indies or born on a southern estate would know plantation creole. Those who worked close to their master as house slaves would, in the words of the advertisements, speak 'very proper English'. No amount of 'proper English' could allay the American slave-holders' fear of what Jefferson called 'domestic insurrection'. When hostilities finally broke out between Britain and its American colonies the black population had to choose sides. The war of independence, indeed, played a pivotal role in the slow and painful process of turning African slaves into American citizens. Paradoxically, it was the British who were, at first, the true liberators.

Partly, they had no choice. The slaves already knew all about the Somerset case, and John Adams's diary describes another kind of primitive linguistic network. 'The negroes', he wrote, 'have a wonderful art of communicating intelligence among themselves; it will run several hundreds of miles in a week or fortnight.' By the autumn of 1775 many of the southern colonies, from Virginia down to Georgia, were in a state of panic about imminent slave insurrections sponsored by the British. These fears were probably well founded. Black preachers were already telling their congregations about a new young English king who had heard the Gospel and 'was about to alter the World and set the Negroes free'.

This garbled news was a long way from George III's strategy. Nonetheless, British forces fighting in the South did enjoy powerful assistance from the blacks. When Charleston fell to General Sir Henry Clinton in May 1780 25,000 slaves escaped from the plantations and headed up the east coast in what the historian Simon Schama calls 'the greatest exodus from bondage in African-American history until the Civil War and Emancipation'. Eventually, in a pattern repeated many times thereafter, these escaped slaves made their way north, especially to New York, which became a kind of haven. The beginnings of African-American liberation in America first occurred not beneath the Stars and Stripes but under that fluttering symbol of colonial oppression, the Union Jack. When the American rebel army withdrew from New York at the end of 1776 incoming British troops observed the blacks hugging and kissing with joy.

In their new metropolitan life, African-Americans could worship in the local Anglican church, be married legally (impossible under slavery) and have their children baptized, a highly symbolic badge of citizenship. For recreation, there was horse racing, bare-knuckle boxing and 'Ethiopian Balls', at which blacks and whites could mingle freely together. They could also attend the theatre: Shakespeare (a notable production of *Othello*) enjoyed a mini-revival during the British occupation of New York. This tantalizing interlude of freedom would, of course, soon be curtailed by the ignominious capitulation of British forces in 1781, but it gave the African-American community a taste of things to come. The black drummers who beat the slow march of the British out of Yorktown were sounding the knell of their own brief hour of liberty, too. Subsequently, there was just one other moment of clemency, when President James Monroe gave his name and his blessing to the settlement of Monrovia in Liberia, a refuge for ex-slaves established by philanthropic American abolitionists in 1822.

Defeat in America and the loss of the colonies inspired a typically English bout of soul-searching whose consequences would also benefit the slaves. The disasters across the Atlantic signalled, it was said, the retribution of the Almighty for a corrupt, 'luxurious' and morally disgraceful national way of life. In this mood, the slave trade became a prime target for patriotic reformers. If God was an Englishman, his people had to have an unblemished contract with him. Only a culture without the stain of slavery could yield political or moral dividends. As the bishop of Durham put it to the peers during an abolition debate, 'we should beware how we forfeited the protection of Providence by continual injustice; for if we did, we should look in vain hereafter for the glories of the Nile and Trafalgar'.

Abolishing slavery would renew Britain's commitment to 'Liberty'. Doing this while the United States was still aggressively a slaveholding society would be all the sweeter. 'In *Britain*,' observed one sanctimonious Unitarian after the abolition of the slave trade in 1807, 'a negro becomes a freeman the moment he sets his foot on British ground.' For the world's English, one vital consequence was the absorption of the language and rhetoric of the slaves into English culture. This redefinition of British national consciousness would have a profound effect on the 'civilizing mission' throughout the following century. Africans were now a global constituency, to be addressed in English. The great black orator Frederick Douglass toured Britain denouncing the crimes of American slavery. 'What to the slave is the Fourth of July?' he thundered. 'Your high independence', he answered, 'only reveals the immeasurable distance between us. You may rejoice. I must mourn.'

By the time Douglass was on the stump, so-called 'Nigger English' was well established in American public discourse. By now, too, 'the Negro dialect' had become widely recognized throughout American society. Mark Twain, a master of the vernacular, put some of this speech into the mouth of Jim in *Huckleberry Finn*, articulating the fear that old Miss Watson would 'sell him down the river': 'Well, you see, it 'uz dis way. Ole Missus – dat's Miss Watson – she pecks on me all de time, en treats me pooty rough, but she awluz said she wouldn't sell me down to Orleans. But I noticed dey wuz a nigger trader roun' de place considable, lately, en I begin to git oneasy.'

The race question was still central to American society. Just before the outbreak of the Civil War, in 1858, Lincoln had faced up to perhaps the greatest threat to American society in a question that reverberates into the twenty-first century. 'When you have succeeded in dehumanising the Negro,' declared Lincoln, 'when you have put him down,' he went on, 'are you quite sure that the demon you have roused will not turn and rend you?' Alongside the cultural fusion of black and white experience in the mid-nineteenth century, there was a constant struggle by the political class to resolve the impossible question that the Founding Fathers had carefully shelved.

Politics had one answer; but culture had another. There was now a market for popular renderings of the African-American experience in which the 'Negro' dialect of American English was not just of sociological interest. Thanks to the Civil War, it found a mass audience in *Uncle Tom's Cabin* by Harriet Beecher Stowe, and in the Brer Rabbit stories of 'Uncle Remus'. The journalist Joel Chandler Harris, the author of these children's tales, exemplifies the complex inter-relationship of standard American culture and slave society: Harris's stories are creole tales collected from the plantations, but he was white, a fact that has tortured the African-American response to his work ever since. Mark Twain gleefully noted that Harris's whiteness was a source of great disappointment to his fans on the rare occasions he could be tempted to meet his audience. 'Undersized, red-haired, and somewhat freckled', Twain wrote, Harris could not even perform his work to a sympathetic audience. 'He had never read aloud to people, and was too shy to venture the attempt now.' Twain regretted this, as one master to another: 'Mr Harris ought to be able to read the Negro dialect better than anybody else,' he wrote, because, 'in the matter of writing he is the only master the country has produced'. Privately, Harris was serious about his representation of slave culture, and paid tribute to the rich tradition of speech and narrative he was trying to preserve: 'If the language of Uncle Remus fails to give vivid hints of the really poetic imagination of the Negro', Harris wrote, then he would have failed to capture its essence.

6

The half-century between the American Civil War and the First World War saw two contrasting, but equally humiliating, sets of experience for black people in the English-speaking world. In Africa, Britain became engaged on an imperial competition, the 'scramble for Africa', with rival European powers that saw the whole continent subjugated to colonial rule. In America, meanwhile, the slaves, finally liberated in December 1865, found themselves catapulted from servitude to legal equality and then reduced to a state almost as degrading as slavery. Four million African-Americans were freed at the end of the Civil War, and an old English legal phrase, 'civil rights', entered the American lexicon for the first time. Once the last Federal troops were withdrawn from the defeated Confederacy, the South hit back, passing 'Jim Crow' laws to limit the rights of former slaves. 'Segregation' became part of the political vocabulary and the final blow to the

African-American community came in the 1880s and 1890s, when the Supreme Court attacked the Civil Rights Act as 'unconstitutional' and sanctioned 'separate but equal' education.

In the South, 'separate but equal' was a formula that kept African-Americans in subjugation as second-class citizens for close on a century after the Civil War, until the appearance of Dr Martin Luther King. Outside the political arena, thanks to a new social mobility, the blacks began migrating north. The immediate consequences for African-American culture of this oppression was the coexistence of North and South, and its expression in music and dance, from jazz to the jitterbug. Especially, it was through the entertainment industry that many blacks worked their way out of the poverty-stricken South and made their way up the Mississippi to Chicago, Detroit and finally New York. Many of these migrants came from the soul centre of African-American culture, New Orleans, bringing with them the music of that city. Originally, 'jazz' was used to mean 'speed up'; by the outbreak of the First World War the word had moved into the mainstream of American culture.

Now white America began the appropriation of African words and style: *jazz, the blues, ragtime, boogie woogie, rock 'n' roll* (in music); the *cakewalk,* the *jitterbug, breakdancing* (in dance); and *cool, jive, hip* and *heavy* (in slang). By the end of 1917, the year the doughboys sailed to Europe to join the allied armies on the Western Front, jazz music and jazz bands were the talk of the town in New York, Paris and London. 'The word jazz', wrote the prose poet of the Jazz Age, F. Scott Fitzgerald, 'in its progress toward respectability has meant first sex, then dancing, then music. It is associated with a state of nervous stimulation, not unlike that of big cities behind the lines of war.' So the black experience was again beginning to engage white imagination (as it had done in the eighteenth century) at the very moment when, more than ever before, blacks were becoming a familiar part of the American urban landscape. Now both blacks and whites were using 'jazz' to mean a particular kind of 'ragtime', music with a syncopated rhythm. In the 1920s and 1930s most blacks living in cities still fitted a white American stereotype. They were maids, cooks, porters and waiters. Or they were boxers and entertainers.

They inhabited their own world, with some highly evolved linguistic conventions. But, in two case studies, the cross-fertilization of black and white had profound consequences for the world's English. By chance, both began in New York City, the first on Broadway, the second uptown in Harlem.

7

In 1926, the young George Gershwin, already acclaimed for *Rhapsody in Blue* and nurturing a deep ambition to compose an American folk opera, was on the lookout for a suitable subject on which to base a libretto. As the story goes, a friend gave him, for recreational reading, a copy of a recent novel, *Porgy*, by DuBose Heyward. A white southerner, Heyward was descended from one of the signatories of the Declaration of Independence, Thomas Heyward. *Porgy* was based on the experiences of some real-life characters from Heyward's native Charleston. Gershwin saw the novel's potential and set out to acquire the rights. At first, the book's success frustrated his hopes: there were already plans for a play (which would reach the stage in 1927), and rumours of silent pictures. But eventually the way was clear for the composer to begin work.

In the summer of 1934 Gershwin, his brother Ira and DuBose Heyward spent several weeks near Charleston, working on the music and lyrics to the opera called *Porgy and Bess*. Gershwin, in particular, immersed himself in the musical culture – the songs and spirituals – of the southern blacks. A celebrated song like 'Summertime' is both a tribute to Black English, but it has also become a universal lullaby.

> Summertime an' the livin' is easy,
> Fish are jumpin' and the cotton is high,
> O yo' Daddy's rich an yo' Ma is goodlookin'
> So hush little baby don' yo' cry.

While Ira and George Gershwin headed south for inspiration, the black jazzmen like Cab Calloway, Count Basie, Duke Ellington and

Louis Armstrong all went north. It's possible to track the movement of a Globish word like 'hip', 'riff', or 'groovy' from Harlem into the American mainstream through the work of a highly popular jazz-band leader, Cab Calloway, who turned 'jive talk' into a popular lyric, 'Mister Hepster's Jive Talk Dictionary':

> If you want to learn the lingo:
> Jive from ABC to Zee,
> Get Hip with
> Mister Hepster's Dictionaree.

Cab Calloway popularized an extraordinary range of jive talk terms, from *Hip*, *cat*, *chick* and *hype*, to *mellow*, *riff*, *square* and *groovy*. In turn these terms were taken up by Louis Armstrong, the darling of young black *and* white American music lovers around the Second World War. One of the youthful veterans from this war, a young writer named Norman Mailer, became so obsessed with 'the near burned-out, throttled, hate-filled dying affair between whites and blacks', which he characterized as 'still our great national love affair', that in 1959 he decided to declare himself a 'White Negro'. Rarely, in the long interaction of blacks and whites, had there been such a bizarre, or telling, formulation.

Mailer had just returned from military service in the Pacific as an enlisted man. Speaking as a veteran, Mailer found it was now man's fate to live with three lethal threats: instant annihilation by atomic war; death by the state (concentration camps); or slow death 'by conformity'. But all was not lost. To meet the challenge of this 'bleak scene' there had appeared a new 'phenomenon' in the shape of 'the American existentialist – the hipster'. Never mind that this entrancing figure bore a strong resemblance to Mailer himself, not least in his quest for the perfect orgasm, the truly interesting thing about this American hipster was that he had 'absorbed the existentialist synapses of the Negro, and for practical purposes could be considered a White Negro'. A White Negro! What greater compliment could the white American writer pay to his oppressed black brothers? James Baldwin was unimpressed but it was, declared Mailer, 'no accident that the source of Hip is the Negro, for he has been living in the margin between totalitarianism and democracy for two centuries'. Specifically, the presence of Hip, and its availability to the would-be hipster, was 'probably due to jazz, and its knifelike entrance into culture, its subtle but so penetrating influence on an avant-garde generation'.

Mailer's invention of the 'White Negro' was a significant curtain-raiser for two generations of black-and-white cultural exchange. Mailer writes that 'the language of Hip is a language of energy, how it is found, how it is lost'. He lists the Hip words 'most likely to last' – *man*, *go*, *beat*, *cool*, *swing*, *crazy*, *dig*, *creep*, *hip*, *square* – but concedes that Hip is 'a special language that cannot really be taught'. And yet Mailer's paean to the African-American experience is a milestone. It signals the 'vastly exciting' capacity of the twentieth century 'to reduce life to its ultimate alternatives' and became an essential manifesto for what would be called the 'Counter Culture'. Mailer also prefigures, with the spooky intuition for which he was renowned, the violent upheavals of the American Civil Rights Movement of the 1960s.

Like Mailer, many African-Americans who had risked their lives for the United States in the Second World War came home as veterans with a new perspective on their situation. They now felt that the white community owed them equal opportunities of the kind they had enjoyed at war, especially as post-war prosperity began to raise national expectations, particularly among the more assertive children of city-dwelling migrants from the South. By the late 1950s the civil rights leadership was symbolized by Dr Martin Luther King. In 1963, at the climax of a 'March on Washington', standing in front of the Lincoln Memorial, Dr King made a speech ('I have a dream'), every bit as quotable and momentous as the Gettysburg Address, that concluded, in a brilliant moment of improvisation, with a specific acknowledgement of the slavery past.

Let freedom ring from the mighty mountains of New York . . . When we let it ring from . . . every state and every city, we will be able to speed up that day when all of God's children, Black men and white men . . . will be able to join hands and sing in the words of the old Negro spiritual, Free at last, Free at last, Thank God Almighty, we are free at last!

But for all the freedom that followed from the Civil Rights Movement (the ending of segregation, and so on), and for all the cross-fertilization between black and white cultural traditions in music, film, literature and dance, the citadels of white power in America remained closed to the African-American community.

8

Until 4 November 2008. The election of Barack Obama concluded some of the unfinished business of the American Revolution, and also signalled the eloquence of the African-American tradition and its global appeal. Obama himself had already begun to weave together the disparate elements of his inheritance in his autobiography, *Dreams from My Father*:

We hold these truths to be self-evident. In those words, I hear the spirit of Douglass and Delany, as well as Jefferson and Lincoln; the struggles of Martin and Malcolm and unheralded marchers to bring these words to life. I hear the voices of Japanese families interned behind barbed wire; young Russian Jews cutting patterns in Lower East Side sweatshops; dust-bowl farmers loading up their trucks with the remains of shattered lives. I hear the voices of the people in Altgeld Gardens, and the voices of those who stand outside this country's borders, the weary, hungry bands crossing the Rio Grande...all of them asking the very same questions that have come to shape my life: What is our community, and how might that community be reconciled with our freedom? How far do our obligations reach? How do we transform mere power into justice, mere sentiment into love?...I find myself modestly encouraged, believing that so long as the questions are still being asked, what binds us together might somehow, ultimately, prevail.

Part of Obama's extraordinary gift is to crystallize the hopes of his audience, to represent their dreams. So, to young Americans he offers 'change we can believe in'; to African-Americans, he becomes the symbol of their struggle for recognition; across the world, he embodies a version of America everyone can identify with – even the Irish, who composed a ballad in his honour, claiming a shared inheritance. 'American Pie', an op-ed column on the front page of the *Indian Express*, captured this perfectly in the days before the election of November 2008. Its author, Manoj K. Das, quoted a Virginian taxi-driver, Rafiq Ogame, as follows: 'No attempt needed. We go on our own. He is our man. Obama is the complete human being. For Christians, he is a Christian. For whites, he has been brought up by a white granny. For Muslims, he is a Muslim. He is everybody, and everybody has a bit of himself in Obama.'

The world's English is the medium through which Obama articulated his appeal. More than one reporter on the campaign trail observed what Mark Danner called 'the absolute clarity and simplicity of his [Obama's] language'. At the same time there was an unmistakable 'tinge of blackness: the Southern tones, the slight mid-Carolina or mid-Southern softening, the falling final g's. He knows these people, each one of them, that's what his grin says – wherever he comes from, he will be this day the local boy made good: *theirs*.' That, for Obama, is only part of his repertoire. He is also Everyman. 'I learned to slip back and forth between my black and white worlds,' he writes in *Dreams from My Father*, 'understanding that each possessed its own language and customs and structures of meaning, convinced that with a bit of translation on my part the two worlds could eventually cohere.' The magic ingredient in Obama's global appeal is his apparently effortless movement between worlds as geographically far apart as Kenya, Kansas, Hawaii and Indonesia.

'Who is the real Barack Obama?' challenged his opponent, John McCain, in tones of mounting frustration, during a long, and bitter, campaign. It was really a pointless question. Obama's candidacy was perfectly timed. As Jonathan Freedland wrote in the *Guardian*, Obama was simply 'the right man for a new and globalised age'. Multicultural in origin, multicoloured in linguistic inheritance, multifarious in education and experience, Barack Hussein Obama, the 44th President of the United States, and the first African-American to occupy the office, holds an appeal that is contagious, adaptable, populist and subversive – in a word, 'globish'. His campaign was the vindication of his slogans 'The Audacity Of Hope' and – more popular – 'Change We Can Believe In'.

Timothy Garton Ash, writing in the *Guardian*, expressed Obama's 'Globish' qualities, though he did not quite put it like that: 'In the way [Obama] thinks about the world,' he wrote, 'and even more in his view of Europe itself, he could not be more different. His mental map goes north–south, not east–west. His roots are in Kenya and the American Midwest; his childhood experience was in Indonesia and Hawaii ... Biographically, he is the personification of a trend the analysts have identified in the abstract: a demographic shift, since the mid-1960s, towards Americans of non-European origin, weakening cultural and historical transatlantic ties.'

PART THREE

Popularizers

8. Rule, Britannia!

How England Became British

The genius of the English language [lies in] its naturalness, which
does not shun either the basest or most monstrous ideas; in its energy,
which other nations might take for harshness; in its daring, which
minds less accustomed to foreign usage would consider gibberish.

Voltaire, Appeal to all the Nations of Europe

1

On 18 June 1746 the bookseller and publisher Robert Dodsley held a
breakfast at the Golden Anchor near Holborn Bar to celebrate the
successful negotiation of a massive contract for a new dictionary of
the English language. The prospective author of this project, Samuel
Johnson, who signed his contract during the breakfast, was the archetypal English amateur. A university drop-out, now aged thirty-seven,
he had published some poetry and a lot of literary journalism, but
had never attempted such exacting work before. Johnson's story is
symbolic of the populist and subversive spirit of English. No one
present at the Golden Anchor could have imagined how significant
this moment would turn out to be, though knowing the author they
might have suspected something special. The trainee lexicographer
was vigorous, fit, tenacious, independent and strong-minded. He
would settle the importance of English in an intensely practical and
typically Anglo-Saxon way, on his own terms. Rather than debate
arguments about English vocabulary with a committee of experts, he
would research and write the dictionary himself.

Dodsley's contract specified an advance of £1,575. With this
money, Johnson set up his 'dictionary workshop' on the top floor of
17 Gough Square. His biographer James Boswell described the garret

where Johnson worked as 'fitted up like a counting house' with a long desk running down the middle at which the copying clerks could work standing up. Johnson himself, no doubt 'with his stockings round his ankles', would be stationed in a rickety chair at an 'old, crazy deal table', surrounded by piles of borrowed books. He was helped by six assistants (five Scots, one an expert in 'low, cant phrases', and an Englishman), two of whom died while the work on the *Dictionary* was still in progress. It was an immense labour. Writing in some eighty large notebooks, and without the benefit of any local library, Johnson wrote the definition of more than 40,000 English words himself, illustrating their many meanings with some 114,000 quotations drawn from English writing on every subject under the sun, from the Elizabethan to his own times. Every line of the *Dictionary* was imbued with a witty, popular and democratic spirit.

Lexicographer: A writer of dictionaries, a harmless drudge.
Oats: A grain, which in England is generally given to horses, but in Scotland supports the people.

Johnson did not expect to achieve complete originality, or to be omniscient. When asked by a lady why he had defined 'pastern' as the 'knee' of a horse, he replied, majestically: 'Ignorance, madam, pure ignorance.' Working to a deadline, he had to draw on the best of all previous dictionaries, and to make his work a heroic synthesis. With hindsight, it was very much more. Unlike previous lexicographers, who had been anxious to 'fix' the language on the page, preserving it in amber, Johnson treated English with the utmost practicality, as a living language with numerous, different shades of meaning. Placing it in the context of everyday, popular usage, he adopted his definitions on the principle of English common law: according to precedent.

Johnson laboured for nine years in Gough Square, as he put it himself, 'with little assistance of the learned, and without any patronage of the great; not in the soft obscurities of retirement, or under the shelter of academic bowers, but amidst inconvenience and distraction, in sickness and in sorrow'. His *Dictionary* was, like its author, very much the product of the world in which he lived. 'I have protracted my work', he told Boswell sadly, 'till most of those whom I wished to please have sunk into the grave; and success and miscarriage are empty sounds.' After many vicissitudes, and the constant money worries familiar to freelance writers, Johnson's *Dictionary* was finally published on 15 April 1755. It was instantly recognized as a landmark. 'This remarkable work', wrote one leading Italian lexicographer, 'will be a perpetual monument of Fame to the Author, an Honour to his own Country, and a general Benefit to the Republic of Letters throughout Europe.' The English could also celebrate the fact that Johnson had taken on the academies of Europe and beaten them at their own game (forty French academicians had just spent forty years producing the first French national dictionary). Johnson's friend David Garrick summarized the metropolitan view:

> And Johnson, well armed, like a hero of yore
> Has beat forty French, and will beat forty more.

The contrast is vital. In France, the process of writing a national dictionary codified, solidified and ultimately fossilized the language. For English, the dictionary process achieved the exact opposite: it gave expression to its contagious adaptability, catchy populism and innate subversiveness. French might be the language of international relations, but its potential as a world language would remain circumscribed by custom, temperament and philosophical preference. The eighteenth century also saw the culmination of England's old war with France. But first, as a decisive curtain-raiser, there was one of the great historical gambles of this story. The Conquest of 1066 had been one; the Glorious Revolution (or Great Rebellion) of 1688 was another. After 600 years of quirky individualism, England had acquired a taste for moderate republicanism.

2

The Glorious Revolution, unlike the Conquest, enjoyed broad domestic support and was progressive in spirit. It began as an expression of insular, Protestant feeling against the absolutist threat of Roman Catholicism in the figure of James II, and the European ambitions of a powerful French king, Louis XIV. Its conclusion surprised everyone: the installation of a Dutch king, a declaration of rights and a reassertion of national pride that was as much *British* as English, and it led to the modernization of an isolated, ramshackle, happily provincial society into an international power.

The events of 1688 will always be debated but their upshot is hardly in doubt: within a generation party politics became the instrument of English government, while the warring kingdoms of England, Scotland and Ireland were finding a new kind of unity beneath British colours. From 1688 to 1815 a succession of Anglo-French conflicts in various theatres across the world meant that there were fewer than three full decades of peace in a hundred years. Britain and France were so constantly engaged in the struggle for world mastery that, for some historians, this is the second Hundred Years War. In 1756 perhaps the greatest Anglo-French conflict, the Seven Years War, broke out across the known world. The expenditure of this war had further global consequences: sharper taxation for the American colonies was followed by the outbreak of war and revolution from 1775 to 1783. The cost of the American War of Independence so nearly bankrupted France that it may plausibly be said to have provoked the French Revolution, which led, in turn, to the Napoleonic Wars, a European crisis that was brought to a conclusion by the Congress of Vienna in 1815. Warfare would be the making of the world's English.

3

The crisis of 1688 began with the news that James II, a zealous Catholic and pro-French king, had sired a male heir. Palace gossip said that the baby was an impostor, smuggled into the queen's bed in 'a warming pan'. In London, the political class that had grown up with Cromwell, and in the Restoration the easygoing figure of Charles II, was faced with an obdurate Catholic dynasty stretching to the crack of doom. But there was an alternative, though it must have seemed like a long shot. James II's daughter Mary (by his first wife) was married to a Dutchman, William, Prince of Orange, a staunch Protestant and, better still, an implacable enemy of France and Louis XIV. In June 1688 a group of seven English patriots sent William an 'invitation' which declared, optimistically, that 'nineteen parts of twenty of the people ... are desirous of change'. On his side, William promised he would, 'preserve and maintain the established laws, liberties and customs' of England. Moreover, he expressed this response in English. It was a shrewd appeal to public opinion.

William's invasion force was Dutch in name and leadership, but wholly European in composition. Five hundred vessels ferried an army of some 20,000 German, Dutch, Danish, English, Swedish, Finnish, Polish, Swiss and even Greek troops across the stormy waters of the English Channel in November 1688. After one false start, due to bad weather, the so-called 'Protestant wind' swept William's fleet down the Channel to an unanticipated landfall in Devon, while at the same time this friendly gale prevented the English fleet from sailing out of the Thames estuary to challenge the invaders. Not that James II's admirals were troubled. Their lively expectation was that, if it was not blown irretrievably off course, William's fleet would be wrecked, as the Spanish had been, a hundred years before.

It was not to be. At Torbay, William was greeted with enthusiastic cries of 'God bless you!' and proceeded to advance steadily into England. In a clever strategy, William's slow march on London sponsored countrywide popular declarations against James II, normalized the idea of another anti-Stuart rebellion and persuaded several nervous English grandees to throw their weight behind the Dutchman. Faced with popular disorder and aristocratic rejection, James panicked. When his generals deserted, he threw the essential instrument of royal authority, the Great Seal of the kingdom, into the Thames, and fled to France. Now the English genius for turning defeat into victory, and catastrophe into government policy, reasserted itself. An armed putsch became first a great rebellion and then a glorious revolution. Factions previously irreconcilable under James formed a united front to promote the idea of William as king, something neither side had ever really intended. After a stand-off between

Parliament and the reserved Dutch prince, William accepted a Declaration of Rights, soon the Bill of Rights, and took the throne as William III, sharing the crown with his wife, Mary II.

Few Britons today celebrate, or even remember, 1688, but it was a vital new chapter in which Parliament achieved some real sovereignty and religious freedom was, in a limited way, secure. John Locke, who had gone into exile during the worst of the recent Stuart reign, wrote that toleration 'has now at last been established by law in our country. It is something to have progressed so far,' he observed. As much by chance as by design, an important theme of English cultural discourse – toleration, compromise and restraint – long recognized by English political philosophy, was now confirmed in a quasi-constitutional arrangement. The English domestic settlement of 1688 was matched, in the wider world, by a *British* foreign policy. Here again, James II, who had the weak man's taste for military adventure, inadvertently played a decisive role. In March 1690 James landed in Ireland with a European army, the first step in the reconquest of his country on behalf of Catholic Europe. His plan was to mobilize an Irish army, cross to Scotland and march south on London. But the Jacobite forces became bogged down in Ireland, and were finally defeated outside Dublin on 1 July 1690 when forced to fight William's army at the battle of the Boyne. 'Madam, your countrymen ran from the battle,' James complained to an Irish supporter. 'Sire,' she replied, coolly. 'You seem to have won the race.' The European importance of this Irish battle is beyond question. Louis XIV and William III, kings of France and Britain, were now at war, and the Stuart claim had become indissolubly linked to the French cause.

4

War with France had always enjoyed popular support in England. Now, associated with repelling the francophile Jacobites, it became a defence of the Glorious Revolution. In the making of the world's English, war with France had at least one vital consequence: it accelerated the emergence of a vigorous, new European entity, Great

Britain, fighting under its new standard, the 'Union Jack'. There was great contemporary pride in this gaudy marriage of conflicting flags. Daniel Defoe composed a bestselling satirical poem, 'The True-Born Englishman', that argued for a vigorous polyglot tradition derived from centuries of immigration:

> From the most Scoundrel Race that ever liv'd
> A horrid Crowd of Rambling Thieves and Drones;
> Who Ransack'd Kingdoms and dispeopled Towns.

The other symbol of England's new self-confidence is the Queen Anne house. Like the monarch herself, who succeeded her brother-in-law William in 1702, this style of architecture was not grand but comfortable, prosperous but never flashy, projecting an air of domestic serenity. Queen Anne houses often stand in the midst of gardens that to the European seem wild and uncultivated. This would be the essential contrast between England and the Continent in the coming century: ebullient, popular nationalism, uttered in a raucous, seemingly anarchic, vernacular against sophisticated *ancien régime* disdain. When the new queen declared, in her first address to Parliament, that 'I know my heart to be entirely English' she set a national agenda for her short reign that would have a decisive effect on the global reach of English.

Within a month of her accession Anne declared war on France. To conduct this campaign she appointed the flawed but brilliant figure of John Churchill, who, at the battle of Blenheim, achieved a victory so brilliant, bloody and comprehensive that French ambitions in Europe were thereafter reduced to sabre-rattling manoeuvres in Spain and the Netherlands. By 1707, the year England and Scotland signed the Act of Union, further annihilating victories gave British forces complete mastery in the Low Countries and made Churchill, now the duke of Marlborough, a national hero. Meanwhile, at home, the newly formed Anglo-Scottish kingdom of 'Great Britain', described by Swift as 'this crazy double-bottomed realm', was uniting its navies and beginning to consolidate its trading position through the promotion of London as a great financial centre. Britannia did not yet rule the waves, but

Tory 'blue water' policy (naval supremacy and fiscal conservatism) ensured that all the right conditions were in place for 'Great Britain' to supersede Restoration England. When the War of the Spanish Succession was concluded at the Treaty of Utrecht in 1713 the London mob rioted, but for no good reason. Britain had won the peace as well as the war, and now held a decisive commercial advantage, operating as the premier maritime power across the globe.

Queen Anne's death in August 1714 handed George, the elector of Hanover and a great-grandson of James I, a united kingdom bursting with commercial potential. The new king showed little interest in his new realm. He landed in England with German advisers, German-speaking Turkish servants and two German mistresses, known from their profiles as 'the maypole' and 'the elephant'. In such a cosy Germanic bubble, George never mastered more than a few sentences of broken English, and was quickly judged 'the Jest, the Contempt and Aversion of the Nation'. Yet, paradoxically, during the long life of the Hanoverian dynasty, a rampant political economy would transplant English and Englishness to some of the most remote and inaccessible places on earth, and give them a new voice.

5

The new British vigour and confidence that are visible in hindsight eluded many observers at the time. Language often acts as a lightning conductor for anxiety about social and cultural change. The more England's monarchy seemed foreign, and England's place in the world in peril of military or mercantile adventure, and the more modernity threatened, the greater were the worries of conservative English writers about the corruption of the mother tongue. The most devastating of such writings are the essays of 'the gloomy dean', Dr Jonathan Swift, whose hatred of change and fear of progress inspired an eloquence on behalf of the English language unique in its history.

A satirist and a pamphleteer whose ferocity made him many enemies, Swift is best remembered today as the author of *Gulliver's Travels*. But when, during the reign of Queen Anne, he addressed his formidable powers to what he saw as the parlous condition of the language, he was devastating. Considering the half-century from the English Civil War to 'this present time', Swift doubted 'whether the Corruptions in our Language have not at least equalled the Refinements of it'. No contemporary author had escaped 'these Corruptions'. Society, for a Tory like Swift, was going to hell in a handcart. Oliver Cromwell's Commonwealth? A 'Usurpation' which had sponsored 'such an Infusion of Enthusiastick Jargon in every Writing, as was not shook off in many Years after'. For Swift, things had hardly improved with Charles II. The 'Licentiousness' which came with the Restoration, having infected 'Religion and Morals, fell to corrupt our Language...' For Swift, the only sure remedy against these 'Manglings and Abbreviations' and against the innovations of 'illiterate Court Fops, half-witted Poets, and University Boys' – horrid words like *sham*, *banter*, *mob* and *bully* – was another ugly word, a quango, an English Academy. Swift proposed the reform of English through a committee, 'made of such persons as are generally allowed to be best qualified for such a Work'. But his ideas lapsed, not least because the idea of such a prescriptive society ran counter to the amateur tradition of English literary scholarship. Swift's fears, however, have been echoed in one form or another by successive generations, notably in Lynne Truss's witty millennial global bestseller *Eats, Shoots and Leaves*. In his own time, by a nice irony, there was one society for whom England and English ways were the source of all that was best in European civilization. Remarkably enough, this was 'that sweet enemy', France. Gallic fascination with the ebullient Englishness of the eighteenth century – symptomatic of Britain's resurgence – is represented by the supreme French man of letters, the philosopher, playwright, poet, novelist and all-round intellectual pest, Voltaire.

6

The young François-Marie Arouet developed his Anglophilia in the 1720s, after a meeting with the exiled Tory grandee Henry St John Bolingbroke, and subsequently from a visit to England in the spring of 1726. Voltaire, who had just enjoyed a *succès fou* in Paris with his play *Œdipe*, was exhilarated by both these experiences. Bolingbroke advised the young man to cultivate his character as he would his garden, and to read Locke's *Essay concerning Human Understanding*. Two years later, in flight from enemies at home, Voltaire landed at Gravesend in perfect sunshine and was at once captivated by the atmosphere of 'freedom' and 'plenty'. England, he decided, was the home of tolerance and reason, a beacon of liberty across the water from a Europe imprisoned in intellectual and spiritual darkness by Catholic priests, absolute monarchs and an intolerant, philistine aristocracy. (There was never much space in Voltaire's thinking for the common man.)

Little is known of Voltaire's visit, but he did meet Dean Swift, William Congreve and two Georges (I and II), dined with Lord Chesterfield and, in a famous faux pas, scandalized Alexander Pope's old mother with his modish use of 'bugger'. He also completed a play, *Brutus*, which contrasted English freedoms with French despotism. The lasting fruits of this trip, Voltaire's *Letters concerning the English Nation*, a ground-breaking new genre – part travelogue, part essay – and written originally in English, would be hugely influential. First published in London in 1733, the *Letters* were a huge success, an 'ode to England' that became the bible of eighteenth-century Anglophilia. The French edition, entitled *Lettres philosophiques*, provoked official fury (burned in Paris by the hangman) and popular enthusiasm. Roast beef, horse racing, gardening, frock coats and English puddings all became the object of the thrilling new phenomenon known as 'Anglomanie', a bourgeois sentiment that would be repeated in Germany throughout the next century.

In both France and Germany, the touchstone of this 'Anglomanie' was Shakespeare. For the first time since his death, the playwright became a national icon abroad. Actor David Garrick, a pioneer of eighteenth-century 'bardolatry', performed scenes from Shakespeare in the Paris salons of the 1750s and 1760s to an audience familiar with English drama through Voltaire's advocacy in his *Letters*. As the historians Robert and Isabelle Tombs have noted, Shakespeare was playing to full houses in Paris during September 1793, at the height of the Terror – in a musical version, *Romeo and Juliette*.

During the later part of his long and contentious life, Voltaire's infatuation with England cooled into something more ironical. In *Candide* (1759), one of the international bestsellers of the eighteenth century, he describes his hero landing in Portsmouth at the very hour of Admiral Byng's execution for dereliction of duty. A puzzled Candide is advised that in Britain it is thought prudent to kill an admiral from time to time 'pour encourager les autres'. Meanwhile, Voltaire moderated his youthful enthusiasm for 'the genius of the English language'. Now he believed it had 'energy' (aka 'harshness') and 'daring', which some 'would consider gibberish'. But 'Anglomanie' lingered at the court of Louis XVI, where it was fashionable to parade occasional snippets of English vocabulary. There was also a frisson, out of the king's earshot, attached to uttering radical new words like *vote*, *opposition*, *jury*, *pamphlet* and *constitution*. The king even translated some passages from Milton, and is said to have studied the history of the Stuarts while awaiting his rendezvous with the guillotine.

In old age, secluded with his mistress at Ferney in Switzerland, Voltaire became an important stop on the Grand Tour: British writers like Edward Gibbon, James Boswell and John Wilkes, en route to Rome and Taormina, would pay homage to the sardonic old Anglophile, now an exotic survivor from another era. By the 1760s and 1770s Britain had long triumphed over France in the Seven Years War, and Britannia's offspring had found a new national icon in John Bull, a boozy, profane xenophobe with a sentimental passion for 'English liberty' and an absolute loathing for 'Popery', Continental foppishness and French contrivance. 'Anglomanie' might flatter national self-esteem in the avenues and courtyards of old Europe, but in the new world of global warfare and global trade, the language now needed a more robust and practical champion. Enter Dr Johnson.

7

Samuel Johnson, born in Lichfield in 1709, was a pioneer who raised common sense to the heights of genius, and a man of robust popular instincts whose watchwords were clarity, precision and simplicity.

But he also revelled in the music of English. One of his tricks, observed by Boswell, was translating plain Anglo-Saxon words into their Anglo-Latin synonyms to ramp up the majesty of his speech. When, for instance, he heard himself say (in perfect Anglo-Saxon phrasing), of a stage production, that 'it hath not wit enough to keep it sweet', he would correct himself and translate it into Johnson-ese with, 'it has not vitality enough to preserve it from putrefaction'. The Johnson who challenged Bishop Berkeley's solipsist theory of the non-existence of matter by kicking a large stone ('I refute it thus') is the same Johnson for whom language must have a daily practical use, and a ready application to the everyday world of the common man.

Despite his formidable reputation as a man of letters, there was always something rather childlike about Johnson. In his awkward, ungainly walk, his carelessness with clothes, unkempt appearance and restless physical movement, he was like an overgrown boy. It is said that he loved to climb trees and to roll down grassy hills. Fanny Burney wrote that 'his mouth is almost constantly opening and shutting as if he was chewing. He has a strange method of frequently twirling his fingers and twisting his hands. His body is in continual agitation, see-sawing up and down; his feet are never a moment quiet; and, in short, his whole person is in perpetual motion.' Johnson's zigzag passage down London's streets was a source of amused wonder to children and bystanders who watched in astonishment at the good doctor's habit of knocking any post with his stick as he passed. 'I never knew a man laugh more heartily,' wrote Boswell; while others said that he laughed 'like a rhinoceros'. Overshadowing this disconcerting exuberance was the cloud of a darker melancholy, reminiscent of Churchill's 'black dog', a sometimes disabling despair. He told Boswell that Robert Burton's *Anatomy of Melancholy* was 'the only book that ever took him out of bed two hours sooner than he wished to rise'.

Out of this troubled psychology, masking a profound inner torment, Johnson found solace in a language that was, in its coarse complexity and comprehensive genius, the precise analogue of his character. With his famous *Dictionary*, the author and his subject achieved a remarkable, unforced unanimity. Both were adaptable, populist and instinctively subversive (or, to put it another way, libertarian). As a result, in the decades after its publication, the *Dictionary* was not seriously rivalled until the coming of the *Oxford English Dictionary*, by which time some of Johnson's definitions had passed into folklore ('*Whigs: The name of a faction*'). The distinctive wit of the *Dictionary* should not obscure its extraordinary grace and clarity. The twelve definitions for a simple, but tricky, word like *Thought* display the fluency and accuracy of an exceptional mind:

1. *The operation of the mind; the act of thinking.* 2. *Idea; image formed in the mind.* 3. *Sentiment; fancy; imagery.* 4. *Reflection; particular consideration.* 5. *Conception; preconceived notion.* 6. *Opinion; judgement.* 7. *Meditation; serious consideration.* 8. *Design; purpose.* 9. *Silent contemplation.* 10. *Solicitude; care, concern.* 11. *Expectation.* 12. *A small degree; a small quantity.*

For all its eccentricities this two-volume work is a masterpiece and a landmark, in Johnson's own words, 'setting the orthography, displaying the analogy, regulating the structures, and ascertaining the significations of English words'. It was an achievement that, in Boswell's words, 'conferred stability on the language of his country', a stability that would be invaluable in the decades to come. But, though it made him famous and well esteemed, the *Dictionary* did not allay his incessant money troubles. In 1759 Johnson was so hard up that he was forced to dash off the potboiling fable *Rasselas*, to pay, he said, for his mother's funeral.

8

Arguably, 1759 is the most important year in British history since 1066. In the words of the historian Frank McLynn, 'the entire history of the world would have been different but for the events of 1759'. This was the year in which Britain established a mastery, at once military and cultural, of a new world. Abroad, there was a succession of victories; at home, there was popular enlightenment. By creating institutions such as the British Museum and Kew Gardens (both founded in 1759), Britain planted the ambition for a public realm in which intellectual and cultural life would be open and accessible to all. This principle would eventually give birth to the BBC and the Open University, and would possibly inspire the World Wide Web, pioneered by Tim Berners-Lee. The significance of 1759 is perhaps reinforced, for the superstitious, by the reappearance of Halley's comet blazing across northern skies in March. To the English, this celestial fire had once been a portent of catastrophe; on this occasion, a year of battles across the known world saw the wheel of historical fortune turn in Britain's favour. In several theatres of war, the seeds of a future lingua franca were being planted by Indians, Africans, Irishmen and even French explorers. The global strategy was deliberate, and self-conscious. 'Ministers in this country,' remarked one British prime minister, 'where every part of the World affects us, in some way or another, should consider the whole Globe.'

In India, throughout January, the French siege of Madras (Chennai) was conducted with horrible ferocity. Madras was a turning point in the Indian theatre of the Seven Years War. By the end of 1759 the French had lost control of the Deccan and had suffered a serious army mutiny. The British East India Company, based in Madras, moved into a position of dominance it would occupy for decades to come. English would be planted in the consciousness of the subcontinent's administrative and commercial native elite, bursting into full, exotic flower in the Victorian English of the Raj. To the eighteenth-century mind, possessions in the East were an inferior prize to the West Indies. Simultaneously with the British victories on the Bengal coast, there were further naval successes in the Caribbean. In the long term, this sideshow would have another significance. At the peace treaty of 1763, Britain traded Guadeloupe for Canada, at once reinforcing the British presence in North America and renewing French sea power in the Caribbean. Eventually, from this base, France would contribute to the American victory at Yorktown in 1781. In such unlikely ways was the Americanization of the New World carried forward in the run up to independence. To British and French military planners alike, Canada (New France), situated at the head of the Ohio valley, was always of great strategic significance. From June to September 1759 Franco-British fighting up and down the St Lawrence river culminated in the battle of Quebec, at which the strange and reckless figure of James Wolfe achieved one of the most spectacular victories in this year of victories, endlessly mythologized in British history books. In Canada, the upshot of this campaign would be 'the two solitudes', the French-speaking third of the country living in uneasy coexistence with their English neighbours. They, in turn, would become culturally colonized by American English. The emergence of Globish (see Epilogue) may sponsor a way out of this linguistic impasse.

The dying Wolfe on the Heights of Abraham became a great imperial icon. At the time, the news of Quebec sent the English-speaking colonies of the eastern seaboard into a delirium of celebration: bells, bonfires and blazing beacons. General Wolfe links the world of warfare to the world of books. According to Robert Southey (who repeated this apocryphal story to Sir Walter Scott), on the eve of battle Wolfe produced a copy of Thomas Gray's poems from his pocket and began to recite the 'Elegy Written in a Country Churchyard'. When his philistine officers responded with silent indifference, Wolfe rebuked them. 'I can only say, gentlemen, that if the choice were mine, I would rather be the author of these verses than win the battle which we are to fight tomorrow morning.' War and literature were also fused in the supreme English bestseller of 1759, Laurence Sterne's *Life and Opinions of Tristram Shandy*. In this classic novel, Uncle Toby, a veteran of the wars against Louis XIV, suffers a comic obsession with siege craft and delights in soldiers' tales from a long-forgotten Flanders campaign in the days of Marlborough. *Shandy*, a word of obscure origin, means 'crack-brained, half crazy', and it expresses the mood of the moment. Tristram himself says, in volume VI of this rambling masterpiece, that he is writing a 'civil, nonsensical, good humoured *Shandean* book'. For Sterne, as for most British readers, this commitment of British troops to a European theatre of war was exceptional, but uninvolving. It was sea victories that thrilled the public. In December, *The Harlequin's Invasion*, a patriotic farce, brought the year to a rousing conclusion with a hit song, 'Hearts of Oak' (words by David Garrick; music by William Boyce), that perfectely captures the nation's exuberant jingoism:

> Come, cheer up, my lads,
> It's to glory we steer,
> To add something more
> To this glorious year
>
> To honour we call you
> As free men not slaves
> For who are so free
> As the sons of the waves...

Throughout the rest of the century, the 'sons of the waves' would consolidate Britannia's rule over her first empire and overcome Britain's intrinsic disadvantage in her war with France. In 1759 the population of the British Isles was scarcely 7 million (against 25 million in France and 140 million in Europe as a whole). Sea power transformed Britain's prospects and restored the balance of power. Before the age of the telegraph, or the internet, a global fleet was the means by which the English-speaking world traded information, gossip, news and luxury. Sea power opened new shipping lanes to four great arenas: North America, Latin America and India, and, ultimately, the Pacific. Sea power begins in the mid-eighteenth century and lies at the heart of an emerging 'Anglosphere'. Between 1750 and 1780 the number of ships at sea increased tenfold. The sea was now, in the words of one awestruck writer, 'a mighty rendezvous' that offered the British traveller immediate and privileged access to one-third of the globe's surface. International commerce and the rise of the slave trade would promote the discovery of more and more new opportunities overseas, but trade was not the only engine of British expansion. There was the exercise of human curiosity – sheer wonder at the world's treasures – and the ever constant dream of a new and better life abroad. Such thoughts were spurred into reality by dramatic improvements in travel: by 1770 almost all of England was within 20 miles of a turnpike.

The result, for ordinary people, in a process analogous with the experience of our own time, was a sharp new consciousness of global connections, facilitated by language. At mid-century the diverse peoples and places of the world suddenly seemed to be connected. This was felt by many European commentators to be something new, though the Greeks and Romans had recorded similar sensations. For some conservative observers such novelty was alarming. In 1777, at the beginning of Britain's American crisis, Edmund Burke declared that 'the great map of mankind is unrolled at once'. Anticipating Thomas Friedman's characterization of the 'flat' world, Burke noted that the global map was 'at the same time under our view'. This was a British perspective derived from its new empire, and one that excited foreign envy. For the moment, British imperialism required some benign cultural underpinning. Here, Britain's cultural elite turned to William Shakespeare.

9

The two-hundredth anniversary of Shakespeare's birth had occurred in 1764, a year after the Peace of Paris carved up the world in Britain's favour, but no one paid much attention. Five years later, inexplicably, a group of amateur bardolaters decided to celebrate a 'Shakespeare Jubilee' in Stratford, on 5 September 1769. It was David Garrick, convinced of his special relationship with Shakespeare, who stepped forward to provide some appropriate verses:

> Now, now, we tread the sacred ground,
> Here Shakespeare walk'd and sung!

This was one of several Jubilee tributes performed by the Drury Lane chorus and orchestra, directed by Thomas Arne, at Stratford's Holy Trinity Church, the shrine of shrines, where the poet's bones are interred. The main Jubilee stage was an octagonal wooden amphitheatre (the Rotunda) erected nearby on the banks of the Avon, the scene of a public banquet, a costume ball and finally a dazzling firework display.

Inevitably, the Englishness of the setting took a hand. On the second morning of the Jubilee it began to drizzle, and then to rain in earnest. The river rose and suddenly the 'soft-flowing Avon' threatened the Rotunda, which was teeming with crowds sheltering from the downpour. But Garrick would not be distracted and delivered a Jubilee Oration in an egregiously melodramatic manner, appalling many observers and culminating in a gesture where he pulled on the gloves – the very gloves! – that Shakespeare was said to have worn on stage.

By the third day of this bizarre occasion many had fled the weather and the bombast, but there was still a Jubilee sweepstake, raced in sodden meadows, and one final ball. Thereafter, Stratford became the focus of a Shakespeare relics industry (gloves, mugs, rings and even pieces of 'Shakespeare's chair'). The *Gentleman's Magazine* published a fine engraving of the Birthplace, the house on Henley Street, but demurred from identifying in which room 'Shakespeare first drew breath'. The Shakespeare scholar Samuel Schoenbaum says that these 'Stratford celebrations contributed to the emergence of Shakespeare as full-fledged culture hero', and now 'bardolatry' began to spread far beyond Stratford or London. 'Let me search for the clue which led great Shakespeare into the labyrinth of human nature,' declared the American revolutionary lawyer (and second President) John Adams to his diary. 'Let me examine how men think.'

Much later, during peace negotiations with the British government after the Revolution, Adams and Jefferson paid a visit to Henley Street, and admired the chair in the corner, where (they were told) the bard himself would have sat. The distinguished tourists were encouraged to help themselves to some souvenir chips of wood from this seat, and Jefferson paid a shilling to see Shakespeare's grave. (Adams later claimed that the author of the Declaration of Independence actually fell to his knees in Holy Trinity Church, and kissed the ground.) Literary shrines are often disappointing. As usual with Shakespeare, the man himself proved elusive. 'There is nothing preserved of this great genius', wrote Adams sadly, 'which might inform us what accident turned his mind to letters and drama.' But this scene illustrates how much Shakespeare's works had penetrated American consciousness. Indeed, there were Shakespeare productions in many colonial theatres across the Atlantic, even after the separation of 1776, and Abraham Lincoln used to derive special pleasure from reading Shakespeare with members of his staff.

10

The Seven Years War redrew the map of the world. In some parts, Britannia's dominion was magnificent, luxurious and corrupt. The East India Company extracted riches from Bengal that were, in the words of William Pitt the Elder, 'a gift from heaven'. Eventually, there was revulsion at heaven's bounty and the governor-general, Warren Hastings, was impeached on charges of misgovernment and corruption. Meanwhile, the American Revolution had relocated the English-speaking world's centre of gravity. Britain, having lost one empire in the West, found a second one in the East. With remarkable foresight, the Scots economist Adam Smith identified this process as early as 1776 in *The Wealth of Nations*. There were, wrote Smith, two milestones on Britain's road to global empire: the settlement of North America and the opening of trade routes to India and the East:

The discovery of America, and that of a passage to the East Indies by the Cape of Good Hope, are the two greatest and most important events recorded in the history of mankind. By uniting, in some measure, the most distant parts of the world, by enabling them to relieve one another's wants, to increase one another's enjoyments, and to encourage one another's industry, their general tendency would seem to be beneficial.

Empire made thoughtful people reflect on the cost to liberty. Adam Smith believed there was an inevitable price. 'To the natives, all the commercial benefits which can have resulted from those events have been sunk and lost in the dreadful misfortunes which they have occasioned,' he wrote. In simple terms, Smith's idea, which trickled down into countless expressions of English colonial policy across the globe, was that Britain should stick to the moral high ground, remain faithful to its explicitly commercial traditions, avoid military commitments and be the thrifty, humane and doughty champion of 'natural liberty' in all its manifestations. It was this idea that generations of independent-minded Scots and Englishmen would take to the four corners of the world. In this way, the world's English became the vessel for a progressive culture and political economy. William Pitt the Younger, the prime minister during the last years of the century, used to quote from Adam Smith in his Commons speeches (while privately admitting that *The Wealth of Nations* was beyond him), popularizing Smith's ideas and placing them at the heart of his government's foreign policy. Yet again, it was war with France that shaped the final decades of Britain's century-long struggle for global dominance.

At first, the French Revolution renewed ancestral Gallic ambitions and, in opposition, stimulated a bruising nationalist temper in Britain. Loyalist mobs yelled slogans like 'Church And King', 'No Popery' and 'No Black Bread'. When, after the shocking execution of Louis XVI, France declared war on Britain (and Holland), traditional roles were reversed. Britain was no longer the admired radical model of constitutional monarchy, but the home of security, sound money and domestic moderation. To patriotic Britons, war with France was now a defence of a way of life against godless, kingless, trouserless revolutionary egalitarians. Pitt's policy would encourage Britain's European allies to engage the enemy on the Continent while using sea power to defeat the French everywhere else.

This strategy was the making of the second British empire and the promotion of the global brand known to cartoonists as 'Britannia', the vindication of every nationalist's hopes. The surge in Britain's fortunes was palpable. In 1792 there were just 23 British colonies; in 1816 there were 43. Similarly, in 1750 the first British empire amounted to some 12.5 million inhabitants, but by 1820 that figure had soared to 200 million. The scale of the fighting involved is important, too. The Napoleonic Wars bore much the same relation to the Seven Years War as the Second World War bears to the First, and they had the same kind of democratizing effect. In India, the West Indies and southern Africa and across the Pacific and the Antipodes, as well as throughout Europe, mankind was mobilized as never before. The

People's Armies (the *levée en masse*) of the French Revolution were never less than half a million men-at-arms, and Napoleon's army was close to a million. In Britain, fears of a French invasion inspired one in twenty Britons to enlist in volunteer militias. British troops had never marched under any ideological flag, but war with Bonaparte's France focused an imperial policy and made conquest as acceptable as commercial exploitation. To be proudly 'British' was to be in the forefront of a civilizing mission on behalf of white, Christian, English-speaking people for whom Magna Carta and the Glorious Revolution were dimly felt to embody eternal British verities. The century-long making of a British imperial identity had reached a climax, remarkably unimpeded by the American War of Independence, but validated in the European theatre of war. The soldiers of Waterloo were the popular emblem of the British triumph over France. Far more significant, in the longer term, was the 200,000-strong army of sepoys, commanded by 30,000 Britons, operated by the East India Company in 1815. The British Raj would become the apotheosis of Britannia's most extravagant fantasies. Closer to home, in Egypt, one enthusiastic traveller reported that 'The French influence is at a low ebb, and the English proudly predominant'. Others saw the development of British power, more typically, as an English estate-management problem, an 'oak planted in a flower pot'.

Perhaps the best barometer of Britain's new and rampant self-confidence, expressed in the cartoon figure of John Bull, was its response to the French Revolution. When the first popular insurrections, symbolized by the storming of the Bastille, broke out in Paris in 1789, many leading lights in the English-speaking world, sympathetic to constitutional reform, became caught up in the ferment of change. Thomas Jefferson, then American ambassador to Paris, discussed Lafayette's drafts for a 'Declaration of the Rights of Man', later claiming that the French Revolution had been fought in his sitting room. The conventional wisdom in London was that the French would simply follow the example of the Anglo-Saxon world, so successfully pioneered during the preceding century. Before the Terror, one English diplomat in Paris wrote that 'the intercourse of the French with the Americans has brought them nearer to the English than they had ever been before'. The British media was playing its part, too: 'The almost unrestrained introduction of our daily publications [has] attracted the attention of the people more towards the freedom and advantages of our constitution.' In Paris, the British ambassador to the French court, England's leading all-round cricketer, the duke of Dorset, was so committed to his sport as a metaphor for life ('beauty the bat, and man the ball') that he assumed the fall of the Bastille marked close of play, not an opening stand. 'The greatest revolution that we know anything of', he reported home, 'has been affected with the loss of very few lives: from this moment we may consider France as a free country; the King a very limited monarch, and the Nobility as reduced to a level with the rest of the Nation.'

But the Revolution was French, not British: there was no appetite for compromise. Events in Paris were spinning out of control. Eventually, to soothe domestic French unrest, and to display British sang-froid, the ambassador proposed a truly British panacea: a game of cricket. Dorset approached a cricketing friend, the earl of Tankerville, who committed himself to sponsoring a team that would feature several famous contemporary players, including William Bedster, formerly his butler and a well-known batsman, and Edward 'Lumpy' Stevens, the earl's gardener and a ferocious fast bowler. Dorset, a fine cricketer, also planned to join the team, from his embassy in Paris, during August 1789. As it turned out, Paris became so unstable, and the British so unpopular, that the duke hurriedly crossed the Channel to Dover, advised Tankerville's team to stay at home, and consoled himself with a Kent–Surrey match instead. So the French Revolution was denied the example of British fair play. Marie Antoinette is said to have kept the duke's bat as a souvenir. Culturally speaking, French would be the language of international relations, but its influence would always be top-down and not, like English, bottom-up.

9. East, in a Western Voice

The People's Empire

And then, before I could open my lips, the East spoke to me, but it
was in a Western voice...The voice swore and cursed violently; it
riddled the solemn peace of the bay by a volley of abuse. It began by
calling me Pig, and from that went crescendo into unmentionable
adjectives – in English.

Joseph Conrad, *Youth*

1

'If you look at a map of the world,' writes Charles Dickens on the
opening page of *A Child's History of England*, 'you will see two Islands'
in 'the left-hand upper corner of the Eastern Hemisphere'. Essential
to the novelist's imagination, 'these Islands' are 'lonely', 'solitary' and
ignorant of 'the rest of the world'. In heroic miniature, this was the
windswept, wave-dashed stage on which Dickens would parade an
extraordinary cast of English historical characters through 'fire and
sword, smoke and arms, death and ruin'. Dickens always displayed
great relish for amateur theatricals; his amateur history would be
similarly melodramatic. It was also quintessentially *English*, teeming
with action, conflict and crowds. But he was wrong about the map.
The great globe itself, not the 'two Islands', was now the scene of the
story; moreover, the plot was unfolding in his lifetime.

Dickens began dictating *A Child's History* in 1843 to his beloved
sister-in-law Georgina when his own son Charley was just six years
old. Part of his ambition was to educate and instruct an impres-
sionable Victorian boy in the achievements of his country, narrating
the dramas of English history – declaring a partiality for King Alfred
and Oliver Cromwell – with a novelist's eye for detail. As well as

celebrating the 'knotted cords' used by Henry II for his penance after the martyrdom of Thomas Becket, or the 'glass of claret' taken by Charles I before his execution, he made no effort to conceal his prejudices. Henry VIII was 'a blot of blood and grease'; and James I 'his Sowship'. Work on *A Child's History* came to a halt in December 1853 when his narrative arrived at the independence of the United States. This, he wrote, swallowing his antipathy, was 'one of the greatest nations on earth'. In truth, the England that Dickens was imaginatively conjuring, and whose historical characters would always seem like walk-ons from his own fiction, had already become replaced by the United States. Dickens knew this. 'Between you and me,' he concluded, 'England has rather lost ground since the days of Oliver Cromwell.' More to the point, his 'England' had become 'Great Britain' and its story was now both imperial and international. There was a new map of the world and much of it would be painted pink in his lifetime.

The empire that provided a massive new audience for Dickens also sponsored international sporting as well as literary opportunities. In 1861 a Melbourne catering company, Spiers & Pond, impressed by the huge success of Dickens's public readings in Britain and the United States, invited the famous writer to perform in Australia. But Dickens was exhausted and unwell, and he declined. In quest of sponsorship, Spiers & Pond moved smoothly from literature to cricket, and decided to ask an English team on tour. A group of senior players accepted an offer of £150 apiece to travel to Australia and play a statewide series of matches. The Spiers & Pond tournament was a great success. In 1863 the Melbourne Cricket Club invited more players. Eventually, the English cricketing establishment reciprocated, with ultimately humiliating consequences for the home team. But it is appropriate that the 'Ashes' series should begin with Dickens, the creator of that supreme proto-Australian, Magwitch, the sombre presence who broods over *Great Expectations*.

For Dickens, as for all the Victorians, the colonies never ceased to be the source of exotic tales, dramatic rewards, bizarre heroism and a constant infusion of strange new cultural experiences, the beginnings of the world's English. These tales of the East begin at the end of the eighteenth century with the settlement of the Antipodes. In January 1788, at the height of the Australian summer, a weather-stained fleet of eleven British ships anchored in Botany Bay after an eight-month voyage from the mother country. Just over 1,000 people disembarked from the First Fleet, three-quarters of them convicts, sentenced for various crimes to a seven-year term in the penal colony of New South Wales. This historic landing marked the beginning of another vital phase in the global expansion of the English-speaking world: the settlement of the British empire.

2

In the next hundred years the English, the Scots and the Irish would take their native language to some of the furthest places on earth: to New Zealand, to Cape Colony in southern Africa, to the country that would become known as Rhodesia (Zimbabwe), to Hong Kong and the China Station, and even to the Falkland Islands in the South Atlantic. Exported English in the nineteenth century had a common stock: these countries were all first settled by the same kind of people within roughly the same generation. To this day the accents of Australian, New Zealand and South African English have a distinct family resemblance, derived from the shared experience of class emigration. The empire was glamorous. For many Victorians at home, the adventures of explorers like David Livingstone in colonial Africa seemed comparable to the exploits of Ralegh and the Elizabethans. Charles Kingsley, the author of many popular fictions, including *The Water-Babies* and *Westward Ho!*, wrote with sentimental brio of a 'brave young England longing to wing its way out of its island prison, to discover and to traffic, to colonise and to civilise, until no wind can sweep the earth which does not bear the echoes of an English voice'.

In the years between the battle of Waterloo in 1815 and the outbreak of the American Civil War in 1861 some 7 million people – soldiers, sailors, traders, missionaries, dissidents, pickpockets, sheep-stealers, settlers and explorers – left the British Isles for overseas, drawn or driven by a tangle of motives, personal, economic or social. Many were casualties of the industrial revolution that was transforming Victorian society. Some were serving the flag. About half went to the newly liberated United States; 1.5 million went to Canada, sponsoring a continuously fraught anglomania; another million went to Australia; the rest were scattered across the globe from Siam (Thailand) to the Transvaal. All spoke some variety of the 'mother tongue'. The nineteenth was, supremely, the century of British English – first the King's and then the Queen's – but it also witnessed the beginnings of the world's English.

Colonial possessions meant colonial wars: the Opium War in China (1839–42 and 1859–60); the Afghan Wars (1838–42 and 1878–80); the Sikh Wars (1842–9); the Maori Wars (1860–66); various wars against the Zulu, Basuto and Matabele tribes in southern Africa (1879–93); eventually the humiliation of the Boer War (1899–1902). These and lesser skirmishes sent 'soldiers of the Queen' across the globe, defending British interests against Pathans, Maoris and Kaffirs, scattering new words into the English lexicon, and planting the roots of Globish in some of the most remote parts of the world. Often, these empire-builders were Irish, especially after the Great Famine of the 1840s, but most were English, the majority of them Cockneys from London and the South-East, the famous 'Tommies' of music-hall song and *Punch* cartoon. For the Londoners and other city folk, and for the other reluctant imperialists, landless labourers, debtors, hustlers and swindlers who headed for the colonies in the nineteenth century, the idea of 'mateship' (the solidarity of 'pals' or 'chums') was fundamental to the experience of exile. 'The bush' could be a harsh environment. You needed friends ('good mates') in adversity.

Not since the Anglo-Saxons landed in Britain, or the Elizabethans arrived in North America, was there such an opportunity for word- and phrase-making. The English-speaking world was enriched with words like *kangaroo*, *bungalow* and *spoor*. This was not so much achieved by the few (poets and novelists, or admirals and colonial administrators), as by the many. From their experience under the tropical sun we get *dungarees*, *guru*, *jungle* (from Sanskrit *jangala*), *juggernaut*, *kedgeree*, *maharaja* and *nirvana*. It was a people's empire of ordinary Britons who subscribed in a highly informal spirit to the now-discredited idea of a 'civilizing mission'. A kind of secular crusade, this mission became the strangest kind of orthodoxy: the British libertarian tradition was at odds with the imperial idea from the beginning. 'The history of empires', declared Edward Gibbon in his first published sentence, 'is the history of human misery.' Even such a passionate conservative such as Edmund Burke could justify the conduct of empire only if it was based on ancient values. 'The British Empire', he wrote, 'must be governed on a plan of freedom, for it will be governed by no other.' This strange clash of English tradition with Victorian ambition resulted in a highly eccentric liberal empire that would be celebrated by its apologists at the old queen's Diamond Jubilee in 1897 as the work of 'the greatest governing race the world has ever seen'.

From a twenty-first-century perspective, the British empire is now long gone, but its power and influence linger in the national imagination. A surprising number of British families will have at least one distant relative who served as a colonial civil servant, or died serving the Union Jack under a tropical sun. Queen Elizabeth II still doles out honours that celebrate an institution that no longer exists. Imperial bric-a-brac pops up on television with the *Antiques Roadshow*. Men and women who have scarcely been east of Greenwich know more about the Raj than Reigate. Today our perception of the empire generally, especially the Raj, comes from the pages of books, the works of Rudyard Kipling, E. M. Forster, George Orwell, M. M. Kaye and Paul Scott. It persists, linguistically, in words like *chi-chi*, *pundit*, *mufti* and *chintz*.

In the immediate aftermath of India's independence in 1947 the idea of empire was denounced, high and low, as oppressive and shameful. A year later the *Empire Windrush* would arrive at Tilbury Docks, carrying 492 passengers from Jamaica who had come, at the invitation of the British government, to start a new life in Britain. Their arrival would be an important landmark in the history of immigration to the British Isles and would be followed in subsequent years by other groups from Britain's former colonies, such as Bangladeshis escaping the war of 1971 or Gujaratis expelled from Uganda in 1972.

Decades later, and while Kipling's stories and poems and J. G. Farrell's fiction vividly conjure up the empire of the past, the effects of that empire continue to imbue the literary culture of the present in equally profound, if very different, ways. In narratives such as Zadie Smith's *White Teeth* and Monica Ali's *Brick Lane*, experiences from North London and Jamaica or Bangladesh are magically braided together. Through many channels, including the educational advancement of second-generation immigrant families, the empire has become part of Britain's national consciousness. In the beginning, however, there was no cultural audit; it was a matter of strategic importance, a kind of unexpected bonus, derived from the defence of the realm.

3

The settlement of Australia was the direct consequence of Britain's humiliation in North America. If the American Revolution played a part in the subsequent French Revolution and, ultimately, in the promotion of Britain at the expense of France, it had an even more direct impact on the development of English-speaking New Holland (registered as 'Australia' in 1817). Before independence, the thirteen colonies of North America had been a convenient convict destination, an outdoor prison (with benefits) to which the criminal poor could be swiftly transported. After 1776 men and women sentenced to 'transportation' found themselves dispatched, not to the New World, but to the ends of the earth, a journey, via the Cape of Good Hope and across the stormy latitudes of the southern ocean, that could take six to eight months. Between 1788 and 1830 some 58,000 involuntary exiles from Britain suffered this fate. Despite these unpromising beginnings, the first governor of the New South Wales penal colony had visions of 'the Empire of the East', though he always protested that the convicts, who were subjected to a harsh local discipline, were emphatically not the 'slaves' of the more privileged settlers.

As in North America, there were painful, even tragic, collisions with the native population. As much as the American Indian, Australia's Aborigines suffered the fate of conquered people, sometimes hunted for sport and even used for dog meat. Less savage, but equally humiliating, their language was distorted and misappropriated. *Kangaroo*, for example, probably derives from Captain James Cook's first landfall in Australia; it was a word he believed to describe the celebrated marsupial. 'Called by the natives *Kangooroo*', he wrote in his journal, it moved 'by hopping or jumping 7 or 8 feet at each hop upon its hind legs only . . . it bears no sort of resemblance to any European animal I ever saw'. Actually, when the First Fleet sailed into Botany Bay a generation later, the new arrivals found that the Sydney Aborigines were already treating 'kangaroo' as a white man's term, and were applying it indiscriminately to sheep (which they referred to as a *patagarang*), and cattle. By a final irony, when 'kangaroo' was used again among the Aboriginal tribes of the Endeavour river area whence it had first come, they did not recognize it as theirs. Its origins remain obscure and disputed.

Apart from the Aborigines, an estimated 300,000 in 1788, Australia was an apparently empty continent, remote, vast, inhospitable and different in practically every way from the colonial motherland, 'a scene too rich for the pencil to portray', in the words of one awe-struck new arrival. For perhaps the last time in the history of the English-speaking world, there was a linguistic emergency in the southern hemisphere which had to be met by the English language. Rarely were so many new words needed so urgently. The settlers were encountering a new flora and fauna (*koalas*, *bandicoots*, *cookaburras* and *wombats*) and experiencing a way of life that was completely different from anything that had gone before. Inevitably, they borrowed from Aboriginal languages, words like *boomerang* and *billabong*. Like the first settlers in North America, the new Australians also turned to their mother tongue. For example, 'creek' and 'paddock', which are now typical Australianisms, have a rather different usage in Britain.

As English-speaking communities go, Australia was far more homogeneous than America's thirteen colonies. This was because the settlement essentially sprang from a single, mostly English source. Two generations after the arrival of the First Fleet, 87 per cent of the population were still convicts, ex-convicts or of convict descent. This was an episode in English life that resonated with all classes. The early chapters of *Great Expectations* illustrate the degree to which this penal experiment permeated white consciousness: convicts like Magwitch hounded by the law, the black prison hulks lying at anchor in the fog on the Thames; an atmosphere of forlorn desperation hanging over those who were about to be shipped off to the 'fatal shore'.

The appointment of a new governor, Lachlan Macquarrie, in 1810, a self-styled 'awkward, rusticated, Jungle-Wallah', saw great improvements in the condition of life in New South Wales. At home, the *Edinburgh Review* optimistically forecast 'a fresh set of Washingtons and Franklins' emerging from the new colony. 'Down under', in a replay of the Anglo-American experience, formerly convict Australians began to demand trial by jury and 'no taxation without representation'. Some hotheads even spoke of a 'Declaration of Independence' by 'the United States of Australia', but republicanism was confined to the fetish of informality (no touching hats to ladies) and a 'culture of opposition', said to derive as much from the example of the French as the American Revolution. 'Australia Felix' (in the confused search for a separate new role, Roman models were also alluded to) was indeed creating a distinctive national identity but, like America before it, the immediate result was to extend and strengthen the English-speaking imperium.

4

From some points of view, Britain had simply traded an empire across the Atlantic for another, more lucrative one on the other side of the world. While the convicts of New South Wales and, later, Van Diemen's Land (Tasmania) took their bearings in the southern hemisphere, the final years of the long war with revolutionary France continued to expand the British empire in the East. When Napoleon invaded Egypt in the summer of 1798, as a stepping stone to a French empire stretching into the Orient, his move inadvertently galvanized British forces. The following year the East India Company marched against the ruler of Mysore, Tipu Sultan, a Francophile Indian prince whose family had been at odds with the British for forty years, and who liked to assert his independence from the East India Company by celebrating French Jacobin successes.

The fall of Tipu Sultan's capital, Seringapatam, in May 1799 was a traditional English military victory, but its aftermath illustrates many new global interconnections. The East had long been the source of hot stuff – spices, perfumes and magic potions – but its influence had been mainly domestic, confined to the kitchen. Now, for Londoners, the spoils of empire suffused Englishness with gorgeous and exotic oriental culture. The storming of the city and the gruesome death of Tipu Sultan inspired plays, pamphlets and coloured prints. On-the-scene sketches of the battle by British officers became the raw material for a massive panorama of the battle by Robert Ker Porter which was exhibited to huge crowds at London's Lyceum in 1800. Much later, in 1868, the opening pages of Wilkie Collins's *The Moonstone*, the first British detective novel, are motivated by the plundering of an accursed diamond from Seringapatam.

The next milestone in the Anglicization of India occurred towards the end of the Napoleonic Wars, in 1813. Once British interests were secure, the East India Company was less important. India now became the keystone of an empire spreading across south-east Asia. To take up 'the white man's burden', a flood of English-speaking administrators – army officers, colonial civil servants, doctors, teachers and missionaries – seeded English throughout the subcontinent. The 'Babu' or 'Cheechee' English of the subject people became the essential means of communication between master and servant, inspiring the transfer of new words like *shampoo*, *pyjamas*, *dinghy* and *cashmere*. Formal instruction in English for the privileged would also give the rising generation access to the science and technology of the West. There were other imperial legacies, as well as language: law, literature and even sport.

In the 1800s a group of Indians in Bombay, adopting the ways of the white master, began to play cricket. Rarely, in the long history of empire, has a ruling power, occupying native lands and oppressing native people, established a sport that would forge such a passionate bond between ruler and ruled. Today more than half the cricket in the world is played in India, by Indians. As the game grew in popularity and became a fixture in the English sporting calendar, it became part of Indian life, too. The Calcutta Cricket Club was founded in 1792, on the site of the present-day Eden Gardens stadium, more or less contemporaneously with the MCC, a matter of some dispute. The first match there was played between Old Etonians and The Rest of Calcutta. Elsewhere in the empire, the game was exported by English public schoolboys turned youthful imperialists. In South Africa, for example, the game was essentially a white man's recreation. Clubs were formed in Pietermaritzburg, Bloemfontein, Kimberley, Pretoria and Johannesburg, but almost exclusively for the ruling class. Across Africa, cricket became something of an obsession among the imperial soldiers. The bestselling novelist Rider Haggard wrote, of the military catastrophe at Isandhlwana (1879), that 'Our generals entered into it with the lightest of hearts; notwithstanding the difficulties and scarcity of transport they even took with them their cricketing outfits into Zululand. This I know, as I was commissioned to bring home a wicket that was found on the field of Isandhlwana, and return it to the HQ to be kept as a relic.' In India, the game really began to flourish not with the sahibs but with the natives, especially in Bombay. According to the historian Ramachandra Guha, it was the Parsees, émigrés from Islamic Iran who had settled on India's western shores, who first adopted the game for themselves, as outsiders. The Parsees were traders and merchants, and had a vital role in the local economy, but they were never fully assimilated into Bombay society. On the cricket field there was the equality and fraternity of the game. So the Parsees played on the *maidan* (field) opposite Fort George, the British headquarters, a huge open space of some 40 acres. Today, as the Azad ('free') Maidan, it remains the home of countless Sunday afternoon cricketing dreams.

5

The way in which a game like cricket became part of everyday Indian life under the empire says a lot about the subtle obliquity of Britain's colonial conduct. Perhaps the empire never needed to be explicitly coercive: it held too many of the political and economic cards. But it was an unusual kind of imperialism, reflecting the contagious, adaptable, populist and subversive character of the world's English. The degree to which westernization occurred at all levels of society is illustrated by this letter to the British government protesting against a plan to set up a school in Calcutta to train the locals in Sanskrit. Raja Ram Mohan Roy was an important Calcutta citizen, and he was distinctly underwhelmed by the idea. 'This seminary', he wrote, directed by 'Hindoo pundits' would be of 'little or no value... The Sanskrit language', he went on, 'is well known to have been for ages a lamentable check on the diffusion of knowledge... I beg leave to state that if this plan [is] followed, it will completely defeat the object proposed.' There is no doubt that western ideas and customs arrived in India thanks to the Royal Navy and the East India Company, and at the point of a musket. Quite quickly, however, there were many Indians eager to acquire western expertise, and willing to jettison their own traditions in the process. In such favourable circumstances, it was not difficult to encourage a policy of bilingualism.

The real beginnings of bilingualism in India occurred in 1835 when the historian Thomas Macaulay, as president of the Indian Committee of Public Instruction, proposed the creation of 'a class who may be interpreters between us and the millions whom we govern – a class of persons, Indian in blood and colour, but English in taste, in opinion, in morals, and in intellect'. Macaulay, whose *History of England* had enjoyed a spectacular popularity with the Victorian middle class, was an out-and-out champion of the superiority of European culture. Raised on the classics, he knew that the Raj, like Ozymandias, was doomed to decline and fall. His idea was to prepare a new class of Indians for independence, so that British civilization would survive in the way that Roman civilization had outlasted the fall of the Caesars. In this scenario, Macaulay decided that the end of the Raj would be 'the proudest day in English history', especially if it left a great imperial legacy, 'the imperishable empire of our arts and our morals, our literature and our laws'. Macaulay's plan for India was adopted. At a stroke, English became the language of government, education and advancement, at once a symbol of imperial rule as well as self-improvement. The results of this policy were profound. English-speaking universities were set up in Bombay, Calcutta and Madras in 1857, the year of the Mutiny. Remarkably, Indian nationalists never seriously challenged the role of English as the lingua franca. Under Gandhi and Nehru it would remain as 'the vernacular of emancipation'. In this Indian context, its historical origins as a 'common tongue' played a vital role in commending it to those committed to overthrowing the British Raj. When the nationalist movement began to gather momentum during and after the First World War, the chosen medium of radical opposition was not Hindi, Gujarati or any of the other local languages, but English.

After Macaulay the English tradition became Indianized at the highest levels of Indian society. By the end of the nineteenth century, after the creation of many more colleges and universities and the introduction of the colonial civil service, English had become the prestige language of India, supplanting all local rivals. Simultaneously, English law, administrative practice and customs became woven into the texture of Indian life. This process was, and remains, a two-way street. Britain's imperial fascination with the people, religions, culture and landscape of India was expressed in the adoption of many Indian words and phrases. Exotic vocabulary from the East – words like *brahmin*, *calico* and *curry* – had insinuated itself into English since the days of Elizabeth I. By the end of the seventeenth century there were more additions (*coolie*, *mantra* and *pundit*), with further infusions by the end of the eighteenth century, from *bandanna* to *veranda*. Throughout the Victorian age, colonial civil servants added more and more local words – for instance, *chutney*, *purdah* and *cummerbund* – and also began to imitate the Indian preference for beards, moustaches and whiskers. This vogue reached a climax during the Crimean War (1853–6), when English barbers would advertise the 'Raglan' or the 'Cardigan', named after Britain's generals. Military whiskers of Indian inspiration became fully an icon of British imperialism in 1914 with Lord Kitchener's First World War recruiting poster 'Your Country Needs YOU'.

The strangeness of Indian life also inspired a flourishing genre of handbooks for the English visitor, with titles like *The Oriental*

Interpreter which advised the 'griff' or 'griffin' (novice) that 'the new arrival in India, ignorant of the language of the country, is puzzled for some time, to comprehend his countrymen, whose conversation "wears strange suits"'. The scale of this English borrowing from Indian speech has had various estimates. The *Oxford English Dictionary* lists about 900 words; a mid-nineteenth-century glossary runs to 26,000. And then there is *Hobson-Jobson: A Glossary of Anglo-Indian Words*, compiled and published in 1886 by Colonel Henry Yule and A. C. Burnell, a classic summary of the mingling of the two cultures before the age of independence. Even its title, described as 'an Anglo-Saxon version' of 'wailings of the Mahomedans' ('Ya Hasan! Ya Hosain!'), reflected the interaction of British and Indian life. The dictionary was intended, wrote its authors, 'to deal with all that class of words which ... recur constantly in the daily intercourse of the English in India, either as expressing ideas really not provided for by our mother-tongue, or supposed by the speakers (often quite erroneously) to express something not capable of just denotation by any English term'. Many of the inventions of Indian English recorded by *Hobson-Jobson* survive into the twenty-first century. This is because the Raj created a bilingual society, Indian English and one (or more) native languages. There were infinite gradations of Indian English, ranging from 'Babu' or 'Butler' English to educated, standard Indian English. Local college graduates would embellish the language of the Raj with exotic, personal flourishes in a process that continues to this day.

6

The fate of Rome as a model for Britannia troubled the minds of the more thoughtful Victorians, from Carlyle and Macaulay to Disraeli and Kingsley. In 1881 and 1882 the Cambridge historian J. R. Seeley gave a series of lectures entitled *The Expansion of England*, which argued, in a surprisingly modern way, that the exploitation of new technology might save Britain from inexorable decline. More than steamships and railways, wrote Seeley, it would be the electric telegraph and submarine cable that would interweave the fabric of empire.

Seeley was a man of his time: the mid-nineteenth century was supremely an age of new technology. In America, Samuel Morse had pioneered his code in 1844. Four years later, the Associated Press began to use the telegraph for its news reporting. In the Indian Mutiny of 1857 the telegraph played an important role in frustrating the sepoy rebellion. These new communications inspired the American writer Herman Melville to recognize their immense potential and to remark, of the United States, that 'we are not a nation so much as a world'. In defence of present British interests, patriots like Seeley believed that the engines of Victorian growth should be linked to the opportunities afforded by the 'civilizing mission' in Africa. Steam and electricity should be put to the service of a 'Greater Britain' in which Africa, the 'Dark Continent', would be purged of slavery by a new trinity: Christianity, commerce and colonization. In such rosy imperial fantasies, 'the Niger will become as romantic as the Rhine'. This notion seems fanciful now, but in the 1860s, to a Scottish missionary like David Livingstone, Africa was an almost holy cause where Britain could usher in a new golden age.

Livingstone's story, which has become a Victorian myth, is symptomatic of the new Anglo-American information nexus. In 1868, James Gordon Bennett, the news-hungry proprietor of the *New York Herald*, ordered his manic star reporter, H. M. Stanley, a naturalized American of illegitimate Welsh origin, to search out and interview the famous missionary-explorer, one of Britain's greatest heroes, who had not been heard from since 1866. After an epic march across 'Fatal Africa', Stanley tracked the shy Scots missionary in November 1871 to the shores of Lake Tanganyika, where, on first meeting, he uttered the much parodied salute, 'Dr Livingstone, I presume.' Thereafter, the threadbare Glaswegian became the kind of homespun imperial celebrity the Victorian media craved.

Livingstone, in contrast to Stanley's crude, and sometimes violent, racism, wanted to transform Africa's prospects through a combination of trade and the Gospel. His actual achievements were limited, but in the longer term his mission and his myth had lasting consequences. The King James Bible, which accompanied his explorations, would be translated into many native languages. The march of Victorian Christianity would seed English grammar and vocabulary into the lives of many natives across tracts of sub-Saharan Africa. After Livingstone died, on his knees, in 1873 he became a secular saint and his mission not far short of a grand humanitarian crusade. In the words of the *British Quarterly Review*, 'his death has bequeathed the work of African exploration and civilisation as a sacred legacy to his country...'

The Christian soldiers of the Anglican Church would always be in competition with the armies of empire. As the century unfolded, the Victorians' efforts to defend British interests in southern Africa would fatally compromise the 'civilizing mission'. George Bernard Shaw, an Irishman who loved to tease Anglo-Saxon self-importance, summarized the state of English world rule in *The Man of Destiny* when he wrote that 'There is nothing so bad or so good that you will not find an Englishman doing it'. Shaw believed you could always rely on English self-confidence. 'You will never find an Englishman in the wrong,' he wrote. 'He does everything on principle. He fights you on patriotic principles; he robs you on business principles; he enslaves you on imperial principles.' In the coming century the legacy of those 'imperial principles' meant that, for the first time in this narrative, speakers of the mother tongue would be far outnumbered by non-native English speakers: Africans, Indians, Chinese, Malays. As such, it became the de facto language of what used to be known as the Third World. In four continents, Asia, Africa and North and South America, and in the ocean basin of the Pacific, English became an official language in some thirty-four countries, from islands as far apart as Jamaica and Singapore, to states ranging from Sierra Leone to the Indian subcontinent. With decolonization, these linguistic shoots would burst into exotic flower in 'Singlish', Caribbean English, Indian English and many other varieties.

That was for the future. At the turn of the century, there was another sign of the imperial frailty feared by historians like Macaulay and Seeley. By 1900 the writing was on the wall: the United States economy was now in the ascendant. US President Theodore Roosevelt commented ironically on the American dominance of world markets in words that still resonate: 'Current advertisements in British magazines', he said, gave 'the impression that the typical Englishman woke to the ring of an Ingersoll alarm, shaved with a Gillette razor, combed his hair with Vaseline tonic, buttoned his Arrow shirt, hurried downstairs for Quaker Oats, California figs and Maxwell House coffee'. After that, the average Briton 'commuted in a Westinghouse tram, rose to his office in an Otis elevator, and worked all day with his Walden pen under the efficient glare of Edison light bulbs'. In 1870 Britain and America were, economically speaking, roughly equal. When the First World War broke out, the US economy was approximately three times larger than Britain's. All was not lost, however. Backed up by some 170,000 nautical miles of ocean cable, and more than half a million miles of conventional wiring, the English language, and its literature, had been transmitted from Cairo to Cape Town, and throughout the East. Alice, Stalky & Co., Sherlock Holmes, Tom Brown, Peter Pan, Toad of Toad Hall and many more had become part of an imaginative landscape familiar to readers from the Caribbean to the China seas. Lockwood Kipling, for instance, marvelled at his son's popularity in words that seem strangely modern:

Owing to the recent development & organising of journalism, syndicates & what not, each new [Kipling] book is more portentous, more widespread and more voluminous in print than the last and it will literally be true that in one year this youngster will have had more said about his work, over a wider extent of the world's surface, than some of the greatest of England's writers in their whole lives.

Moreover, there was still the 'invisible hand' of global capitalism in Britain's favour, combined with the imperial self-belief inspired by the Jubilee celebrations of 1897, the sixtieth anniversary of Queen Victoria's ascent to the British throne.

10. 'At the Top of the World'

The Imperial Swansong

> The 'decline' of England seems to me a tremendous and even, almost,
> an inspiring spectacle, and if the British Empire is once more to shrink
> up into that plethoric little island, the process will be the greatest
> drama in history.
>
> Henry James, 1877

1

The Jubilee of 1897 was a worldwide festival in which about 400 million people, a quarter of mankind, celebrated a universal *jamboree*, a new word for 'a large festive gathering' imported from some imperial outpost, no one knows quite where. In Hyderabad, writes James Morris, the supreme historian of Britain's greatest imperial moment, every tenth convict was set free. There was a grand ball at Rangoon, a dinner at the sultan's palace in Zanzibar, a gunboat salute in Table Bay, a Sunday School treat in Freetown, West Africa, and a performance of the 'Hallelujah Chorus' in Happy Valley, Hong Kong. Bangalore erected a statue of the queen, one of thousands across the empire. In Ottawa, columns of schoolchildren marched through the streets, waving the Union Jack; and in London, the eight-year-old Arnold Toynbee watched a parade of camel troops from Bikaner, Gurkhas from Nepal and hussars from Canada. Later he recalled the atmosphere: 'It was: "Well, here we are at the top of the world, and we have arrived at this peak to stay there forever..."' Toynbee was not alone in this supposition. Even in France, *Le Figaro* conceded that Rome itself was 'equalled, if not surpassed' by an empire that encompassed Canada, India, Australia, the China seas, Egypt, central and southern Africa, and also the Atlantic ocean. More remarkable, perhaps, the *New York*

Times so far forgot itself to declare, in an outburst of Anglophilia, 'We are a part, and a great part, of the Greater Britain which seems so plainly destined to dominate the planet.'

By the rhetorical standards of June 1897, this was tame stuff. Elsewhere, otherwise sensible people were losing their heads over the empire. To the poet Kipling, God himself had favoured English middle-class boys over all others. To the historian Sir Alfred Lyall, the British empire was the work of the Almighty. Lord Rosebery, prime minister from 1894 to 1895, believed that the empire was 'human and yet not wholly human' and exhibited in its global majesty 'the finger of the Divine'. When Queen Victoria gave thanks for her reign, and paid homage to her Anglican God in St Paul's on 22 June, the *Daily Mail* found it wholly appropriate: He was now the only Being more majestic than the Queen Empress.

In London, the world's capital, the Jubilee pageant was a spectacle of almost unimaginable splendour. The streets of the city were garlanded with banners and bunting, and many of its prominent buildings draped with massive VRI symbols. Before taking the imperial state landau to St Paul's, in a procession that included several maharajas and eleven colonial premiers, the Queen Empress telegraphed a short electric message to the 'beloved people' of her empire in an apt marriage of imperial propaganda, the English language and the new technology. But behind the huzzas and the trumpets and the intoxicating nationalism lurked a typically English melancholy, the apprehension of imminent and inevitable mortality. It was Kipling whose famous poem 'Recessional' caught the mood, noting how the 'pomp of yesterday' would soon be 'at one with Nineveh and Tyre'. The fleet might steam in three columns for 30 miles in line astern at Spithead, but France, Russia and, most especially, Germany were building rival battle fleets.

For many Britons, the new century, which would be dominated by world war, was also mediated by memories of empire, a plangent chord in the great imperial symphony. As Elizabeth Buettner has shown, if the subjects were 'oppressed', the oppressors' lives were no less scarred, albeit to a different degree. The ex-imperial English middle class suffered psychologically from the emotional wounds incurred in its imperial duties. After Kipling, who mythologized his childhood in the story 'Baa Baa, Black Sheep' and the memoir *Something of Myself*, it became commonplace to contrast the warmth and brilliance of India with the dank drabness of metropolitan England. In fact, far more damaging in the long term, it was not the weather but the strength of the child's identification with, and understanding of, Indian society that made the return home so difficult. Even more traumatic was the separation of the child from its overseas parents. Colonial separation was poignant. Buettner writes that 'a discourse of family sacrifice runs through countless family letters, fictional works, and other contemporary commentary on British life in the empire'.

Letters, diaries, novels, stories: the empire sponsored a mass of literary activity whose afterlife still lingers in the collective memory. As well as Kipling, it certainly inspired writers like Orwell and Saki (H. H. Munro). Orwell's father, Richard Blair, sent the young Eric home in 1904, aged one. He did not see his son again until 1911, by which time the boy had been scarred by the horrors of prep school, reproduced in his essay 'Such, Such Were the Joys'. No surprise, then, that the more sensitive children should escape imaginatively into a fantasy world of castles in the air. In the place of parents, the motherless and fatherless children of empire were brought up by a monstrous regiment of aunts and governesses. Empire families came to accept as utterly normal conditions of astonishing emotional deprivation. Kipling coolly observed that 'Children tell little more than animals, for what comes to them they accept as eternally established. Also, badly-treated children have a clear notion of what they are likely to get if they betray the secrets of the prison-house before they are clear of it.'

Perhaps it was not all in vain. By a nice irony, when the British empire went to war against the Kaiser and then against Nazi Germany, dispatched its armies and navy to defend a way of life as well as its far-flung possessions, and also evacuated its young ones from the cities, the children of empire were prepared. Years of colonial service from Calcutta to Hong Kong had schooled successive generations in 'maternal deprivation trauma'. The People's War, in Angus Calder's ringing phrase, changed Britain externally, and transformed the world's English. Internally, the People's Empire already possessed a natural resilience. Britain would be well equipped for a century of world war.

In 1901, when the old queen died, the future held few terrors for the benevolent imperialist. Indeed, the spreading power of English merely sponsored patriotic calls for its universal adoption. 'What should prevent this language of the ruler in every zone, in every clime, and the merchant of every market', declared one enthusiastic late-Victorian pamphleteer, 'from extending and supplying the necessities which are growing in their urgency and importance wherever our sails are unfurled?' In 1907, in a similar spirit, a certain E. H. Babbitt guessed that the year 2000 would see 1.1 billion English-users, spread around the world, a surprisingly accurate forecast. Others went further. In 1908 Albert William Alderson argued that warfare could be abolished 'in perpetuity' if the world spoke a common language. Not surprisingly, he proposed English for this task in his visionary scheme: 'The United States should use every endeavor and strain every effort', he wrote, 'to cause the whole of the New World [North, South and Central America] to speak English.' If Britain would do the same in Canada, South Africa and India, the result would be the extinction of all other rival languages – and universal peace would reign. Alderson was both wrong – and right. English was no pacifier. The next century was to be one of the most violent in history. But it was also the century in which English finally became the international language of the developing world.

Today, underpinning the world's English, there is a roster of new Englishes, heirs of empire, expressed in portmanteau words that describe local variants from Japlish (in Japan) to Spanglish (on the Costa del Sol, and across the Iberian peninsula). Some of these are genuine mixed languages (like Hinglish – English and Hindi); some are examples of heavy code-switching between English and another language (like Benglish – Bengali English); some are local dialects used by first-language English speakers; some are simply non-native pronunciations of English (like Franglais). There are also, according to Loreto Todd of Leeds University, as many as 61 different English creoles, spoken by some 200 million people worldwide. This patchwork is always changing as new varieties of language live and die; moreover, it has transcended its origins, long ago leaving the imperial hang-up behind. Here again, the New World has played its part. The century that followed Britain's imperial moment would be essentially American, and the figure who would influence this next episode in the world's English was the impetuous child of an Anglo-American marriage.

2

Winston Churchill haunts almost every aspect of the coming American century: as a soldier and journalist; as a politician and historian; finally as a war leader who 'mobilized the English language and sent it into battle', like Alfred the Great or Henry V, to defeat an enemy that threatened ancient habits of freedom derived from a thousand years of independence. 'Words', he once said, 'are the only things that last', and English words would be his weapons. The young Churchill was a creature of his times. After a brief military-imperial apprenticeship, Churchill discovered that he could make a living in the new mass media. When the Boer War broke out in South Africa, he wangled an appointment as the chief war correspondent for the *Morning Post*. At the end of his career, speaking on his eightieth birthday, he recalled these beginnings: 'I have always earned my living by my pen.'

In this, the first media war, the press made all the difference to the conduct, and the perception, of the conflict. Foreign correspondents from all the main titles (*Morning Post*, *Chronicle*, *Times*, *Mail*) were an essential part of the campaign, sending home their dispatches with the help of the latest technology: telegraph, typewriter and even the new-fangled telephone. Back in London, newspaper copy from some 6,000 miles away was prepared for high-speed linotype presses and dispatched along the great Victorian railways to the lower-middle-class readership of the imperial cities and suburbs. During the Boer War, news from the English-speaking empire was delivered direct to the nation's breakfast tables. Churchill's appetite for self-advancement did not need this mass audience for inspiration, but it did him no harm. When he was caught up in a Boer railway ambush, was captured and subsequently escaped, as the *Morning Post*'s fearless correspondent he became a national hero. He was rarely out of the headlines thereafter. 'Youth seeks Adventure. Journalism requires Advertisement,' he writes in *My Early Life*. 'Certainly I had found both. I became for the time quite famous.' Aside from young Winston's adventures, the Boer War, a catalogue of strategic disasters, limped towards peace negotiations. When the old queen died, it seemed as if the glorious age to which she had given her name had died with her.

Her son Edward VII's reign began in a mood of obsessive national self-excoriation. The army was incompetent, the navy was obsolete, the game was up for the empire, and Britain's traditional European enemies, led by Germany, were planning to invade. The change in mood touched every level of society and nowhere more so than in the bestselling adventure stories of Edwardian England. For decades, adventure fiction had celebrated the thrills of empire in spellbinding narratives set in exotic locations across the world. Classics in this genre included H. Rider Haggard's *King Solomon's Mines* (1886) and *She* (1887); and the works of G. A. Henty, whose military historical series (*Under Drake's Flag*; *With Clive in India*) dramatized the imperial saga through the eyes of young English boys caught up in decisive British historical moments. In this first decade of the twentieth century the threat to the empire on which the sun never set, for so long concentrated in villainous despots in faraway lands, would be located across the North Sea in the Kaiser's Germany and its rapidly expanding fleet of battleships. Paranoid British nationalism inspired a new genre of popular thriller, the spy story. Typically, dashing young English amateurs would foil evil Continental (aka German) plans for the imminent invasion of Britain. From Erskine Childers (*The Riddle of the Sands*), to John Buchan (*The Thirty-Nine Steps*) to Eric Ambler (*Journey into Fear*), it is a short step to Ian Fleming (*Casino Royale*).

The Edwardians inhabited a world remarkably similar to our own: global capitalism, massive industrialization, especially in the United

States, conspicuous consumption, international instability, astonishing technological change and widespread anxiety about the imminent future. Almost for the first time since the Conquest, the traditional enemy (France) had been replaced by a new, naval foe, Germany. This rivalry between former allies was a serious business, with unprecedented consequences. In 1902, for example, in another break with tradition, Britain signed its first peacetime alliance for centuries – with Japan. Now, finally, global interests demanded a global strategy. But what came to be known as the 'special relationship' was still strikingly absent. In world affairs, the United States was a remote, apparently unimportant, spectator; and in British consciousness, America was also distant. Not until 1912 did *Whitaker's Almanack* place its data on the United States ahead of information about 'Foreign Countries'. Economically speaking, however, America was becoming the dominant partner. Between 1860 and 1914, thanks to the completion of the great transcontinental railroads, America's imports had increased fivefold, and its exports sevenfold, and the New York Stock Exchange was booming. Moreover, there was a reckoning on the horizon. In the making of the world's English, it is impossible to overestimate the consequences of the four years that were about to unfold in the fields of France, a truly international conflict, the First World War.

3

When war broke out in the summer of 1914 the common language and culture of Europe was either German or French. Paris and Berlin were the capitals of the arts and sciences, twin magnets for ambitious and cultivated young Englishmen. By the time the first American President in history sailed into Cherbourg, en route to Versailles, in 1918, to negotiate a peace treaty that would conclude four and a half years of senseless and bloody fighting in which about 950,000 Britons (and some 10 million combatants of other nations) had been killed, Europe had already begun an Anglicizing process that continues to the present day.

The war to end all wars began as an imperial conflict. When Britain declared war on Germany, the first British military units to respond to the urgent telegraph message were based in Melbourne, Australia. Opposing the Allies, the Berlin that mobilized in 1914 was the hub of an empire based on Germany's pre-eminence in Europe. Inspired by Britain's example, some educated Germans nurtured aspirations for a German Europe (dubbed *Mitteleuropa* by Friedrich Naumann in a famous bestseller) in which the remnants of the Austro-Hungarian empire, scattered from Poland to Turkey, would form a loose affiliation with the fatherland something like the later British Commonwealth. There was certainly no escaping the powerful web of alliance and consanguinity linking Europe to a common fate in the mud and horror of France. Once the assassination of Archduke Franz Ferdinand on 28 June 1914 had set in motion the juggernaut of European mobilization, a European war conducted in German quickly became a world war conducted in half a dozen of the world's oldest languages: Japanese, Russian, French, Italian, Chinese – and English. The First World War saw the annihilation of imperial costumes, medieval fortresses and the cavalry charge. It also hastened the mass production of telephones, typewriters, gramophones and linotype presses. In June 1917 there was also the first disembarkation of the American 'doughboys', farmhands from the Midwest and former clerks from the big cities having their first experience of a world outside the United States. This was an important military manoeuvre, and a cultural earthquake.

On the first declaration of war, the American response had ranged from the lukewarm to the downright hostile. William Randolph Hearst, the pugnacious newspaper baron, declared, in a signed editorial, 'This is a war of kings, brought on by the assassination of a king's nephew, who is of no more actual importance to modern society than the nephew of any other individual.' Once it was obvious that the war would not, as many had predicted, be 'over by Christmas', American opposition to the conflict in France centred on the Allied blockade, especially the free flow of goods and services. When the Germans launched unrestricted submarine war and, in a dreadful blunder, sank the passenger ship *Lusitania* with the loss of 1,198 lives, including 159 Americans, the United States protested as vigorously against British as against German naval conduct. In the presidential election of 1916, Woodrow Wilson, the Democratic nominee, had to tread carefully on the issue of America's involvement in the war. When the United States did finally declare war on the Central Powers, it did not join the Allies, but fought in France on its own terms.

American intervention was decisive in the outcome of the war, and in the shaping of an English-speaking world. For the first time in the history of the world, an empire based on one set of literary, linguistic and cultural assumptions was replaced by another based on essentially the same inheritance. The uneasy cessation of hostilities from 1919 to 1939 marked the generation in which American values began to supplant British ones. The United States was the outright victor of the First World War: all its territory was intact, and it had become the chief creditor of the exhausted belligerents. Britain's economic indebtedness to the United States would soon be matched culturally and socially. In May 1917, the young Aldous Huxley, glimpsing the future, wrote in a letter that 'France is really a first class power no longer. We [Britain] shall go on till on a level with Haiti and Liberia.' As Paul Fussell puts it in his classic study *The Great War and Modern Memory*, 'The economic ruin uncomplete by the Great War was finished by the Second, which necessitated a replay, but much magnified, of immense indebtedness to the United States. The Americanization of Europe from 1945 to the late sixties was the result.'

In 1919 the idea of such 'Americanization' was still as exotic and intoxicating as ragtime or the dry martini. When Woodrow Wilson sailed for France in December 1918 he declared, with all the sanctimony of his Scots Presbyterian heritage, 'We are to be an instrument in the hands of God to see that liberty is made secure for mankind.' Enthusiasm for American language and culture swept through Gay Paree; Gertrude Stein and Alice B. Toklas took up residence in 27 rue de Fleurus; George Gershwin composed *An American in Paris*. By the time Wilson sailed back to New York, in the summer of 1919, to sell his dream for a League of Nations to a sceptical Congress, post-war cynicism and the 'Jazz Age' had begun. But, more than that, so had the American century. This was something new, and thoughtful people could see it. 'France was a land,' F. Scott Fitzgerald reflected in one of his *Notebooks*, 'England was a people, but America, having about it still that quality of the idea, was harder to utter — it was the graves at Shiloh and the tired, drawn nervous faces of its great men, and the country boys dying in the Argonne for a phrase that was empty before their bodies withered. It was a willingness of the heart.'

Practically speaking, through international relations, this 'willingness of the heart' became focused on Woodrow Wilson's obsession with the League of Nations. 'Once that is a *fait accompli*,' he told his aides, 'really all the serious difficulties [in the post-war settlement] will disappear.' Inevitably, the Allies used Wilson's penchant for the League to extract concessions. As the Australian prime minister Billy Hughes put it, 'give him the League of Nations and he will give us all the rest.' During the negotiations in Paris, the League seemed to represent 'the final enterprise of humanity'. Then the US Senate rejected it as a contravention of the right of the Congress to declare war, expressed in the US Constitution. Thereafter, both the League and the Treaty of Versailles were dead, with grave international repercussions in the run-up to the Second World War. De facto, America was now a world power, with global interests. Britain projected an illusion of world mastery that would become cruelly exposed by the conflict with the Third Reich.

PART FOUR
Modernizers

11. 'A Willingness of the Heart'

The American Century I

The Americans are doing what the Elizabethans did – they are coining new words. In England, save for the impetus given by war, the word-coining power has lapsed.

Virginia Woolf, *American Fiction* (1925)

1

When the American delegation sailed from New York to arbitrate the settlement that would end wars for ever, there were hooting tugs, cheering crowds and a symbolic release of pigeons with messages of peace. Wilson placed his hopes for peace in the League of Nations. Others, less optimistic, identified a more practical solution. Sir Robert Borden, the Canadian prime minister, told Lloyd George that they should look for a union between 'the two great English-speaking commonwealths who share common ancestry, language and literature, who are inspired by like democratic ideals, who enjoy similar political institutions, and whose united force is sufficient to ensure the peace of the world'.

Surprisingly, Wilson had no time for this sentimental vision. At a gala reception in Buckingham Palace he advised one startled British official, 'You must not speak of us who come over here as cousins, still less as brothers; we are neither.' He dismissed talk of an Anglo-Saxon world. So many Americans came from other cultures, he said, that it was foolish to harp on about the English-speaking traditions of Britain and America. 'No,' he went on, 'there are only two things which can establish and maintain close relations between your country and mine: they are community of ideals and of interests.' Wilson's realism did not go down well in the British circles. 'There was no glow of friendship,' wrote one observer. But with hindsight his response defines the terms on which the American century should be understood. Language would always be subordinate to 'ideals and interests'.

As America became increasingly dominant, the English tradition, a contradictory weave of libertarian instinct, insular nationalism and international savvy, now became the object of misty-eyed nostalgia. If the present was a 'waste land', in the words of T. S. Eliot, then an obscure Anglo-American poet working in a City of London bank, the past could furnish the vision of a world in which the English and their Englishness were still important. One evening in the spring of 1924, Stanley Baldwin, the prime minister and a true blue Conservative, addressed the Royal Society of St George on the subject of 'what England means to me'. Typically, he was full of regrets about a paradise lost, and the march of cultural uniformity.

Time was, two centuries ago, [he began] when you could have told by his speech from what part of England every member of Parliament came. He spoke the speech of his fathers, and I regret that the dialects have gone, and I regret that by a process by which for want of a better name we have agreed among ourselves to call education, we are drifting away from the language of the people and losing some of the best English words and phrases which have lasted in the country through centuries, to make us all talk one uniform and inexpressive language.

Then he moved to address the question posed by his speech. 'To me,' he said, 'England is the country, and the country is England.' And if he wanted to conjure up this world, he went on, warming to his theme, it came to him through the senses of eye and ear, and 'through certain imperishable scents'. There was more to come ('the tinkle of the hammer on the anvil, the corncrake on a dewy morning, the sound of the scythe against the whetstone...'), but it was less a political analysis than an elegy for a world whose time was up. So sure was Baldwin's grasp of the national mood that he would dominate the inter-war political scene as few others could. Britons, unlike Americans, basked in the warm glow of nostalgia; Americans wanted nothing to do with the past and its dirty secrets.

The contrasting moods of the British and American people in the 1920s explain why the two nations, with so much in common, reluctantly brought closer together by the experience of war in France, had sharply different responses to the opportunities of peace. In Britain, the long imperial sunset inspired an appetite for global adventure, and the flexing of imperial muscles overseas, where possible. In America, the popular will was for isolationism, and for a fresh start unspoilt by grubby Old World compromises. In 1920 the symbol of starting over was the handsome but vacuous (and deeply corrupt) figure of Warren Harding, who, mangling his syntax, introduced a new word – 'normalcy' – into the Anglo-American political lexicon. 'Normalcy', under Harding and his successors, Coolidge and Hoover, came to mean three things, each of which internationalized American culture on a scale hitherto unimaginable: the motor car, the film business and the stock market. The worldwide promotion of automobiles, movies and money now made the American language intrinsic to the global economy as never before. Eventually, it would also proliferate through fast food (McDonald's), popular music (from the Beach Boys to Eminem), teenage fashion (blue jeans and Nike trainers) and the catchy inflections of California's 'Valley girls', who pioneered a vocabulary and a style of speech that has become universal. Many aspects of Valspeak would have been strange to a 'flapper' of the 1920s, but some of its vocabulary, for example *max* and *barf*, *jive* and *vicious*, derived from black street talk, would not have been so strange or unfamiliar.

2

In the early days, when American mass culture first arrived, it often rolled into view on four Firestone tyres. Henry Ford's Model T had been launched in 1909, designed and manufactured with a mass market in mind. By 1915 the millionth car was rolling off the production line, and some 28 million cars were produced by the end of the 1930s. The inter-war motor car inspired a network of national freeways, unifying the country and intensifying an American identity that was now ready for export. If the English-speaking world has a sense of America in the 1920s it is because, for the first time, there was a means to communicate this identity: the newsreel and the Hollywood movie.

The American movie industry had begun in California years before the First World War, at the turn of the century. Hollywood had been established by east coast Jewish immigrants who discovered there was money to be made in selling the myth of America back to a mass audience. Once peace was restored, the troops brought home, and a new young audience with an appetite for entertainment had come of age, the business began to boom. Capital investment in American films hit £2 billion by the mid-1920s; at the end of the decade there were no fewer than twenty studios producing about 800 films a year, a figure never surpassed since. This phase, with the transition from the silent to the talking picture, was the making of the dream factory we know today and led to the great years of the business, 1930–48, often described as the 'Golden Age of Hollywood', the age of stars like Clark Gable, Rita Hayworth, Cary Grant and Katharine Hepburn.

Films and newsreels needed American heroes, men and women who could advertise the American achievement to the world. These new Hollywood movie legends – men like John Wayne and Errol Flynn – would speak in American English, and inspire a new fascination with a language and a culture that, in the final decades of British imperialism, was sometimes as much a source of hostility as admiration. Fittingly, the great American superstar of this new interconnected world was the first man to fly the Atlantic single-handed, Charles Lindbergh.

Now that the Atlantic could be shrunk to ever-shorter aeroplane journeys, Great Britain and the United States would move closer together in culture and language. This American century is the essential precursor to the Globish millennium. It was a two-stage process. First, there was the worldwide development of a common print culture, in which American language and cultural values became widely available. Secondly, the IT revolution and its infinity of data globalized these resources while at the same time splicing them with a multiplicity of competing traditions.

One important indicator of the inter-war surge in American influence, as the critic Cyril Connolly perceptively noted, was to be found in literature. 'Imagine', writes Connolly, 'trying to deliver a lecture on the influence of American literature on Kipling, Hardy, Shaw, Yeats, Conrad, Bennett, Galsworthy or George Moore. It would be a very short lecture.' Contrast this with the age of Waugh and Greene, Huxley and Auden, and, says Connolly, 'the difficulty now would be to name any major English writers who were *not* deeply influenced by America.' This vigorous new American voice was as vulnerable to the vicissitudes of capitalism as any other. Before the Great Depression, according to F. Scott Fitzgerald, money and power 'had fallen into the hands of people in comparison with whom the leader of a village Soviet would be a gold-mine of judgement and culture'. In 1929 the Jazz Age bubble of optimism, energy and excess finally burst. On 24 October the New York Stock Exchange crashed as never before, and swept away the savings and livelihoods of thousands, from corporate bankers and fat-cat lawyers to taxi-drivers, shoeshine boys, farmers and hairdressers. Then, out of this disaster, came one of those miracles that punctuate this story. It was all the more miraculous for being so unexpected.

The man who was elected to tackle the Depression – silent banks, empty factories, millions out of work and a pervasive air of national bankruptcy – was an American aristocrat who happened to bear a famous name. Before Franklin Delano Roosevelt came to the White House, few held out much hope. Walter Lippmann, a great newspaper columnist, described FDR as 'an amiable man without very strong convictions', and added, in words that he would soon want to eat, 'He is no tribune of the people; he is no enemy of entrenched privilege. He is a pleasant man who, without any important qualifications for the office, would very much like to be president.' On the morning of Roosevelt's inauguration, an overcast day at the beginning of March 1933, the inadequacy of this verdict became evident from the moment, inside the Capitol, the new President levered himself out of the wheelchair to which his polio usually confined him and descended the steps to the inaugural platform, supported by steel braces, the arm of his son and his own incandescent inner determination. From its opening clarion call ('The only thing we have to fear is fear itself'), the speech that followed lifted the nation's spirits. With ringing clarity, Roosevelt spoke of 'action', 'action now' and 'lines of attack'. But he also reaffirmed that, even in this great crisis, the repub-lic's institutions were still intact. 'Our constitution', he said, 'is so simple, so practical that it is possible always to meet extraordinary needs by changes in emphasis and arrangement without loss of essen-tial form...It has met every stress of vast expansion of territory, of foreign wars, of bitter internal strife, of world relations.' In fact, for the first two terms of his presidency FDR concentrated on his domestic programme, to the exclusion of 'world relations'. This lat-est exercise in American reinvention – the New Deal – would begin at home. Another world war would cement America's command of the century. While the United States was seized with the Depression, its future as a global superpower was obscured by domestic crisis. There was no appetite for international relations in Kansas or Nebraska while men were out of work and millions of families were on the breadline. There was, however, a potential in the economy that FDR's policies rejuvenated, the engine of the American indus-trial heartland, from Pennsylvania to Chicago. It would take another war to mobilize these forces, and harness them to the American cause. For the first time since Britain's industrial revolution, Europe would no longer play a decisive part in shaping the global future, and Britain itself was in decline.

3

And so, by a strange irony, these two decades before the next out-break of world war witnessed not the apotheosis of American dom-inance, but the continued swansong of British imperial power and influence. To those like Adolf Hitler, scrapping with his opponents in the streets of Munich and dreaming of world rule, Britain in the 1920s was still 'the greatest power on earth'. This was partly derived from the habit of empire, and partly from a now instinctive appetite for power that trumped all rivals. In theory, the League of Nations was to be a dynamic world forum for international self-determination (Woodrow Wilson's dream). In practice it was a talking shop, dom-inated by the British. At Locarno in 1925, and throughout the 1920s,

Britain exercised effortless superpower control over a weakened and divided Europe and, until Nazi Germany began to set a disturbing new agenda from 1933, dictated foreign policy with scarcely a reference to Washington or the White House. In 1922 the newspaper baron Lord Northcliffe noted with satisfaction that 'Britain's greatness and our vast possessions make Uncle Sam "sit up and take notice" '. The upshot was fierce inter-war jockeying for world supremacy between Britain and America in two fields of competition: credit and fleets.

To the United States, Britain's reluctance to repay its massive war loans was a constant source of puzzlement and irritation. 'They hired the money, didn't they?' fumed President Coolidge. Not until the Depression, when payments were suspended, was the British government free of this nuisance. Ideally, the British government would, in Curzon's words, have 'no business with America at all'. There was also the naval rivalry. To Britain, the Royal Navy and its command of the high seas was the cornerstone of foreign policy. But the credit squeeze meant that, as the First Lord of the Admiralty admitted, if the United States 'chose to put all their resources into the provision of a larger Navy, we should in the end be beaten from the point of view of finance'. This Anglo-American rivalry inaugurated nearly two decades of rancour and controversy. Relations between the two countries sank to an all-time low. Even Churchill, who was half American, thundered against Coolidge, 'a New England backwoodsman [who would] soon sink back into the obscurity from which only accident extracted him'. The problem was further complicated by the British empire of the 1930s. It had reached a zenith, from which it could only decline, commanding 'one continent, a hundred peninsulas, five hundred promontories, a thousand lakes, two thousand rivers, ten thousand islands'. The final years of the empire inspired a new appetite for global experience.

4

As so often in this story, it is the writers who epitomize the national mood. The British literary diaspora, described by the critic Paul

Fussell as 'a flight from a real or fancied narrowing of horizons', took Robert Graves to Majorca, Somerset Maugham to the South of France, Aldous Huxley to California, P. G. Wodehouse to the Riviera and Hollywood; and several lesser figures anywhere from Beijing to Tenerife. It was both a requiem and an escape – and it was repeated on a smaller scale in the lives of a million late-imperialists watching the sun set over the empire on verandas from Kuala Lumpur to Trincomalee. In this sultry, gin-fuelled imperium, the English of Shakespeare and the Bible was now being taught in thousands of colonial classrooms, shaping the imaginations of successive generations of colonial children. This last gasp of empire posed one of the most profound questions of all, one that would reverberate into the millennium: how can one be original in a foreign tongue? As V. S. Naipaul puts it in his essay 'Reading and Writing', 'I had begun to put together an English literary anthology of my own ... I wished to be a writer. But together with the wish there had come the knowledge that the literature that had given me the wish came from another world, far away from our own.' Out of this limbo, the world's English begins to emerge.

Now, in another decisive extension of English influence, the launch of the British Broadcasting Company (later, Corporation) ensured a way for 'nation to speak peace unto nation' – these words are chiselled into the portico of its London headquarters – and to do this chiefly in BBC English. The years 1919–39 were the heyday of radio in Britain and the United States, the years of Prime Minister Baldwin's homespun broadcasts, and President Roosevelt's fireside chats. The BBC was the world's first broadcasting service, and its founding was a milestone in the making of an English-speaking world. As one of the BBC's first executives wrote, 'The broadcasting of aural language is an event no less important than the broadcasting of visual language [printing], not only in its influence on human relations, but in its influence upon the destinies of the English language.' From the first, the BBC had a global, quasi-imperial, attitude towards English language and culture. 'BBC English', as it became known, was broadcast by eight so-called 'Empire announcers' and was intended to unite the colonies, later the Commonwealth. Its first test, as a national communicator, came sooner than expected, with the outbreak of another world war.

The Second World War began, like the First, as a conflict about Germany's European ambitions but ended as a turning point in the making of an English-speaking world. It achieved this in two quite distinct ways. First, nationally, it placed a modern master of English prose in command of Britain's resistance to Adolf Hitler and the propagandists of National Socialism. Secondly, internationally, it created a situation in which an English-speaking alliance, made up of the United States and its dependencies, Britain and the Commonwealth, inherited responsibility for world governance in the aftermath of world war. After 1945, across an unprecedented area of the world, Anglo-American power and influence would stem directly from the events of 1941–5.

12. 'The Unity of the English-Speaking Peoples'

The American Century II

A. Ah bet tha heard Churchill.
B. Aye – I did.
A. He doesn't half give it to them. I corn't go to sleep when he's on.

Conversation in Bolton, October 1939

1

The weekend before the Second World War broke out, Churchill was at home in Chartwell, his Kent manor house, working on the proofs of *The History of the English-Speaking Peoples*. This was an overdue volume for which his London publishers were beginning to agitate. Within the following week Churchill would be swept up in a tide of events every bit as momentous as any passage in the grand narrative history he was finally putting to bed (or so he thought). On the afternoon of Friday, 1 September 1939, just hours after Hitler marched into Poland, Churchill was summoned to see Prime Minister Neville Chamberlain and offered a place in Britain's War Cabinet. Within two days he was once again installed as First Lord of the Admiralty, a job with real executive power in the prosecution of the war. It was his first government post in ten years and dramatically ended the period of his life known as the 'wilderness years'.

The transformation of Churchill's fortunes in 1939–40 has occasionally obscured the fact that, preoccupied as he was with politics, he never ceased to be a professional writer conscious of deadlines, and a tireless champion of English-language culture. Throughout his career he wielded both the pen and the sword. At times he was certainly a hack, but he was also capable of rare inspiration. For example, *My Early Life*, published in 1930, is a masterpiece of English autobiography. Self-taught, and steeped in the English tradition, his response to the emergency of 1940 unites many themes of this book. In person, he would lead the defence of the realm in the warrior spirit of his forebears. He would champion 'freedom' against Nazi 'tyranny'. And he would rally the nation, partly by example but more particularly through his electrifying speeches. Looking back on this moment, Churchill would later say that, '[Britain's] will was resolute and remorseless and unconquerable . . . It was the nation that had the lion's heart. [*pause*] I had the luck to be called upon to give the roar.' In retrospect, Churchill's defiant stand against Nazism, when much of the West was supine, or actually capitulating, was a moment of true greatness that stirred even sceptical Americans. Roosevelt's secretary of state Cordell Hull wrote in his memoirs, 'Never have I admired a people more than I admired the British in the summer and autumn of 1940. Even the children seemed to realise that upon their indomitable spirit depended not only their own fate but also that of the whole democratic world.'

Churchill was also busy confounding those critics who whispered that, pushing sixty-five, he was past it. In September 1939 a brilliant short speech in the House of Commons contrasted favourably with Chamberlain's colourless performance at the dispatch box. One observer noted that 'Churchill brought himself nearer the post of Prime Minister than he has ever been before'. Next, getting into his stride as the most prominent member of the War Cabinet, his BBC radio broadcast one Sunday evening in October sounded the first chords of a patriotic defiance to Nazism that would reach a climax in the year ahead. He told his listeners that 'You may take it absolutely for certain that either all that Britain and France stand for in the modern world will go down, or that Hitler and the Nazi regime and the recurring German and Prussian menace to Europe will be broken and destroyed'. These were sentiments that could have been uttered by William Pitt, or Elizabeth I, or Henry V – and he knew it.

By mid-December 1939, in a Churchillian feat of concentration, he had completed *The English-Speaking Peoples*, some 500,000 words. His publishers, however, were not happy, complaining that the manuscript ended too abruptly, with the assassination of Abraham

Lincoln when it was supposed to run up to 1914. After much negotiation, Churchill agreed to supply a 10,000-word conclusion addressing the empire, the growth of democracy in Britain and the United States and Anglo-American relations before the First World War.

Churchill's work on English history, combined with the continuing wartime crisis, possibly inspired the tone of another Sunday evening broadcast on 20 January 1940. He reported to his BBC listeners that 'Things are not going badly after all – indeed, they have never gone so well in any naval war.' He went on to survey the resistance of neutral Europe to Hitler. 'The Dutch, whose services to European freedom will be remembered long after the smear of Hitler has been wiped from the human path, stand along their dykes, as they did against the tyrants of bygone days...' He concluded with sentences that both echo the King James Bible and anticipate the rallying cry: 'The day will come when the joy-bells will ring again throughout Europe, and when victorious nations... will plan and build in justice, in tradition, and in freedom, a house of many mansions where there shall be room for all.' In the words of his biographer Roy Jenkins, he was not yet prime minister, but 'he had without question made himself the orator of the government'. Churchill was now on the threshold of greatness.

2

Churchill's rise to supreme power, in the aftermath of the disastrous Norway campaign, was propelled on a tide of rhetoric. Now, it was as if all the players were conscious of performing roles in a dramatic historical moment. After Chamberlain had been replaced, on 10 May, the very day Hitler launched his blitzkrieg against France, Churchill addressed the House of Commons with his celebrated credo, 'I have nothing to offer but blood, toil, tears and sweat.' This was followed by his report on the conduct of the war to Parliament. 'The battle of France is over,' he said, 'I expect that the battle of Britain is about to begin.' Then he moved to a stirring passage, resonant with Shakespearean echoes:

Hitler knows that he will have to break us in this island or lose the war. If we can stand up to him all Europe may be free, and the life of the world may move forward into broad, sunlit uplands...Let us therefore brace ourselves to our duties and so bear ourselves that if the British Commonwealth and Empire last for a thousand years, men will still say, 'This was their finest hour.'

Later, in his own history of the war, a masterpiece of personal myth-making, Churchill wove these lines into a gorgeous, multicoloured advertisement for his heroic efforts, a necessary legend about Britain's defiance. His propensity for the stirring sentence and the grand historical pose, always hovering somewhere between self-parody and legend, also inspired a – possibly apocryphal – rallying call to his Cabinet, inspired by Cicero, in the depths of May 1940: 'We shall go on and we shall fight it out, here or elsewhere ... If this long island story of ours is to end at last, let it end only when each one of us lies choking in his own blood upon the ground.'

Did he *really* say that? It hardly matters, and it does not do, now, to be too cynical. These 'days of May' *were* a 'finest hour'. Without Britain's refusal to make terms with Hitler, twentieth-century Europe would have been a very different place, and not just politically. If the Nazi Fatherland had prevailed, varieties of German might have been spoken from Athens to Archangel, and the English-speaking world confined to a much diminished 'Anglosphere'. When the crisis was over, the evacuation of Dunkirk concluded and the 'battle of Britain' won, Churchill's collected speeches were published under the title *Into Battle* (in America, *Blood, Sweat and Tears*), a volume that sold well on both sides of the Atlantic. Perhaps not since Alfred the Great had there been a British war leader who so exploited the power of English to unite and galvanize his people and sustain his own victorious narrative.

For the moment, however, Britain was still more or less alone, and desperate to secure American support. On 15 May 1940, five days after becoming prime minister, Winston Churchill addressed a begging letter to President Roosevelt in which he warned that the burden of fighting alone against Germany 'may be more than we can bear'. Churchill, steeped in the eighteenth century, understood that a long war would turn on sea power. He asked the President for 'the loan of forty or fifty of your older destroyers to bridge the gap between what we have now and the large new construction we put in hand at the beginning of the war'. This was the beginning of an Anglo-American alliance that would decisively shape the course of late-twentieth-century history. He told the President with typical bluntness, 'we shall go on spending dollars for as long as we can, but I would like to feel reasonably sure that when we can pay no more you will give us the stuff all the same.' Two days later, in language that would become a refrain in his correspondence, Churchill writes that 'if American assistance is to play any part it must be available soon'. The wooing of American support continued; at this early point in the war Churchill was new in his job and still widely distrusted as too old, too unreliable and, too often, too drunk. As the historian John Lukacs puts it, 'Roosevelt's trust in and friendship with Churchill were not yet strong. There was still a distance between their minds.'

Events moved rapidly, and now the American position began to shift too. In June France capitulated. On 16 July Hitler ordered the invasion of England. Three days later he made a victory speech in which, as well as attacking Churchill, he made one last offer of peace. Churchill was implacable. On 31 July Hitler told his generals to prepare for war against Russia. Hitler, for one, saw England's future options clearly. England, he said, had only two hopes, America and Russia. If Russia were defeated, England would have no European ally and America, fully preoccupied with the threat of war in the Pacific, would offer no help. By chance, on the same day, 31 July, Roosevelt prepared to bypass Congress and offer Britain the use of fifty ageing destroyers, a move that would mark a significant reversal of American neutrality.

On 31 December 1940, once the election was over and FDR safely re-elected, Churchill wrote to Roosevelt, another wide-ranging letter intended, as he told his staff, to make the newly re-elected President feel that 'if we go down, the responsibility will be America's'. Roosevelt pondered Churchill's appeal and came up with the

Lend-Lease Act, declaring that America was now 'the arsenal of democracy'. It was also a global superpower-in-waiting. 'Thanks to lend-lease,' writes A. J. P. Taylor, 'Great Britain virtually ceased to be an exporting country. She sacrificed her post-war future for the sake of the war.' In the words of J. M. Keynes, 'We threw good housekeeping to the winds. But we saved ourselves, and helped to save the world.' One unintended consequence of this failure of 'good housekeeping' was to see American trade and culture in many fertile markets of the former British empire maturing into the beginnings of post-war culture.

British and American public opinion was still fiercely nationalistic. Then, on 7 December 1941, out of a clear dawn sky, the war planes of the Japanese first fleet bombed Pearl Harbor. The next day both Britain and the United States declared war on Japan. On 11 December the Axis Powers (Germany and Italy) declared war, in turn, on the United States. With Britain and America in alliance at last, it was a decisive turning point in the evolution of the world's English.

It was, crucially, no longer an alliance of equals. From the execution of Operation Overlord (the D-Day invasion of June 1944) to the summit conferences of Yalta and Potsdam (February and July 1945), the United States was increasingly the dominant partner in a relationship that has always been more 'special' to the British than the Americans. By 1945, and the dropping of the atomic bombs on Hiroshima and Nagasaki, the United States had become a truly global force, with Britain reduced to merely regional significance. However, in the exercise of 'soft power' Britain was about to excel itself. Once again, the lead came from Winston Churchill.

3

Typically, it was a coup that Churchill executed, on his own, through the medium of a platform speech. In August 1945, after his shock defeat at the polls, he had muttered to one of his secretaries, 'I wanted – I wanted to do the Peace too.' There is little doubt that, while he licked his wounds in the aftermath of electoral humiliation, he was looking for a way 'to do the Peace' in his own inimitable way. It was in such a spirit of brooding introspection that he took off for a winter vacation to Florida in the New Year of 1946. 'It may be', he said, wistfully, 'that Congress will ask me to address them. I'd like that.' Actually, he already had the American speaking engagement he needed. In October 1945 the president of Westminster College in Fulton, Missouri, had invited Churchill to give a series of three or four lectures. The offer had come with a postscript from Harry Truman: 'This is a wonderful school in my home state. Hope you can do it.' That was enough for Churchill. If President Truman introduced him, he could be sure of the audience he craved. As the months passed the significance of this occasion grew in his imagination.

It was to be a moment of decisive importance for the world's English, as much for the unintended consequences of his words as for his literal message. The historian David Reynolds writes that there were 'four sound bites' in Churchill's Fulton speech. Most famously, there was the phrase 'the iron curtain' ('From Stettin in the Baltic to Trieste in the Adriatic an iron curtain has descended across the continent'). On one side, in Churchill's vision, there was a free Europe, on the other Soviet satellite Communist parties aiming for 'totalitarian control'. This was to define a sphere in which European liberal and democratic values were to be promoted, and led to Churchill's second point: the 'lessons of appeasement' were that Communism, like fascism, should be vigorously opposed. Moreover, the home of liberal democracy was not just Europe. There was, he argued, making his third point, an important role for 'the fraternal association of the English-speaking peoples'. Having created what would later come to be called an 'Anglosphere', Churchill sent it, rhetorically, into battle. This bastion of anti-Communism, he said, should be based on 'a special relationship between the British Commonwealth and Empire and the United States'. In fact, this 'special relationship' was exceptionally recent and exceedingly fragile. But Churchill gave it a new impetus and provoked, among America's liberal establishment, a critical reaction to the old war leader's ferocious drum-beating.

Churchill's Fulton, Missouri speech is often interpreted as the starting gun for the Cold War. At the time, however, the press response ranged from lukewarm to hostile. In America, the *New York Times* was critical, and the *Wall Street Journal* stated coldly that 'the United States wants no alliance, or anything that resembles an alliance, with any other nation'. Elsewhere, the *Chicago Tribune* was so hostile to what it dubbed 'the poisonous doctrines' of Fulton that Churchill angrily pulled out of a serialization deal for his speeches. Ironically, it was Stalin, in a rare interview with *Pravda*, who rebutted Churchill's appeal to 'the unity of the English-speaking peoples...whose vocation is to control the fate of the world'. That, said Stalin, would make war 'inevitable'. If Churchill's speech did not entirely achieve what he intended, on a longer view it drew the boundaries of the post-war world that would slowly morph into a landscape hospitable to Globish. At the very least, Stalin's response made it certain that Churchill's words would go down as uniting the English-speaking world against the emerging Soviet bloc, a rallying cry in a crisis to equal his rhetoric in 1940.

4

In the hour of victory after a long and costly war, the United States had experienced a heady moment of triumph in which the world seemed to be at its feet. Then came the hangover: food shortages, labour unrest, black-market racketeering, civil disorder and the threat of Communism. In the first half of the American century English language and culture in the world had looked to the influence and support of Britain. Now, finally, the United States could no longer evade the burden of global responsibility. On 5 June 1947 General George Marshall made the speech in which he announced his plan to deal with the latest European crisis. The New World had an obligation to help sustain the Old, he said, identifying the ties of affinity between Europe and America that would find expression in the idea of 'the West'. There were concerted efforts, he went on, 'to change the whole face of Europe as we know it, contrary to the interests of free mankind and free civilisation'. Truman's administration saw the *pax Americana* in grand, classical terms. Secretary of State

Dean Acheson observed that the United States had 'arrived at a situation unparalleled since ancient times. Not since Rome and Carthage had there been such a polarisation of power on this earth.' To hard-pressed Americans, grappling with an unaccustomed quasi-imperial role, the English writer who seemed to understand the implications of this 'unbridgeable ideological chasm' was the great English libertarian George Orwell. In June 1949 Orwell's new novel, *Nineteen Eighty-Four*, was launched in America and quickly became a best-seller, in the wake of his popular 'fairy story', *Animal Farm*.

Away in California, the Psychological Warfare Workshop (PWW), the undercover Hollywood operation of the Central Intelligence Agency (CIA), which included the young novelist Sidney Sheldon, loosely affiliated to the 'Militant Liberty' programme, began to take an interest in Orwell's work. Shortly after Orwell's death in 1950 two members of the PWW travelled to Britain to meet Sonia Orwell and secure the film rights to *Animal Farm*. This improbable contract was sealed with a promise to introduce Orwell's widow to her hero, Clark Gable. The ensuing animated version of *Animal Farm* was financed and distributed worldwide by the CIA as part of the agency's extraordinarily far-reaching campaign to promote 'freedom' and American cultural values as part of the battle against Soviet Communism.

5

Also in the aftermath of war, there were other characters, equally flamboyant, just as eager to exploit the world stage. On 23 April 1953 the recently appointed special consultant to the US government on cinema, Cecil B. De Mille, strode into the office of the local CIA director, who reported that De Mille 'is quite rightly impressed with the power of American films abroad'. De Mille had every reason to be impressed. At that moment there were no fewer than 135 United States Information Service posts operating across 87 countries. By mid-1954 among the films scheduled for release behind the Iron Curtain as part of the war against Communism, were: *Peter Pan*, *The Caine Mutiny*, *Executive Suite*, *Roman Holiday*, *The Glenn Miller Story*,

Little Women and *Show Boat*. More impressive still was the roster of top Hollywood executives lining up to support this initiative of 'soft power': Darryl Zanuck (from Twentieth Century Fox), Nicholas Schenck (MGM), Harry and Jack Warner (Warner Bros.), Barney Balaban (Paramount), James Grainger (RKO), Milton Rackmil (Universal), Harry Cohn (Columbia), and Walt and Roy Disney. Motivated by anti-Communist zeal, this powerful group would play a crucial role in the dissemination of American cultural values, and language, across the world. It was the beginning of post-war Globish.

The drive to insert the idea of 'freedom' into American movies acquired a new momentum in December 1955 when a secret meeting, convened by the joint chiefs of staff, placed the idea of 'Militant Liberty' at the top of a covert Hollywood agenda supported by a posse of anti-Communist directors and stars led by John Ford and John Wayne, no less. To demonstrate how to insert the Militant Liberty programme into the movies, Wayne invited the meeting to his house. After dinner one evening two movies (*They Were Expendable* and *The Quiet Man*) were screened to demonstrate the 'free-world cultural programme' that had been introduced into the films. 'I want to show our people their country,' said one diner, 'and also to make certain that the rest of the world learns more about us.' The movies of the *pax Americana* would not only spread the American language, they would proselytize the American way of life, aims now intrinsic to the world's English.

'Militant liberty' has a Churchillian ring. They could not know it, but these movie moguls were articulating a programme whose origins can be found some fifty years before in Winston Churchill's first platform speech. Speaking of 'the English-speaking peoples', at the age of twenty-three, to a Conservative Party fringe organization, the Primrose League, young Winston declared that 'the vigour and vitality of our race is unimpaired' and that, as Englishmen, 'our flag shall fly high upon the sea, our voice be heard in the councils of Europe, our Sovereign be supported by the love of her subjects', whose duty was to 'carry out our mission of bearing peace, civilisation and good government to the uttermost ends of the earth. [*Loud cheers*]' In parts, the cultural agenda of the Cold War derives from late-Victorian liberal imperialism.

The United States was now the world's English-speaking policeman. Not only did it possess the bomb, in 1945 it had hosted a conference in San Francisco devoted to a discussion of world government,
an attempt to learn from the tragedy of the League of Nations.
America, a clear winner in the world war, was fully conscious of its
new global responsibilities. A sign of the times, Wendell Willkie,
Roosevelt's Republican opponent, had already published *One World*,
an American bestseller that argued for US participation in the future
maintenance of world peace. Before he died Roosevelt had wrestled
with the future of the United States in global affairs. He told Anthony
Eden, 'we have no idea of three or four Great Powers ruling the
world', but when the talking was over, the new world government
reflected the de facto situation.

The charter of the United Nations contains two highly significant
assumptions. First, in handing power to the Security Council (France,
China, the USSR, the United Kingdom and the United States) it
assumed that the wartime alliance would continue to shape the post-
war world. Secondly, in giving two seats on the Council to Britain
and America, it tilted world government decisively in an English-
speaking direction. Lip-service would be paid to the old diplomatic
language of French. In the field, however, the international community had become Anglo-American. This trend was further reinforced
by a third development: the establishment of NATO, the North
Atlantic Treaty Organization. For 'North Atlantic' read 'Anglo-
American'. Now the United States and Europe were united militarily
in defence of liberal democracy. Finally, and crucially for the financial underpinning of global Anglo-American culture, there was the
International Monetary Fund, the invention of J. M. Keynes that
would, he said, 'lock the United States into a rule-based post-war
financial order'. UN – NATO – IMF: these would be the pillars of
a resurgent English-speaking world from 1950 to 1989. And more
shadowy, in the background, was the CIA and its covert programme
of 'Militant Liberty'.

The shaping of this new world order reflected Churchill's strongest instincts. Throughout the 1950s Churchill's rhetorical powers
waxed as his political strength waned. He might no longer be prime

minister, but his words and ideas resonated more widely than ever. Even in retirement, he continued to champion the 'special relationship', though he was never so foolish as to use the expression. After some significant post-war revisions, his *History of the English–Speaking Peoples* was finally published in four volumes in 1956–8. On publication, the first volume alone, *The Birth of Britain*, sold some 220,000 copies, and the subsequent three volumes each had printings of 150,000. Together with massive newspaper serialization, this was an impressive bully pulpit from which Churchill could continue to popularize his notion of the 'English-speaking world': 'For the second time in the present century [he recalled] the British Empire and the United States have stood together . . . Vast numbers of people on both sides of the Atlantic and throughout the British Commonwealth of Nations have felt a sense of brotherhood. A new generation is at hand . . . Every nation has its own tale to tell . . .' Perhaps, he concluded, his history might 'play some small part in uniting the whole world'. This veteran's rhetoric is almost a mission statement for the world's English. Churchill's words, moreover, were reinforced by the polarizing experience of the Cold War.

6

Prolonged through different phases, from 1945 to 1989, and in many different spheres of action, the third world war of the American century – the Cold War – was decisive in the evolution of the world's English. At first, the opposition of the United States and NATO to the threat of the USSR and the Soviet bloc divided the international community into two halves, anglophone and non-anglophone. Of course at the local level local language and culture continued to flourish but now, with the spread of television, radio and the movies, there was an alternative cultural narrative available. In this 'hot' phase of the Cold War, the American mobilization of an anti-Communist campaign, led by the CIA, inspired a full-scale culture war that pushed the English language, in all its varieties, into the front line. 'By 1953,' writes Tony Judt, 'at the height of the Cold War, US foreign cultural programmes employed 13,000 people worldwide and cost $129m.' This struggle for hearts and minds sowed the seeds of the world's English in parts of the world previously unreceptive to British or American cultural colonialism.

The Russian response only intensified the hothouse atmosphere. On the Communist side, the 'Fight for Peace', as it was called, was conducted, culturally, by the 'Battle of the Book', through the agency of Communist Party organizations across Europe. To this, the United States responded with 'America Houses' (sixty-nine in Europe by 1955). In Austria alone, for example, some 134 million copies of English-language books were distributed nationwide, while the study of English replaced French and the classics as the preferred choice of Austrian secondary students. In Britain, the conservative novelist and broadcaster J. B. Priestley coined the term 'admass' to characterize this new consumer society. With American culture came American capitalism in all its gaudy brashness. When from 1947 to 1949 the Coca-Cola company began to open new bottling plants across Europe, from Italy to the Netherlands, the French reacted very badly. They were already defensive about the future of their language and culture in the post-war settlement. In 1950 the news that Coca-Cola planned to sell 240 million bottles of Coke in France alone provoked a national debate about 'coca-colonization' and a surge of nationalist hostility towards 'Anglo-Americans'. Eventually, under President Pompidou, French opposition to an inexorable cultural tide would be passed to the Académie française and its campaign against abominable terms like 'jumbo jet', 'software' and 'fast food'. 'We must not let the idea take hold', declared Pompidou, 'that English is the only possible instrument for industrial, economic and scientific communication.' French and European fury against the 'Anglo-Saxons' was only intensified by the realization that, among the new post-war generation of baby boomers, Anglo-American culture was exceedingly desirable. It was probably a futile protest; today it has been calculated that about one-twentieth of day-to-day French vocabulary is composed of *anglicismes*. For example, a McDonald's hamburger is simply a 'McDo'.

After the Berlin Wall and the Cuban Missile Crisis of 1962, the Cold War moved into a more stable phase, while the United States (but not

Britain) fought the threat of Communism in South-East Asia. Britain, meanwhile, had divested itself of almost all its colonial possessions, letting the 'winds of change' blow through Africa. Within a decade the 'self-liquidating empire' had exchanged hard political power for soft cultural influence. Mass tourism replaced imperialism as an engine of global linguistic transactions. Simultaneously American capitalism was beginning to export Anglo-American popular culture through television, movies, fashion and, above all, rock 'n' roll.

By the late 1970s the Soviet and American stand-off was nearing its final phase, occasionally referred to as the 'second Cold War'. Now the Anglo-American hegemony – often hotly disputed by anti-American liberals – was wholly underpinned by rampant capitalism, represented by Margaret Thatcher's premiership in Britain and Ronald Reagan's two-term presidency in the United States. After the fall of the Berlin Wall in 1989 this new global culture would morph into the worldwide cultural revolution that would become Globish. The eerie decade that preceded the crisis of 2001 was the first in a century in which the world was no longer in the shadow of war. Francis Fukuyama declared 'the End of History'. It was during this unreal and optimistic hiatus that the little term coined by Jean-Paul Nerrière in 1995, 'Globish' – simple, inelegant and almost universal – first gained currency. Now Globish began to emerge, in the words of *The Times*, as 'the language of the present and the future', the world-wide dialect of the third millennium.

13. 'The World At Your Fingertips'

From Google to Globish, 1989–2009

> Because it amplifies our potential in so many ways, it's possible that
> the long-term impact of the Internet could equal that of electricity,
> the automobile and the telephone all rolled together.
>
> Bill Gates, chairman of Microsoft, in December 2000

1

In Christopher Hampton's play *Savages*, one of the characters, a guer-
rilla, wittily defines capitalism as 'the process whereby American girls
turn into American women'. By the last decades of the twentieth century capitalism seemed to be turning everything American, especially
in the UK, from movies and fashion to rock 'n' roll and musicals.
From the eighteenth century there had always been anxieties about
America's 'corruption' of Britain's cultural life, usually focused on
language, neologisms like 'belittle' and 'hospitalize'. In 1959 Alistair
Cooke complained that 'the English vocabulary seems to have suc-
cumbed to Americanisms since the war at an unprecedented rate'. In
the aftermath of the Vietnam War such anxiety was changing into
panic and anger. It was not sufficient that mandarin intellectuals in
ivory towers could purr soothingly about Britain being Greece to
America's Rome; across the board, the Americanization of England,
from *Friends* to McDonald's, seemed to threaten a way of life. In 1998
the former editor of the *Guardian* Peter Preston expressed this fear in
the title of his novel *The 51st State*. Actually, the cultural traffic was
flowing both ways. There were just as many expressions of American
anxiety about British influence, especially on Broadway. The rivalry
was natural. Britain and America were, in the formula of John Le
Carré (the spy writer whose fiction defines these years), 'cousins'.

France wanted no role in that cultural family. Instead, in the centuries of conflict between France and the Anglo-Saxons, the moment in the spring of 1992 when the Disney Corporation launched its state-of-the-art amusement park, EuroDisney, some 20 miles outside Paris, became one nadir of Gallic pride. 'Mickey, Go Home!' chanted the demonstrators at Marne-la-Vallée, protesting against what they called 'neo-provincialism'. This was Agincourt, Blenheim and Waterloo, and all the more humiliating because it was a cultural as much as a socio-economic defeat. In 1994, in an attempt to assimilate the theme park into French culture, the name was changed to Disneyland Paris, but the hurt lingered. The same year the government proposed a quota for francophone content (50 per cent) on radio, following a logic already applied to films. Many legislators were alarmed at the emergence of radio stations with names like 'Skyrock' and 'FUN'. Ever since Georges Pompidou had charged the Académie française with finding pure French synonyms for such hideous Anglo-Saxon imports as *jumbo jet* and *software*, French cultural superiority had been on the defensive against the American cultural domination of television series like *Dallas* and *Friends*. Pompidou had defended the French language as integral to European consciousness ('Should French ever cease to be the primary working language of Europe, then Europe itself would never be fully European'), but the opening of the theme park was the last straw. French outrage settled on the news that Disney's American managers required English to be spoken throughout Mickey's new French domain. *Le Figaro* hoped, 'with all its heart', that 'the rebels would set fire to EuroDisney'. The French theatre director Ariane Mnouchkine went further. EuroDisney, she announced, would be 'a cultural Chernobyl'.

These declarations were partly the expressions of a traditional French reflex, but also an indication of a wider European dismay at the unipolar world that took shape after the fall of the Berlin Wall. The logical culmination of the American century, the 1990s seemed to presage the death throes of a distinctive European culture. So this final decade began with increasingly vehement outbursts of anti-Americanism. In July 1992, with the wounds inflicted by EuroDisney still raw, some 250 French personalities and intellectuals, including novelists and poets, signed a petition demanding that Mitterrand's government enact a law announcing the mandatory use of French in all meetings, seminars and conferences, in all French-sponsored films – indeed, in all transactions conducted on French soil. The alternative was too horrible to contemplate. 'Les angleglottes', declared the petitioners, slamming the door on Anglophilia, 'will have us all speaking English, or rather, American.'

A fierce assertion of the anti-Americanism that later intensified during the Iraq War, and a restatement of an old French anxiety, this petition came too late. The European Community's bilingual policy (in which French and English were its two official languages) was already disintegrating in the face of the world's English, a widespread preference for a workable lingua franca. I recall a visit I made to the European Commission in the mid-1990s. At the bar, in the nearby Parliament building, Dutch, Swedish, Spanish and Irish delegates were all arguing – in English. Across the street, in the Commission, the (Italian) deputy head of commission, then President Signor Prodi, liked to season his conversation with popular lines from the BBC sitcom *Yes, Minister*. 'That was a courageous argument,' he would say, with a knowing wink at any adjacent British MEP. When I spoke to anglophone parliamentarians, I was told that delegates from, for instance, Greece or the Czech Republic who could not speak English had 'a miserable time in Brussels'. Across Europe, there were countless examples of a decisive tilt towards the world's English. *The Times* reported that 'British interpreters are now so rare in Brussels that most official EU translation is being done by non-native speakers'. In Holland, some students at the University of Amsterdam were taking their courses in English rather than Dutch. In linguistically fragmented countries like Switzerland or Belgium, English was increasingly being used for communication between a Swiss German- and a Swiss French-speaker, or between Walloons and Flemings. In Canada, the Quebec government, following France, felt compelled to launch a cultural policy aimed at resisting Anglo-American influence. At the international level, this has been reinforced, since 2002, by France requiring the CIA to use French as a working language for the new liaison office it shares in Paris with the Delégation générale de la Securité Exterieure, the French version of the CIA. More startling still, in the Basque regions of Spain it was becoming fashionable for the younger generation to learn Catalan at school, in deference to the separatist agenda, but to pass their leisure hours speaking 'English', in a complex adolescent mixture of rebellion and self-improvement. There was no question of a flight from Catalan, but there was now a local rejection of the national language, Spanish.

Higher up the food chain, in European business circles, there had long been an awareness that English was a more efficient means of internal corporate communications. The multinational truck and van manufacturer IVECO, a Fiat subsidiary with headquarters in Turin, had been established, in English, as long ago as 1975. The finance for IVECO came from France, Germany and Italy, but the company's lingua franca was always English. Throughout the 1990s, as the smoke began to clear after the upheavals of 1989, more and more European companies began to follow the IVECO model. In Germany, for instance, the great engineering giant Siemens declared English to be its inter-company language. And within the borders defined by the watch-towers of the now defunct 'Iron Curtain', in the territory once occupied by the Soviet Union, there were newly invigorated societies like Poland, Hungary and the Czech Republic in which English was becoming the natural expression of the would-be European. The later enlargement of the European Union in 2005 was a triumph for the European ideal, but it would also turn out to presage a decisive victory for a language that remained contagious, adaptable, populist and subversive.

2

The most unexpected thing about the unipolar world that followed 1989 was not that it should advance the spread of Anglo-American culture but that, notwithstanding the unhappiness of the French and their anti-American flourishes like the opposition to EuroDisney, there should be such widespread enthusiasm for the language of the surviving superpower. There are, perhaps, three reasons for this. First, it made sound economic sense. It was hard to gainsay the potency of Starbucks and Microsoft, or Google and IBM. Secondly, as we have seen, English has always had this subversive capacity to run with the hare and hunt with the hounds, to articulate the ideas of both government and opposition, to be the language of ordinary people as well as the language of power and authority, rock 'n' roll *and* royal decree. Finally, the collapse of the USSR did not see the United States step forward as an ambitious or sophisticated global superpower on the Roman, French or British model. In so far as the United States exercised global leadership in international relations, it was confined to farcical interludes, like the Parsley Crisis.

In the summer of 2002, when Europe was on holiday, the government of Morocco dispatched a platoon of twelve soldiers to invade the island of Leila, 250 yards off its coast in the straits of Gibraltar, and fly the Moroccan flag. Apart from some goats, Leila is uninhabited and almost barren. The only vegetation is the wild parsley from which it takes its alternative Spanish name, Perejil. The Spanish government protested against the invasion, and airlifted a counter-force of some seventy-five troops to pull down the Moroccan flag, unfurl its own royal standard and expel the impertinent North Africans. At this, the Moroccan government denounced an 'act of war', and rallied its young men on the streets of Rabat, who chanted 'Our souls and our blood are sacrifices for you, Leila!'

This comic opera could have turned nasty, causing an ugly Mediterranean crisis, but now there was urgent international mediation. US Secretary of State Colin Powell, who speaks neither Arabic nor Spanish, began placing high-level calls to Rabat and Madrid, pushing hard for a compromise. Eventually, Powell sat down at his home computer, drafted an agreement, persuaded both sides to accept it, and faxed it to Spain and Morocco. Soon after, the two warring countries agreed to leave Leila unoccupied and begin talks about its future. They also issued statements thanking the United States for its mediation. The goats of Perejil were possibly among the few to benefit from the exercise of American influence after the Cold War.

Unipolarity turned out to be so brief as to be a will-o'-the-wisp. The United States, with its anti-colonial tradition and constitutional aversion to foreign wars, had no appetite for an enhanced role as the world's policeman. Long before the administration of George W. Bush declared war on Iraq, there was, it seemed, little but disdain for international agreements on a range of subjects from global warming to world trade. President Bush's subsequent contempt for the Geneva Convention was part of a broader picture. Moreover, the American ethos favours the individual in competition. When issues of global foreign policy were brought to Washington, the American response was often strictly American. In the absence of an American mission, apart from the almost meaningless 'War on Terror', the world was left to get on with its own multifarious business. All this had the vital effect of decoupling the English language from what cultural conservatives would always see as American imperialism. This, too, was greatly to the advantage of the world's English. Now the lingua franca was flourishing globally, more and more independent of its history and associations. But first, for an understanding of the new international infrastructure, we must go back to 1989.

3

The Berlin Wall began to crumble after a GDR press conference on 9 November 1989 at which the GDR ministerial stooge Gunter Schabowski announced the lifting of travel restrictions between East and West Germany. This moment was symbolic of a new dynamic in the flow of information. During the next two decades television, radio and then the internet would set the pace of social and cultural change by breaking global news 24/7. Founded in the early eighties, CNN pioneered the non-stop news cycle with its coverage of the first Gulf War in 1991, and followed up this initiative with the launch of its news websites in 1995. The opening of the Wall also had a metaphorical force. The distinguished Indian economist Amartya Sen has noted that 'global' ideas derive from global perspectives. 'If I celebrate the fall of the Wall,' Sen has said, 'it is because I am convinced how much we can learn from each other. Most knowledge is learning from the other across the border.'

After the Wall came down, there was a seismic shift in the balance of world power, economically, politically and culturally. Where once there had been the clash of competing ideologies – loosely, capitalism vs. communism — now a formerly divided world became united, economically speaking, in the common enterprise of global capitalism. For better or worse, every country under the sun was in the same world market, trading on unequal terms, but trading nevertheless. In the short term 1989 inspired a boom that was more than just a 'peace dividend'. In the next two decades, 1990–2008, the global economy would grow from $23 trillion to $54 trillion, and global trade would increase 133 per cent. About half this global growth came from 'emerging markets'. Estimates vary, but after the collapse of the Soviet Union some two billion people would join the world market. Inevitably, these new consumers sought a reliable means of global communication. The more global capitalism boomed, the more English developed as its preferred medium of communication: contagious, adaptable, populist and subversive.

The world's English does not just answer to an economic imperative. This free-market boom also had immediate political consequences, stimulating a worldwide trend towards democratic change and democratic vocabulary. Rickety autocratic regimes from Asia (South Korea) to Latin America (Chile), which had been in the habit of governing in the selfish interests of a ruling clique, were now forced to take a path that was more consensual, transparent and consumer-friendly. Global culture and economics, the English language and global banking, began to achieve some remarkable transformations. The privatization of geriatric planned economies liberated western-style entrepreneurship and promoted a new interest, among aspiring capitalists, in acquiring control of the mass media, the essential means of market manipulation. British and American English now became the default position of the international media. This did not always mean the automatic extension of the world's English. For instance, when Star TV was established in Hong Kong in 1991 its intention was to broadcast English-language, western-style programmes to an Asian middle-class audience. In practice, Star TV fragmented into thirty popular local channels, broadcasting in eight languages. Still, during this period the ownership of global media (newspapers, television, film and advertising) became concentrated in the boardrooms of ten major companies, which controlled about two-thirds of the communications industry.

A global information network, and a global market, require a global language, but one that is not, overtly, the instrument of empire. In the Middle Ages, and exclusively in the West, this language had been Latin. As the millennium approached, there was an obvious appetite, and need, for another lingua franca to fulfil this role. Immediately after 1989 British and American English were often spoken of in such terms, but they were still perceived as the tool of an Anglo-American hegemony. With the spread of new information technology, however, and the emergence of new, popular regimes with anglophone inclinations, the English language began to lose its colonial connotations. Now, in keeping with its long history, English began to morph into a supranational means of global communication at the approach of the new millennium.

The engine of this change was economic, but it was also technological. Although, in the words of Michael Lewis, 'the Internet boom triggered one of the most astonishing grabfests in the history of capitalism', it also sponsored a global data revolution. Information could be spread in English (or any other language), but much more freely if there were fax machines, personal computers and mobile telephones to speed the transfer. Here the interplay of money, science and politics becomes fascinating. The Windows-driven IBM PC of 1990 enabled its myriad users to share their 'content' more freely and universally than ever before. Music, photographs and, finally, video could be transmitted digitally, something that totalitarian regimes could not readily prevent. Just as important, the Highway Code of this teeming information freeway was written in American English. In the fulfilment of Bill Gates's mantra, the acronym TWAYF ('The World At Your Fingertips'), this was the brave new world of 'connectivity', and its first consequence was to make the labour market dramatically more mobile. If the workers could not always go to the work, at least the work could now go to the workers. The 1990s saw the beginning of outsourcing and the transformation of local economies by the magic of broadband, as a new generation – the so-called 'Generation Y' – took advantage of the opportunities offered by the internet. Where, as in Ireland or India, there was already an indigenous English-speaking population, the opportunities for growth would be almost limitless. Ireland had been at war with Britain for eight centuries. In the 1990s a deep, ancient enmity became anaesthetized by Globish consumerism – Gap jeans, Benetton fashion and Dell computers. Above all, it was the personal computer, like the printing press of the 1460s and 1470s, that would create the new environment in which Globish, the dialect of Generation Y, could flourish.

4

Tim Berners-Lee, who invented the World Wide Web, called it 'an abstract (imaginary) space of information'. 'On the Net', he said, 'you find computers. On the Web, you find information. The Web could not be without the Net.' In 1995 the potential of the Web was transformed by the launch of Netscape, the first commercial browser. Two weeks after Netscape went public, Microsoft launched Windows 95. The combination of Netscape and Windows 95 started the next Californian Gold Rush, the dot.com boom. In five years, by the turn of the millennium, the whole world was wired together. Trained in the world's English, outsource workers in Belfast could now communicate with partners in Bangalore or Bogotá.

Netscape pioneered the democracy of the Web, liberating the mass global forces that resulted in the dot.com bubble. Netscape's development of 'open protocols' meant that the key consumer question vis-à-vis the new technology was not 'How do we get onto the internet?' but 'What can we do with the internet?' In turn, this was stimulated by digitization and the boom in fibre-optic cabling. This, in the words of Thomas Friedman, created 'a whole new global platform for collaboration'. In his now celebrated formulation, Friedman writes that 'this was the genesis moment for the flattening of the world'. In the course of the next generation there will, no doubt, be many more tipping points in global communication, some of them utterly unforeseen, but this was the vital first step. It is hardly a coincidence that Jean-Paul Nerrière identified the concept of 'Globish' in 1995, the year Netscape marketed its first commercial browser. In this 'new new world', the internet could now become a forum for worldwide communities to share information electronically. Enter the 'people's encyclopedia'.

Wikipedia marries a Hawaiian word meaning 'quick' (*wiki*) and the classical Greek for 'education' (*paideia*). This project was a creature of the new millennium. It began when Jimmy Wales, the founder of a now-abandoned plan to produce a free encyclopedia, began to discuss with Larry Sanger ways of supplementing his brainchild Nupedia with a more open system of contributions. The upshot was Nupedia's first *wiki*, which went online in January 2000. Within three years Wikipedia was scoring 2–3 billion hits a month. By March 2007 'wiki' had become a recognized English word, waves of non-English wikipedias had been launched (in Chinese, Dutch, Esperanto, Arabic, Hungarian, Afrikaans and Russian, to name a few) and the online family of free-content initiatives had been collected under the umbrella of the Wikimedia Foundation.

Wikipedia has attracted the satirical attention of late-night television comics and has provoked the disdainful outrage of librarians, pedants and sticklers, but they miss the point. Wikipedia is democratic, fast and light, with low overheads: as recently as October 2006 the Wikimedia Foundation had just five employees. In line with its goal of producing reference material free to all people, this team now operates Metawiki, where matters inpinging on all projects, global discussions and global policies can be formally documented. Some of these include international data collections related to soccer, cricket and basketball. Here Globish was becoming more viral than ever.

5

Modern sport, especially soccer and cricket, is often identified as a symbol of contemporary globalization. This is half true. In the history of sport, there have been a number of important transformative moments. As far back as the fourth century BC to the second century AD there was the slow emergence of a unified 'sports culture' stretching from Roman Britain to Roman Palestine. Chariot racing was its football, the most popular spectator sport throughout the ancient world, with notoriously rowdy fans quite the equal of any football hooligan: one chariot race in Constantinople in AD 532 started a riot that left 30,000 dead. Another great transformation of sport took place during the nineteenth and twentieth centuries, when team sports like football and baseball began to be exported from England and the United States. In this phase, Anglophile Latin Americans adopted football while modernizing Japanese took up baseball.

What separates modern sport from its antecedents is the mass media dimension. In the final decades of the twentieth century the corporate owners of the mass media joined forces with the corporate owners of international sports teams to attract billions of viewers to 'mega-events' like the Olympic Games, the Superbowl and the World Cup. Here, the pace of change accelerated exponentially. For instance, when skateboarding was first invented by disaffected American teen-agers in California it soon spread like wildfire among urban youth the world over. Innovation in sport can become a global fad in a matter of weeks, even days. But when we take a closer look at one of the great corporate sports – football, for instance – its original English-ness becomes highly significant in the sporting arena.

FIFA claims football as 'the world's language', and points to the more than 200 million men and women who play the game competi-tively across the globe. FIFA itself has more national members than the United Nations, and, although it is based in Zurich, its default language is English or, more accurately, Globish. This reflects the game's medieval English origins, when it was a violent village sport played on Shrove Tuesday. The international dimension is compara-tively new. Football became professional in England only with the launch of the FA Cup in 1872. By the end of the nineteenth century there was a Football League and many professional players, and the game had become a working-class passion. Now it was exported abroad, at first to the ports of Italy, Spain, Argentina and Brazil. In 1904, a Frenchman, Robert Guérin, organized the Fedération Inter-nationale de Football Association (FIFA), a Franglais organization that took its inspiration from the Olympic ideal of Baron Pierre de Cou-bertin, an eccentric Anglophile who believed in cold baths and cricket. Football became at last truly international in 1930, when another

French sporting enthusiast, Jules Rimet, promoted the first World Cup in Uruguay. Initially, there were just four European competitors, including the Italian team, whose instructions from Mussolini were 'Win or die'. (They lost.) By the 1950s football had become truly global, but not yet Globish. FIFA had seventy-three members, and the game was dominated by the great Latin American teams of Brazil and Argentina. Eventually, the game took off in the Far East, Africa and, finally, the United States, which hosted the World Cup in 1994. In Japan, the dominant local team, Tokyo Verdy, had a fan club which sang a dreadful anthem written by none other than the great Pelé:

> Olé, Olé, Olé, Ola
> Hey, Verdy, Fantastic Technique!
> Come everyone, and have a good time together,
> Together with Verdy – kick-off time!

6

Japan, the setting for the movie *Lost in Translation*, is both a showcase for contemporary Globish and a striking alternative to the British example. Protected by the sea, Japan developed a strong local culture free from foreign rule. In contrast to English, which was always a hybrid, Japanese stands alone, essentially unconnected to any neighbouring language families. Its characters may be almost interchangeable with Chinese, but its grammar is unique and its syntax quite distinctive. Even its distant relationship to Korean is disputed. For centuries Japanese was remote, mysterious and separate. But this special linguistic inheritance does not seem to have made Japan proud of its culture, as it did in Britain. Paradoxically, a nation that is assertive in business and commerce is unconfident in language and culture. The annihilating defeat of 1945, and the 'Honeymoon occupation' by the Americans that followed, contributed powerfully to Japan's preference for American language and culture. Ever since Commodore Perry's appearance off the coast of Tokyo in 1853, and long before Hiroshima, there had occasionally been suggestions from leading Japanese that the country should adopt English, or even French, as the national language. Many older Japanese, Nobel laureate Kenzaburo Oe for example, are fluent in French, and well versed in French culture, a hangover from French colonial days. After the Second World War it was felt that, to modernize fully, Japan had to retool its factories and interact with the world's language. Some of the influence flowed outward: terms like *CD*, *DVD* and *Walkman* originate in Japan's high-tech breakthroughs of the 1980s, which also generated quasi-English brand names like *Panasonic*, *Sony* and *Pioneer*. Moreover, whereas English has certainly borrowed from Japanese in words like *geisha*, *ju-jitsu*, *soy*, *honcho*, *tycoon* and *sushi*, the Japanese have appropriated hundreds of words and phrases for their own use, and continue to do so. In Peter Carey's *Wrong about Japan*, the writer meets a teenage Japanese named Takashi in Starbucks, and has this exchange.

'You like muffin?' asks Takashi. '*Miruku?*'

The *u* ending suggested an English word recently adopted by the Japanese, but in the case of 'milk', that made no sense at all, so I asked Takashi was there no other word for 'milk'.

'Oh yes, of course.'

'So why do you call it *miruku?*'

'*Miruku* is more modern.'

'But what's the matter with the other word?'

'Not so hygienic.'

'How is that?'

'The other word is *gyuunyuu*.' He wrinkled his nose. 'It means liquid from udder. *Miruku* is better.'

Carey also meets the manga author Yoshiyuki Tomino. In response to Carey's questions about Mr Tomino's apparent lack of interest in national identity in his characters, the translator replies that Mr Tomino 'has always tried to make his characters as standard and as universal as possible by *not* giving them local colour or national colour or ethnic colour'.

The post-1945 annihilation of old Japan's manners, customs and traditions by a new generation of Japanese students determined to modernize is one of the themes addressed in the novels of Kazuo Ishiguro, including *A Pale View of Hills* and *An Artist of the Floating World*. Ishiguro was raised in England, writes in English and has only a rudimentary knowledge of Japanese, but he is one of Japan's most admired contemporary writers. The achievement of having won that supreme English-language literary trophy, the Booker Prize, in 1989, makes his success all the more complex for the Japanese. On the one hand, there is pride in a writer of Japanese origin succeeding abroad; on the other, there is anxiety that this indicates some wider cultural failing. Ishiguro's experience represents a moment of transition. Since 2001 young Japanese have begun to display a less uncertain response to the impact of English, which is now generally welcomed as an essential element in Japan's interaction with the Anglo-American hegemony. According to Mark Abley in *The Prodigal Tongue*, 'The hybrid speech that many young people now favour in Japan may well embody the most radical incursion English has yet made on another widely spoken language.' This, in turn, is another symptom of Thomas Friedman's 'flat' world; or, to put it another way, a global society equally interconnected regardless of the traditional restraints of time and space.

Friedman's 'Eureka moment', he writes, came in Bangalore when Nandan Nilekani, the CEO of Infosys, used the phrase 'the playing field is being levelled' to describe the new opportunities available to the India-based computer company. London, Boston, San Francisco, Kuala Lumpur, Bangalore: in the new knowledge economy, all these cities could be linked simultaneously, offering a new challenge as much for a modernizing India as for a globalizing America. 'My God,' exclaimed Friedman, 'he's telling me the world is flat.' Armed with this insight, Friedman mobilized himself to explore the many economic aspects of globalization, from Wal-Mart to Yahoo!, that were contributing to this flattening process. For Friedman, the fall of the Berlin Wall, the rise of the PC, Netscape, outsourcing and 'off-shoring'. – his 'flattening' forces – combined to enhance a new global awareness.

Millions of people [he writes] on different continents suddenly started to feel that something was new. They couldn't always quite describe what was happening, but by 2000 they sensed that they were in touch with people they'd never been in touch with before, were being challenged by people who had never challenged them before, were competing with people they had never competed with before ...

In the new millennium 'what they were feeling', he concluded, was the 'flattening of the world'. At first for an urban minority, but increasingly for a new generation, this new world was no longer the vertical, top-down society of old, but increasingly horizontal, and animated by words and concepts like 'collaboration' and 'consensus'. The new technology was beginning to dismantle old frontiers, lubricate social frictions and facilitate global interconnections. But technology alone would not be enough. There had to be a language to humanize the software, a language that was adaptable, collaborative and populist: part English, part American, part global. There is nothing aesthetically sentimental about this; it was the practical response to a practical need. At the interface of technology and global capitalism, the world's English responds to specific, local imperatives, as Jean-Paul Nerrière understood when he coined 'Globish' in 1995.

The rise of an educated middle class is not merely a feature of the new India but of South-East Asia as a whole. In cities like Bangalore, Kuala Lumpur, Chennai, Jakarta and Bangkok, IT graduates-turned-entrepreneurs began to exploit a combination of the world's English and the new media to market their expertise across the developed world, and especially America. Among countless examples of the world's English in action during this decade there is, for example, the case of Dell computers setting up operations in Nashville, Tennessee, Penang, Malaysia, Xiamen, China, Eldorado do Sul, Brazil, and Limerick, Ireland. (On an average day, Dell will sell approximately 150,000 computers, orders that are placed by email or over the telephone – in the world's English.) Hewlett Packard – based in Palo Alto, California – employs some 156,000 workers and has a billion customers in about 170 countries. The majority of its employees and customers are found abroad. More dramatically, there is Lenovo, the former IBM subsidiary, a worldwide PC company, with factories in Beijing and Raleigh, North Carolina, listed on the Hong Kong Stock Exchange, and all the Asian stock exchanges, with a headquarters in China, and a US-educated chairman of the board. In Britain, the blue-chip company Rolls-Royce has about 39,000 (approximately 45 per cent) of its workforce outside the United Kingdom, part of a global operation that reaches from Shanghai to Singapore to Seoul; to New Delhi; and also to Italy, Spain, Germany, Japan and, finally, the United States and Canada.

In this arena, Globish becomes more than just an essential means of communication: it embodies a contemporary aspiration, one that expresses a willingness to innovate, to adapt old uses and to enfranchise new people. Language is intrinsically neutral. The history of the world's English, however, puts it on the side of the individual confronting a demanding new challenge about his or her place in society. Inevitably, it is an imperfect solution, with many loose ends and much unfinished business. But it is precisely the imperfections of English that are part of its enduring strength. Social conservatives who point to scare headlines about the decline of, say, British or American literacy among Asian, Hispanic or African immigrant populations overlook the fact that, for the simple purpose of communication, the world's English remains brilliantly adaptable. Besides, for every split infinitive, misconstrued verb and clumsy malapropism there will be a dozen faultless executions of expressions with complex grammar and syntax. Chinese, Indians, Mexicans and Poles who are ambitious to succeed in the 'flat' world will acquire the language skills necessary to achieve their goals. In the words of the German publisher of the *Frankfurter Allgemeine Zeitung*, speaking to the *New York Times*, 'It is not that we are becoming more Anglo-Saxon. It's that we are having an encounter with reality.'

7

Like any language, the world's English has both a written and a spoken dimension. As a global phenomenon, shaped by contemporary international conditions, the written expression is influenced by cyberspace – the internet, text messaging (txting) and numerous online slang conventions like 'lol', 'lmao', 'fyi', 'omg' and 'wtf'. The linguistic commentator David Crystal estimates that we send more than a trillion text messages a year, though he considers that they amount to little more than 'a few ripples on the surface of the sea of language'. Perhaps. But if the fluttering of a butterfly's wing in the Amazon forests can cause a hurricane in the Caribbean, then these trillion textings must make some contribution to the English language, however small. Allowing for the fact that such abbreviations occur in all the world's main languages, including Chinese, which uses the Pinyin convention, the requirements of texting have begun to make a decisive contribution to Globish. In China today, for instance, the popularity of the BlackBerry has had a dynamic, transformational effect on upwardly mobile, middle-class Chinese who have enthusiastically embraced Globish to exploit the opportunities of the BlackBerry keypad. Before the advent of the BlackBerry, Rob Gifford, author of *China Road*, described Chinese texting as follows: 'Write the character you want in romanised letters (*mao*, *xia*, *zu*, *wang*, or whatever), then hit Return, and a selection of all the characters that fit that sound comes up, and you highlight the one you want, and hit Return again. It's laborious, but the best way to do it for a non-alphabetical language.' Gifford notes that 'the Chinese are inveterate text-messagers'. Seventeen billion texts were sent as greetings over Chinese New Year 2008. During 2007/8 some 592 billion texts were sent in China. That is 1.6 billion texts a day, coming from about 600 million mobile phone subscribers. 'In China,' adds Gifford, 'texting has inspired loads of text slang – and Chinglish.' In a country in which 350 million are learning English, a geometrical explosion of the world's English cannot be far behind.

Worldwide, for the mobile or cellphone, English is functional and fashionable, and well suited to the witty reductions of the keypad. The average English word has only five letters, where the average Inuit word, by contrast, has fourteen. English has few inflections and almost no diacritical marks. As the language of the world's popular culture, English will be the default position for the younger generation for decades to come. According to Crystal, all the world's texters use 'lol', 'gr8' and 'u', irrespective of their mother tongue. The French apparently prefer *now* to *maintenant*, and the Dutch write '2m' for 'tomorrow'. The astonishing speed of technological change in the world of information will eventually relegate texting to a quaint footnote, but, in the short run, it is an important development in our language.

For example, the now-defunct British mobile phone company Dot Mobile pioneered the publication of the classics in text format. Traditionalists will deplore the witty text rendering of Hamlet's most famous line (2b?Ntb? = ?), but it hardly compromises Shakespeare's thought or imagination, and only makes the Prince of Denmark a character to whom a younger audience can more easily relate. Dot Mobile went out of business, having discovered that the students at which it was aiming its services had neither an interest in the product nor the money for its classic summaries. There is, perhaps, no need to panic. Some studies have shown that this apparent dumbing down is not a sign of the western tradition going to the dogs but, on the contrary, evidence of a modest linguistic renaissance. In a world where 175,000 new blogs are launched every day, to argue about the cultural validity of text-Shakespeare is a bit like arguing about your bill in the saloon bar of the *Titanic*. It is also to confuse a linguistic with a pop-literary innovation. Texting operates within quintessentially linguistic parameters: it is playful, concise and universal.

It is important to distinguish between culturally specific and more broadly linguistic innovations. The freedom of cyberspace has certainly, in the words of one Amazon.com president, poured 'gasoline on the human imagination' (that's a linguistic revolution), but rhyming 'ecstasy' with 'texting me' is strictly a Globish phenomenon. In evaluating the transition from the culture of the printed book to what Sven Birkerts has called 'the culture of electronic communication', it is important to remain clear-sighted about real and fundamental changes in the function of language and about more superficial, but equally impressive, changes in contemporary usage.

In summary, then, the extraordinary IT revolution of the new millennium has accelerated time, globalized information, dissolved traditional frontiers and liberated the workplace. It has also begun to influence textual language, as much written as oral communication. Any visit to Facebook or YouTube confirms this observation. As we move from the immensity of cyberspace to the enthralling kaleidoscope of Globish, this is a good moment to acknowledge the influence of British and American English. While this book, *Globish*, argues that the Anglo-American hegemony is yielding to the supranational hegemony of a new lingua franca, at the same time we must concede that, at an immediate village level, the real surge in communication is in local languages and local media. For instance, to take a random page from the *New Indian Express*, published in Kerala, listing the available television channels, we find, in October 2008, programmes in English, Hindi and as many as ten regional languages. So of course there will be the Discovery Channel and Kids' Corner with its hours of *Tom and Jerry*, but there is another channel, Potpourri, broadcasting in Malayalam. In China, the state-run broadcaster CCTV and the provincial and municipal stations offer a total of about 2,100 channels and the availability of non-domestic television is limited. AOL Time Warner, News Corp and Phoenix TV (based in Hong Kong) are allowed to transmit via cable in Guangdong province. In Africa, there is the example of Ghana: the television transmits in English because that is the national language. Local radio, however, broadcasts in local dialects (*twee*, *eweh* and *gah*) and some local television programmes are extremely idiosyncratic.

This is a new phenomenon, responsive to the flattening effects of Globish. As recently as 1989 the world was still defined by the great Anglo-American television networks (ABC, BBC, CBS, NBC and CNN) or by international magazines like *Time* and *Newsweek*, or American newspapers like the *New York Times* and the *Washington Post*. Today, a British website like *Guardian Unlimited* can record 29 million hits a day. Increasingly, the new technology enables local cultures to define themselves on local terms through local media. For the world's lingua franca, the stronger the local loyalty, the more urgent is the need for the supranational advantages of the world's English.

The two decades after 1989 marked a transition period in which the economic infrastructure was remodelled, and both British and American English came to mirror the respective power of the UK and US economies. For the first time in many decades there was now a fairly precise equivalence between national, and superpower, importance, on the one hand, and international cultural significance on the other. Globish, meanwhile, began to enjoy its supranational momentum, fulfilling its destiny as 'the worldwide dialect of the third millennium'.

PART FIVE

Globalizers

14. One World, One Dream

'Conquer English To Make China Strong'

China is the elephant in the room that no one is quite willing to recognize. As a result, an extraordinary shift in the balance of global power is taking place sotto voce, almost by stealth.

Martin Jacques, *When China Rules the World*

1

About 20 miles to the east of Beijing in Tongzhou district, just beyond the fifth ring road, is the Beijing International Book City. This can plausibly claim to be the Largest Bookshop in the World, so vast that it comes with both a massive car park and its own hotel, where visiting booksellers can spend the night adjacent to the actual bookshop.

The Beijing International Book City says a lot about the place of English in contemporary China. Its first task is to stock the latest books from several hundred Chinese-language publishers, with names like the People's Press and the China Population Publishing House. But, as you pass through the turnstile from the spacious car park, the first sign you see is a banner with the slogan 'Open Up Your World', promoting a gaudy English-language section, as much British as American. Here, you might be in Barnes & Noble or Waterstone's. The staff have displayed what they describe as the leading 'professional bestsellers', Chinese style, in elegant swirling pyramids of print, often shrink-wrapped: Michael Crichton, Eoin Colfer, Charlie Higson, Homer's *Odyssey*, and a book you have never heard of, *The Success Principle*.

Modern China is all about success. Such is the obsession with the transforming power of the marketplace in the new China that the eager young booksellers I spoke to were concerned to know more about likely British 'bestsellers'. The idea of a little book making its way through word of mouth and the quiet accumulation of devoted readers is foreign to this generation of English-language readers. Bestseller-readers in China are Globish readers. They are being willingly coerced by the soft power of a global force, and by Globish prose, a universally accessible style and story. Today, during my visit to Beijing, the dominant example on display is Harry Potter 7: *The Deathly Hallows*. By the time you read this, J. K. Rowling will have been replaced in Beijing International Book City by another global bestseller.

In 2010, if there is one nation whose modernizing mission should benefit from Globish, it must be the new China. But how exactly, and when? The beginnings of the new China are to be found not in the Communist takeover of 1949 but in the prelude to the Third Plenum of the Eleventh Central Committee, which met in December 1978. Mao Zedong had been dead for just over two years but his revolutionary heirs still held the reins of power. So it was all the more remarkable that the new party chairman, Deng Xiaoping, a feisty survivor of the Cultural Revolution, should make a speech in advance of the Third Plenum arguing that the reality of the world economy, not narrow party ideology, should govern China's future policy and direction. 'It does not matter if it is a black cat or a white cat,' Deng observed. 'As long as it can catch mice, it is a good cat.' This homely incitement to pragmatism launched the Chinese economic miracle of the last three decades.

2

How to convey the awesome scale of China's self-transformation? In 1949 there were five cities in China with populations of more than 1 million; by 1990 there were ninety-nine. From many astonishing statistics about cellphone usage and DVD ownership, one startling figure stands out: in 1978 China made some 200 air conditioning units per annum; in 2005 it manufactured 48 million. Indeed, for thirty years its economy has grown at a rate of more than 9 per cent per annum. Today, even with the worldwide recession, this growth is still awe-inspiring in its scale. Thus, for example, China in 2008 exported in a single day more than it exported throughout the whole of 1978. A good part of this is accounted for by Wal-Mart, which imports about $12–18 billion worth of goods from China each year. (It is estimated that more than half the world's clothes and shoes will now have a 'Made in China' tag.) In the Republic itself, on the domestic consumer side, Starbucks estimates that by 2010 it will have more cafés in China than in the USA.

On my visit to Beijing in March 2008 I checked into a high-rise Sofitel luxury hotel that had just been built at top speed, to the finest international specifications, during 2004–6. At three in the morning, disturbed by jet lag, I looked out of my twenty-second-floor picture window into the smoggy Beijing night. Across the ceaseless highway, in the near distance, was the distinctive outline of the as-yet-uncompleted CCTV tower, the headquarters of China's English-language television. Disembodied high in the gloom was a flickering light like a child's Christmas sparkler: a moonlighting Chinese construction worker was welding rivets through the night in urgent completion of this landmark project. For me, far more than the rhetoric and the statistics, that solitary blowtorch fizzing through the darkness is the unforgettable symbol of China's determination to modernize.

What happens in Beijing is also happening in Shanghai, Chongqing and other Chinese cities: at least twenty of the world's fastest growing urban centres are found in China. And in Beijing, the renewal of the capital has been compared, inadequately, to Haussmann's rebuilding of Paris after the 1848 revolutions. In fact, the run-up to the 2008 Olympics (the most expensive in history) saw something else again, a radically overhauled infrastructure: six brand new subway lines; a 26-mile light railway; the world's largest airport terminal; and, of course, Beijing's Olympic Park with its Bird Cage and National Aquatics Centre, Shuilifang, commonly referred to as the Water Cube. In a piquant historical touch, part of this Olympic development was designed by Albert Speer jun., the son of Hitler's architect. China's slogan for its Olympic brand was expressed in Chinese characters that translated into the simple and optimistic motto 'One World, One Dream'. Amid this seismic growth, there is the Beijing International Book City, proving that there is still, astonishingly, a place for books, beyond the fifth ring road, in this world of the future.

Printed English in China will usually attempt, with inevitable lapses, to follow internationally recognized norms. To reach the goal of full participation in the world of Globish, the would-be student must negotiate the path that traverses the wild terrain of Chinese English, or Chinglish. This variety, which is the subject of fierce debate and scrutiny inside and outside China, has been a feature on the linguistic radar for many years. One American expat in Beijing, David Tool, aka Du Dawai, a retired US army colonel, has strong views about Chinglish, and has made it his mission to eradicate broken English in Beijing, especially where it appears on public notices. Locals call him the 'sign police professor'. Tool says: 'When foreigners come here, I want them to understand Chinese culture, not laugh at it.'

China's soaring ambitions and booming economy have changed the dynamics of Chinglish. During the preparations for the Beijing Olympics a new phenomenon – 'Crazy English' – began to attract international attention. A vivid contemporary example of Globish at work, this is the single-handed creation of the 'Elvis of English', Li Yang. This rampant entrepreneur, according to the *New Yorker*, is 'the world's only language teacher known to bring students to tears of excitement'. Li Yang has made a business empire out of exploiting China's obsession with acquiring the language that Mao and his acolytes denounced for its association with 'the running dogs of capitalism'. Li Yang has an opposite motto, but an equivalent patriotism. One of his slogans is 'Conquer English To Make China Strong'. In teaching methods, there is a direct link between the students of the 'English corner' and Li Yang's classes. Both learn English through raucous repetition. 'I am', declares the instructor. 'I am', yells the class. 'Going to come', cries the teacher. 'Going to come', they repeat. 'To Your'. Another mass repetition. 'To Your'. 'Beautiful House', concludes the teacher. 'Beautiful House', roars the class. Part preacher, part sergeant major, part pedagogue, Li Yang also teaches this way, often to groups of ten thousand. His operation is run from a head-quarters in Guangzhou. From here, the Crazy English team market books, audiotapes and videos. There are also software programmes like 'Li Yang's Crazy English Blurt Out MP 3 Collection'. Li Yang has also published a memoir, *I Am Crazy, I Succeed*.

This mania – that is what it is – reflects the spirit of the new China, but it is hardly new. The last time China fell under the spell of a language guru it was in the 1980s, and she hosted the BBC English-language programme *Follow Me*. Her name was Kathy Flower, and she was, and still is, more famous in China than almost anyone else alive. When we filmed her for *The Story of English* we showed her weekly programme being watched by waiters in restaurants, part of an estimated audience of 50 million. 'You would go into a shop,' she remembers, 'and find two sixty-year-olds practising the dialogue from *Follow Me* the night before.' Kathy Flower now lives in the French Pyrenees, but keeps in touch with China, where she is still greeted as 'Teacher Flower'. She remains sceptical about Crazy English, but concedes that

the Chinese have already assimilated English *culture* much more than I would have thought possible twenty years ago, largely in the form of American cartoons and films (90 per cent pirated). Language is another matter, though, and the linguistic impact of the English language on Chinese is minimal. There isn't even the borrowing from English into Chinese which characterizes Japanese.

But what about the English-language slogans the visitor sees on all sides? 'They exist in a parallel universe,' she says, 'and they don't really creep into everyday speech.' And yet western education, of which English is a vital part, is essential to the new China. Kathy Flower remarks that 'It's almost impossible to overstate the importance of education to the Chinese family, especially the ones who have stuck to the one-child policy and therefore have only one child to spend their money on, and only one on whom to pin their hopes for the future'. But she is not optimistic about profound change. 'Until [the authorities] do something about the 60,000 Chinese characters which an educated person is supposed to learn (as they did in Vietnam), I don't think it's ever going to change places with English. When you leave the cities and go into the countryside you find millions of people for whom even basic education in the mother tongue is a lifetime's achievement.' Compared to India, for example, China has no anglophone reservoir of colonial history to draw on, even if the inhabitants of the Middle Kingdom were interested in such a thing, which is doubtful.

This belief that the Chinese languages reflect a self-contained and aloof civilization with no real interest in any cultural exchange with outsiders is held by many observers and must temper any excitement about the power and influence of 'Crazy English' in the aftermath of the Beijing Olympics. In *China Road*, his account of a seven-year stint in Beijing, the journalist and China expert Rob Gifford writes of the link between 'the unassailable fortress of the written Chinese character and the unassailable fortress of the imperial (and then Communist Party) state'. Economic factors are vital to this equation and world trade can achieve remarkable transformations. As Timothy Garton Ash recently wrote in the *Guardian*, 'This is not the 17th century. The prospects for the Chinese economy [in 2009] depend directly on what happens in the American and European markets for Chinese exports.'

If the state continues to modernize and to develop, then Globish is likely to be part of the process, but that remains a big 'If'. Conversely, could a Chinese economic superpower persuade the world to acquire Mandarin, in population terms the world's Number 1 language by a factor of 2 to 1? Probably not. The omens are unpromising. The Chinese language, like Chinese civilization, is self-contained and difficult to penetrate. As Rob Gifford writes in *China Road*, 'getting into the language (learning how to read, write and pronounce characters) is by far the most difficult part of learning Chinese.' After that, he says, it is 'much simpler than English'. This simplicity might seem to be a virtue, but it has a flip side, notes Gifford. 'The fact that characters cannot change gives the whole language an inflexibility that even Chinese scholars admit can stunt originality.' In *When China Rules the World*, Martin Jacques takes an opposite view: 'the

Chinese enthusiasm for English in no way reflects a decline in the popularity of Chinese. English remains a strictly second language, an interlocutor language for the young, well-educated and ambitious urban elite.'

3

As Kathy Flower implies, the larger question posed by China's obsession with the English language is simple: how will it affect China? Will the manufacture of hairdryers and hatchback saloons inspire an appetite for free expression? Can rampant capitalism be married to state control? More fundamentally: can China assimilate Globish to its modernizing purposes as a giant economy in the twenty-first century? The same question must be asked of India, its great rival, but with much surer answers. What is fascinating about China's Globish question is that, though it is far from academic, and will have long-lasting consequences for billions of people in decades to come, it is also a subject that occupies some of the country's best minds. The China-watcher Mark Leonard writes that there is 'a hidden world of intellectuals, think-tankers and activists, all engaged in intense debate about the future of their country'. For the contemporary thinker in China, the issue is: how can we enjoy the benefits of global capitalism, represented culturally by Globish, while protecting China from the creative instability such forces could unleash on its rigid economic and political system?

For some, it is not enough to be passive participants in globalization. According to Leonard, some Chinese intellectuals are actively trying 'to challenge the flat world of US globalisation with a "walled world" Chinese version'. This contemporary recapitulation of China's historic international stance is supported by a long tradition. But that is not the whole story. China is more than capable of conducting a Sino-intellectual takeover of western ideas, as Mao's uniquely Chinese brand of communism suggests. Maoism, of course, is history. Now, in the twenty-first century, the challenge for China will be how to integrate Globish values into the alien matrix of the Chinese tradition. Some commentators, like the *Observer*'s Will Hutton, do not believe it can be done. In *The Writing on the Wall*, Hutton declares: 'for all China's success to date, ultimately the system that the communists have created is structurally unstable.'

China's 'new left', who support the market reforms inaugurated by Deng Xiaoping in 1979, disagree with this bleak diagnosis, which they see as uninformed, and talk instead about institutional innovation, with frequent references to low-price health care, green development programmes and the reform of property laws to incentivize workers in the state's project. According to Leonard, 'the balance of power in Beijing is subtly shifting towards the [new] left'. In the 11th Five Year Plan of 2005, for instance, Hu Jintao and Wen Jiabao were happy to describe a blueprint for a 'harmonious society' rather than insisting on a forced march towards more economic growth, previously China's great ambition. The 11th Five Year Plan offers a gradualist reform process rather than shock therapy. This plan seems to accept that the market, with all its unpredictability, will drive China's development in the near and medium future.

Theory is one thing; practice is something else. The irony of Mao's Communist experiment is that the Chinese are natural, and rather brilliant, capitalists who love the thrill of investment. Elsewhere, the example of post-colonial Hong Kong, a universal market for everything from pig futures to plasma-screen televisions, offers a demonstration of Globish in action. But it is the changes on the mainland that are truly impressive. When you witness the global market in action in Beijing, the Benetton and Samsung stores, the videos and DVDs sold on street corners, and the rows of BMWs, Audis and Hondas gridlocked on the third ring road, you see a society embracing global capitalism and its attendant Globish with the fierce enthusiasm that the Chinese always bring to their endeavours.

This has some surprising manifestations. Shen Yan has a nine-to-five job as an education officer in the Cultural Section of the British Embassy. He is young and hip and alert to Globish culture. In his spare time, he is also the lead singer in his own rock band, The Tumbleweeds. How would he describe his music? It is his own invention, he says, and adds that, in homage to his favourite Heavy Metal, 'I call it "Love Metal".' Shen Yan's song 'Change' contains the following lines:

Live for today as if there was no tomorrow
Live for today, and there will be no more sorrow

But if the influence is American, the language in which Shen Yan will habitually sing this song is still Chinese. In the Middle Kingdom, even Globish has its limitations.

4

China's interaction with English is effecting an impact not just on its millions of domestic consumers. There is an international dimension to consider, too. For example, it is in the heart of Africa that the supranational power of English could be decisive. The continent has the vast, untapped resources of the oil and natural gas that China needs to fuel its dash for growth. Beijing and African governments like Colonel Qaddafi's Libya can do business because there is no ideological or colonial hangover to inhibit the development of trade, now growing at about 50 per cent per annum. When some African states expressed resentment at what they saw as an exploitative relationship, Beijing at first launched Globish diplomacy. In November 2006 President Hu Jintao hosted a Sino-African conference on international relations. Forty-eight African countries, from Botswana to Zimbabwe, attended the largest African summit ever to be held outside the continent. To sweeten the dialogue, China undertook to double aid to Africa within two years, provide $5 billion in loans and credits, cancel a large portion of Africa's debt to China, train 15,000 African professionals (doctors, teachers and lawyers) and build new hospitals and schools. As the unprecedented scale of China's largesse began to sink in, Ethiopia's prime minister Meles Zenawi declared ecstatically, 'China is an inspiration for all of us.'

The inevitable reckoning came soon after, in February 2007, when Hu Jintao announced the creation of a new economic zone in Zambia. This was a neo-colonial statement, but with a difference. China would transplant its growth model to Africa by connecting the copper, cobalt, tin and diamonds of Zambia to the People's Republic, by rail, road and shipping links. There would also be a 'trading hub', based on Mauritius, and a 'shipping hub', possibly located in Tanzania. Few Africans, of course, speak or read Mandarin Chinese, and even trained Chinese bureaucrats would be utterly ignorant of African languages like Hausa, Yoruba and Swahili. Inevitably, most of the negotiations and international press coverage of this highly significant initiative was conducted in the world's English. CCTV, China's English-language television channel, has broadcast many of the key Sino-African encounters in this extraordinary transaction. Globish, inevitably, became instrumental in bridging the cultural chasm between the two traditions, African and Chinese.

Massive and unprecedented as China's contribution to African development has been, it was surely dwarfed by its commitment to its own 2008 Beijing Olympics, an investment of nearly 300 billion yuan ($44 billion). This was a turning point, a matter of huge national pride. To host the Olympics was to put China in the same socio-economic and even cultural league as the United States and the great powers of Old Europe. The Beijing Olympics made China a player on the world stage.

That might seem to place it on a collision course with the United States. Certainly, some members of the Pentagon saw China's global renaissance as a threat, not an opportunity. Some hawkish neo-cons will even speculate about a war over Taiwan. Other observers believe that this is to misread the situation. As the China-watcher Joshua Cooper Ramo has put it, 'The goal for China is not conflict but the avoidance of conflict.' For China, true success in its strategy, in which Globish must have a role, involves the successful manipulation of the situation to achieve an outcome that will inevitably favour Chinese interests. This policy, writes Ramo, emerges from the oldest Chinese strategic thinker, Sun Zi, who argued that 'every battle is won or lost before it is ever fought'. Many Americans will feel roughly the same about Globish as most Britons felt about American English in 1776. China – and Globish – is still a long way from such a moment, but it needs to be considered carefully. We have the means to compare. Closer to home, there is another modernizing society for which Globish is – and has been for decades – in play: India.

15. 'Virtually Running America'

India, the Far East and Beyond

Our nation, though it has no drinking water, electricity, sewage system, public transportation, sense of hygiene, discipline, courtesy, or punctuality, *does* have entrepreneurs. Thousands and thousands of them. Especially in the field of technology. And these entrepreneurs – *we* entrepreneurs – have set up all these outsourcing companies that virtually run America now.

Aravind Adiga, *The White Tiger*

1

Bangalore, the Silicon Valley of the new India, twinned with San Francisco, is almost literally the gateway to a brave new world. Visitors who remember dingy airports, oppressive bureaucracy, long lines at customs and immigration, and sweltering chaos en route to a battered taxi, will be astonished at the smooth and airy efficiency of twenty-first-century Bangalore airport with its marble halls and spacious arrivals concourse. It is like landing at Denver, Colorado. Outside, beneath bright, clear skies – at 3,000 feet above sea level, Bangalore is cooler and less humid than other parts of the subcontinent – rows of Honda and Toyota SUVs reinforce the illusion of being in the American Midwest. Only when you leave the airport perimeter do you step back in time to the old India of dirt, destitution and decay. Bangalore is a former garrison town from the Victorian Raj, popular with British officers looking for relief from the heat and dust of the Indian plains. The Bangalore Club, a faithful Pall Mall replica, proudly displays one of Winston Churchill's unpaid bar bills. But Bangalore is not just a museum of the imperial past. It is also at the leading edge of India's newest transformation. The city is the home of Infosys, Microsoft, Texas Instruments, Accenture, Bosch, Siemens, Verizon and India's astronaut training centre.

When, in contrast to China, you try to identify the architects of this astonishing renewal, you find that the state has almost nothing to do with it. Unlike China, its government has played no direct role. India has followed the development path pioneered by its former British masters: accidental, wasteful, free-spirited and democratic, with a lavish top dressing of outright chaos. As Aravind Adiga writes in *The White Tiger*, there is no shortage of would-be entrepreneurs in India and the socio-economic climate is hospitable to their efforts. One reason they prosper is that, as a direct result of the 150-year Raj, they have instant access to Globish.

The world's English is intrinsic to the growth of contemporary India, which is now the world's third largest English-language book market, after the USA and UK. On dozens of streets in a city like Bangalore, Calcutta or Mumbai, you will find advertisements for 'English Centre' or 'Career English', the passport to a better future. In Bangalore, I climbed a rickety outside staircase to the offices of 'Easy English' (advertising 'Spoken English, Call Centre Training, Placements') to learn about the programme on offer to the would-be student. 'Easy English' turned out to be a husband-and-wife team, operating out of four rooms (and a tiny kitchen), with a clientele of barely a dozen students who were paying 1,500 rupees a month, a substantial commitment, to acquire enough English to apply to one of the call centres. How long, I wondered, had 'Easy English' been in business here. 'Six months.' The proliferation of such training rooms happens at the end of the Globish food chain. Infosys, Microsoft and the other big corporations will train thousands of high-quality graduates to operate in North American, Australasian or British markets. Nonetheless, the shabby, hopeful offices of 'Easy English' are symptomatic of a hunger for opportunity.

Sayad Aga, a young Indian graduate, formerly employed in a Bangalore call centre, describes the acquisition of 'voice and accent training' as 'a kind of gold rush' among young Indians. Having been schooled by one of the city's big companies, like Infosys or Microsoft, the call centre graduate can work in what Sayad calls 'global communication', that is, outsourcing, for many multinational and American corporations – Citibank, IBM and the like. Sayad Aga's training gives him versatility in the global market. 'When you talk to someone over the phone,' he says, 'you automatically mirror him.' He adds that in conversation with British clients he will use words like 'bloke', where 'guy' would be more usual in dealing with Americans.

Modernizing India mirrors the West in other ways, too. In Bangalore, the journey to the Infosys campus takes the visitor down a teeming highway typical of old India – cows, beggars, potholes, shanties and an interminable jam of hooting traffic. After several miles of tortuous driving to the outskirts, you reach Electronics City. Here, there is a right turn into a shady road lined with taxis, and in a few moments you pull up outside a security checkpoint. A PR woman comes to meet you and suddenly you are in ... California! There are shady lawns, plashing fountains and well-kept walkways; crowded cafés, a lovely open-air swimming pool set among cypress trees, a Domino pizza concession and even an outdoor theatre. A kind of oasis, the Infosys campus occupies an 83-acre plot dotted with sleek, modern buildings and workers' recreation areas (a gym, a bookstore). After the heat and dust of the city, the atmosphere is cool and tranquil. Infosys employees stroll about in shirtsleeves or ride in golf carts from department to department.

Sayad Aga and his friend Ayaz Ali, graduates from Infosys, have a wide experience of India's outsource culture. Both are at home within many varieties of English, and recognize Globish as 'the worldwide dialect of the third millennium'. They confirm how intimately familiar India's new managerial class has become with western business trends. 'We have no need for translators or cultural guides,' comments Sayed. They read about computers, management theory, marketing strategy and the latest innovations in science and technology as easily as they follow the progess of the Indian cricket eleven. As Fareed Zakaria has put it, both 'speak globalization fluently'.

Globish is essential to India's globalizing ambitions. This is not the Indian English of *Hobson-Jobson* and the bazaar or the standardized American and British English of the universities, but the emerging supranational lingua franca that enables a call centre in Bangalore to answer impossible queries, or sell new products, as far afield as Cheltenham in the UK, Cedar Rapids in the United States or

Co. Cork, Eire. Many major cities in India now have call centres, with a dynamic effect on the local economy (call centre employees enjoy a salary as much as five times the national average). The road to Electronics City is symbolic of old India, but the Infosys campus, barely five miles from the centre of the city, is an oasis of Globish. Each of the 21,000 employees, with an average age of 25 to 26, is an exponent of Globish culture. The lifestyle of the Infosys campus takes its inspiration from global capitalism: in the atrium of the headquarters building there is a snappily dressed receptionist wearing headphones. The ambient sound of water in a marble fountain mingles with the hum and ping of elevators. Sunanda Jayaseelan, the Infosys publicist assigned to my visit, is typical of the new class here in Bangalore. Formerly a journalist with a local paper, she has embarked on a career with Infosys that will allow her to work flexible hours, raise a family if she wants to and enjoy above-average earnings. The competition for such jobs is fierce. Sunanda reports that last year there were some 1.3 million applicants for about 30,000 Infosys jobs, all of them graduates using Globish to advance their careers.

At the heart of the Infosys campus, I was ushered into the offices of CEO and managing director S. Gopalakrishnan, known as Kris, who was working in shirtsleeves at his laptop. For Infosys, the market in China is an important opportunity. Kris notes that the lingua franca of the interaction between Infosys offices in Bangalore and Shanghai is the world's English, but, he says, the company is also using local languages to accelerate the local growth of the company. Globish is developing exponentially. 'Every new intake speaks and uses better English than the previous year. Every new intake makes better inter-company connections,' he says, explicitly comparing this Globish to Latin, and describing it as an essential tool of his company's expansion programme.

The roots of this programme lie deep in colonial India.

2

India's independence from Britain came in 1947, two years before China's declaration of its People's Republic. Just after midnight on

15 August, Prime Minister Jawaharlal Nehru uttered the landmark words that would set his country on its new path: 'A moment comes, which comes but rarely in history, when we step out from the old to the new, when an age ends and when the soul of a nation, long suppressed, finds utterance.'

For all the excitement at the novelty of independence, there were two factors – language and religion – that ensured a certain continuity in Indian life. In the first place, the country's elite had been steeped in English language and culture for more than a century. Educated Indians grew up reading Dickens and P. G. Wodehouse and also playing cricket; some of them went to English public schools and universities. In law, literature and everyday life their habits were refracted through the English language. The journalist Malcolm Muggeridge used to joke during the 1930s that the last Englishman would be an Indian. At the same time – especially after Partition – the dominant religion was Hinduism, contributing a unique perspective on the wider world.

It is an Indian paradox that the language of the former colonial masters is both a vehicle for originality and free expression, as well as a unifying national force. For instance, in the south of India, which is still profoundly resentful of the Hindi northern states centred on the capital, Delhi, English becomes a default language among people who need to find a means of communication that is acceptable (and intelligible) to all speakers. As a result, you find that multinational advertising campaigns will marry both idioms, Indian and English. Pepsi's 'Ask For More' became *Yeh dil maange more*, meaning 'The heart wants more'. In response, Coca-Cola retaliated with 'Life Should Be Like This', or *Life ho to aisi*. And in Mumbai, the novelist Salman Rushdie likes to say, the people of his native city speak something called 'Hug-me', his witty acronym for the Mumbai mixture of Hindi, Urdu, Gujarati, Marathi and, finally, English. 'Hug-me' is more localized than 'Hinglish', but you will find alternative urban variations of it all over India.

In the twenty-first century the fusion of the English and the Hindi traditions, cultural and religious, together with many other Indian customs, is creating a society uniquely equipped to contribute to, and benefit from, the development of English. The country is modernizing with a vengeance. There are so many examples, but the success of Pre-Media Global, a publishing-service firm based in Chennai (Madras) and founded in 2005 by the brother-and-sister team of Kami Narayan and Kapil Viswanathan, is emblematic. Kami is a graduate of India's National Law School, with an MBA from Harvard; Kapil also has a Harvard MBA but trained as an engineer at Stanford. Both are equally at home in East or West. The service PreMedia Global offers is essentially a co-ordinated outsource operation for design, production and editorial. Its clients include McGraw-Hill, Thomson, Houghton Mifflin, Pearson, Wiley and Reader's Digest. 'They supply the content,' says Kapil; 'we edit and compose the text for printing and electronic publishing.' In their dealings with non-English clients, they rely on Globish. Video conferences enable the company's 1,000 Indian and American employees to cross linguistic and cultural gaps.

PreMedia Global offers a paradigm for an English-language economy. By the middle of the first decade of the new millennium India had just enjoyed more than ten years of sustained and peaceful economic growth. The demons of the past were slowly being exorcized. Relations with Pakistan were normalized; the near-derelict infrastructure was being overhauled; Indian democracy and global marketing were becoming wired together. Where, in the past, young Indian high-flyers sought advancement and new opportunities in the UK or California, now the new generation was committing itself to exploit the opportunities of India's surging private sector, at home. Fareed Zakaria, a symbolic figure from this transitional decade, an Indian educated in Britain and the United States, who has made a distinguished journalistic career in the United States, notes approvingly that 'India now has more billionaires than any other Asian country, and almost all of them are self-made'.

3

Globish does not merely have a business or a diplomatic application, though that can be important. There is plenty of evidence that it is flourishing at a more popular level, too. One of the vital characteristics of India today is that its educated middle class – its managers, travel agents, salespersons, secretaries, clerks, and the like – has a new appetite for literary entertainment. Their taste falls between the elite idiom of the cultivated literati, as seen in the novels of Amitav Ghosh or Salman Rushdie, and the Indian English of the street and the supermarket. Consider the case of Chetan Bhagat.

The author of the romantic comedy *One Night @ the Call Centre* is one of the biggest-selling writers in India. His work is only available in India, and certainly never considered for the Man Booker Prize. Yet it is known to almost every college student on the subcontinent and has sold about 1.5 million copies in all editions. According to the *Guardian*, Bhagat's latest novel, *The 3 Mistakes of My Life*, 'sells a copy every 17 seconds'. The key to Bhagat's success is that he addresses the everyday concerns of India's middle-class youth, does this in a language they can relate to and also consciously strives for a mass appeal. Bhagat's books sell at 95 rupees (£1.20), the same price as a cinema ticket, and are aimed at supermarkets. 'We don't have bookshops in every town,' he says. 'We have supermarkets. I want my books next to jeans and bread. I want my country to read me.'

Bhagat writes in the quick-fire campus idiom that young Indians use, and exploits a brash populism (scorned by some critics as 'toilet reading') to reach the widest possible market. His first novel, *Five Point Someone*, adopted a breezy, ironical tone to explore the lives of the exam-oppressed students who cram to get into the Indian Institute of Technology (Delhi) and then rebel against the stultifying atmosphere of academic competition. *Five Point Someone* features soft drugs, binge drinking, and an affair between a student and his professor's daughter. *One Night @ the Call Centre* is a romantic comedy set in a call centre office where bored young Indians try to resolve the mindless enquiries of midwestern American technophobes. Bhagat says that his novel reflects a generational divide in India. His model society is China, not the modernizing China of Deng Xiaoping, but the radicalizing China of Mao Zedong. 'India needs a cultural revolution to change mindsets,' Bhagat told the *Guardian*. 'In China it was bloody, but India needs to learn that the old ways are not always the best ways.' *One Night @ the Call Centre* has already sold almost half a million copies. In October 2008 it reached a new audience when a Bollywood film adaptation went on general release.

Bollywood is another example of Globish in microcosm, and a vital barometer of linguistic and cultural change in India today. The industry, based in Mumbai, actually produces about 800 films a year, in various languages. Most of the English used in Bollywood movies is confined to scenes of business and professional life, but there are changes afoot. American movie tropes – action, sex, violence, on-screen nudity – are becoming adopted, to the fury of conservative Indian commentators who object that 'traditional' Indian culture is being crushed by the West, specifically America.

Actually, the pundits are wrong: Bollywood holds all the aces. Just on its own terms, India's domestic entertainment and media market was worth $15 billion in 2008, and is projected to grow to $25 billion by 2013. There is an international dimension, too. Elsewhere, according to the *New York Times*, Bollywood's worldwide fan base numbers 3.6 billion, and Hollywood, led by Disney and the financier George Soros, has begun to invest. The Indian entertainment group Eros International already has some lucrative joint ventures. Kishore Lulla, chairman of Eros, told the *Observer*: 'India's entertainment industry is growing rapidly, and it will soon be a powerhouse. In a couple of years a Bollywood film might take $50 million at the box office in India alone.' Bollywood operates in a skein of languages, but the alliance with Hollywood will yield a Globish dividend. The Bollywood star Akshay Kumar (more famous, to half the world's population, than Brad Pitt, Tom Cruise and Bruce Willis put together) has just completed *Kambakkht Ishq*, a film co-starring Sylvester Stallone and Denise Richards. Kishore Lulla says, 'A lot of [US] companies have already approached Eros International, very interested in Bollywood. I think *Slumdog Millionaire* was a large part of that.'

In 2003, inspired by the British television quiz show *Who Wants to Be a Millionaire?*, a would-be writer named Vikas Swarup, an Indian diplomat from Allahabad, completed a first novel about a quiz show winner from the Mumbai slums, accused of cheating his way to a million. Entitled *Q & A*, it was published in 2005, to favourable, but hardly ecstatic, reviews. In an overcrowded bazaar, *Q & A* might have joined that melancholy heap of promising debuts which drift into oblivion. Instead, in a twist of fate, the novel caught the attention of the British company Film4, which took an option. The author of *The Full Monty*, Simon Beaufoy, was commissioned to write a script. Finally, in a cinematic ripple-dissolve, *Q & A* became *Slumdog Millionaire*, a Globish movie. The dialogue was simplified; any dialogue in local languages was given subtitles. Many local references were airbrushed for a world audience. Friends became brothers. The denouement became a cliffhanger. Names were changed. Ram Mohammad Thomas became Jamal Malik, vibrantly portrayed by Dev Patel. In most other respects, Swarup's original, which has the simplicity of a good yarn, was faithfully rendered on the screen.

Q & A is popular fiction at its best and brightest, Globish storytelling for a Globish audience. The magic that Beaufoy brought to *Q & A* was, essentially, to streamline the narrative and make it a full-blown love story. In the book, Swarup's hero, Ram Mohammad Thomas, does fall in love with a beautiful Indian girl named Nita, but she is a *bedni* (a prostitute): that old standby, the tart with a heart of gold. In the film, Nita becomes the infinitely more appealing Latika. For his part, Ram's emotional compass does not extend much beyond 'I knew in my heart of hearts that she was my princess.' His relationship with Nita, whom he marries in the book's Epilogue, gets lost in the resolution to the film's quiz show plot. *Q & A*'s other cinematic secret, unlocked by Beaufoy and director Danny Boyle, is not only that it is set in Mumbai's classic slum, Dharavi, but also that its author, and his puppets, are obsessed with Bollywood, like many slum-dwellers. The trick of the book, and the movie, is to marry an archetypal tale of rags-to-riches with the Bollywood genre of storytelling that revels in violent scenes, bizarre and implausible coincidences and outsize villains. *Q & A* teaches us that Bollywood is to the suspension of disbelief what the Indian rope trick is to Newtonian physics. Apart from a few routine nods to the richness of Indian English in the use of local terms like *eve-teasing*, and words like *chai wallah*, *chawl* and *lathi charge*, Swarup writes in standard British English, as you would expect from a career diplomat in the Indian Foreign Service (IFS). But his market is a Globish one.

4

The spread of the world's English in sport, advertising, films, tourism and international finance continues to enjoy a supranational momentum. Open any newspaper, and there are countless examples of Globish at work. Consider, for example, Misha Glenny's study of international crime networks, *McMafia*, first published in Britain and the United States in 2008. Glenny's subject had wide international appeal and was translated into thirty-one languages, including Portuguese, Dutch and Russian – the 384-page text, that is. Glenny's catchy title, which is almost a brand name, has required no translation. It has become, in the author's words, 'widely accepted shorthand for international organised crime'. But where does it derive its inspiration? From a multinational fast-food chain of Scots-American origin (McDonald's), married to a Sicilian slang word for a secret criminal society. Contagious, adaptable, populist and subversive, Globish will always display this capacity to animate inert linguistic fragments into striking new configurations, like iron filings around a magnet.

The publishing history of *McMafia* is just one example of Globish in microcosm. On a much larger scale, there is the case of Rwanda, a small, landlocked African republic with a tragic recent history. Colonized by the Germans in 1884–5 and then by the Belgians in 1923 under League of Nations supervision, Rwanda has been francophone for at least a century. Not any more. In 2008, in a decisive bid for a new national direction in the global economy, the government of Rwanda officially abandoned French. Instead, it adopted English as its language of international communication, and the language that would be taught in schools, even to children whose mother tongue was Kinyarwanda or Urunyaruanda. Rwanda did not have just linguistic reasons for breaking with its francophone heritage. It still blames France for failing to prevent the Hutus from massacring nearly a million Tutsis in 1994.

But the real reason was commercial. 'French is spoken only in France,' said Rwanda's trade and industry minister, with withering disdain, 'some parts of West Africa, parts of Canada – and Switzerland.' Enough said. That would be of no use to Rwanda's business ambitions. On the other hand, the minister continued, 'English has emerged as a backbone for growth and development not only in the region but around the globe.' By 2009 Rwanda had formally applied to join the British Commonwealth, following the example of Madagascar and Algeria. It would be hard to find a more vivid example of the post-colonial appeal of Globish in the new millennium.

The upsurge of Globish in the Iranian elections of June 2009 demonstrated both its role and its limitations. Cellphone photographs of English-language slogans and innumerable tweets from Twittering westernized Iranians communicated the strength of the emergency to the West, and possibly contributed to the instability on the streets. The tragic death of one demonstrator, Neda Agha-Soltan, a terrible story transmitted globally on Facebook, was fundamentally an internet phenomenon, but much of the subsequent international commentary was conducted in Globish through many media. The regime's determination to retain power at all costs proved too strong for the opposition, however. Globish could internationalize the Iranian struggle, but Globish could not transform its prospects locally.

At the same time as the crowds were demonstrating on the streets of Tehran, an infinitely more sober transfer of power was taking place north of the 60th parallel: the people of Greenland were celebrating their independence after nearly three hundred years of Danish rule. Greenland is an Inuit society and its colonial masters come from a small Nordic state on the north-west perimeter of the European Union. When the world's press arrived in Nuuk to report on the independence day festivities, the English language became the inevitable means of communication. Greenland was asserting its Inuit identity, for instance, proudly referring to its new government by its Inuit name, Naalakkersuisut. But the new prime minister, Kuupik Kleist, described the balance of power between Greenland and Denmark in good old English terms that would have been intelligible to Caxton and Chaucer. 'From today,' he said, comparing the situation to a marriage in which the wife bosses a henpecked husband, 'the man in the house has as much say as the wife.' Iran and Greenland are the latest contemporary examples of Globish in action. Both are indicative of a lingua franca at work, unhindered by the Anglo-American past. In the Far East, there is an even more dramatic example of Globish power. Singaporean English (Singlish) owes its existence to the British empire. At the same time it has come to embody the ambitions of a modern city state to participate in the global marketplace.

Thirty years ago, in the 1970s, Prime Minister Lee Kuan Yew instituted his 'English First' programme as a way of guaranteeing that Singapore would enjoy a vital membership of the international community. In those days, with memories of the empire and the Second World War still green, the local population of about 2.5 million was a mixture of Malay, Chinese and Indian. The many mother tongues of the island included Mandarin, Cantonese, Malay and Tamil. To one and all, English was the language of the ex-colonial power. Still, to unite the people in the common purpose of modernization, Lee Kuan Yew, a proud graduate of Cambridge University, placed his considerable authority behind what he called 'clear, clean English', one of the first state-sponsored expressions of Globish. He argued forcefully that just because it was not a mother tongue, there was no reason it could not become part of Singapore's traffic with the international community. 'There is this naive belief', he told me in an interview in 1984, 'that because the language is English, therefore it is not part of me, so I cannot learn to use it as well as an Englishman. This is utterly wrong.' Privately, he deplored vagaries of Singlish, for instance the typical Singapore habit of ending a sentence with 'lah', as in 'He is big-sized, lah.'

Lee Kuan Yew was running an authoritarian city state. So the customary interplay between English, free market capitalism and the steady adoption of democratic procedures did not really apply to Singapore. In the heyday of his power Lee was determined to modernize the economy while keeping the society under his thumb. To a surprising extent, he succeeded. But, as Marx instructed, rigid political systems will rarely resist the liberalizing effect of the market. So, even in Singapore, there was change. Now a fully Globish society, playing a crucial role in global capitalism, Singapore has become socially more open and more free than many rival Asian countries.

At the same time, because of the unique conditions of Singapore and its people – a kind of natural language laboratory – the emergence of a recognizable Singaporean English in accent, vocabulary and idiom has yielded a vivid, local cultural dividend. Local writers began to represent Singlish in their work. For richness of expression, they could never surpass the local variant. Lee Kuan Yew was not happy. In 1978 he went on television to debate the Singlish question. 'The English we are beginning to hear our people speak', he said, 'is a very strange Singapore pidgin, a Singapore dialect in English which is not ideal.' The prime minister, however, was a pragmatist. This new 'pidgin' was 'not ideal' but it was, he said, 'the best for the time being'. He concluded by suggesting that 'we can improve upon [it] if we can concentrate our effort and considerable resources'. Shortly after this intervention Lee's government changed tack. In 1979 Singapore launched a 'Speak Mandarin' campaign, an attempt to limit the use of various other Chinese idioms (for example, Hokkien, Teochew, Cantonese and Hakka). The 'Speak Mandarin' initiative did not last long. By 1987, under pressure from rampant globalization, the government decreed that all Singapore's children − Chinese, Malay and Indian alike − should be schooled in English.

Twenty years on, this programme has morphed into twenty-first-century Singlish, a powerful and distinctive local variety of English that resists all government efforts to systematize its self-expression. So rooted has Singlish become in local experience that there is now a *Coxford* [sic] *Singlish Dictionary*, not a regular lexicon that Oxford would recognize, but a maverick compendium of local idiom ('Save our Singlish! Buy it before the Gahmen bans it!'), the fuzzy end of the linguistic lollipop. Singlish works in the home and on the street. More formally, for their transactions in the wider world, educated Singaporeans will default to Globish. This reality was actually put into words by Lee Kuan Yew's son, Prime Minister Lee Hsien Loong, in a speech given in 2005 to launch a 'Speak Good English' campaign. 'I believe we should all make the effort,' he said, 'and consciously speak good English − at home, at work, or in social gatherings.' Defining his terms, he went on, 'Speaking good English does not mean using bombastic words or adopting an artificial English or American accent. We can speak in the normal Singapore tone, which is neutral and intelligible. But speak in full sentences, and cutting out the "lahs" and "lors" at the end of each sentence.'

Neutral and intelligible: this is an exact description of Globish. As we have seen, it is the residue of empire, but reinvigorated by its traffic with the global community. In the twenty-first century Globish will continue to develop the supranational momentum it exhibits today. Recession may slow the expansion of the global economy, but it will have little or no impact on the world's linguistic transactions, which, facilitated by technology, will continue to expand exponentially. In many instances, economic crisis will merely intensify the impetus towards a workable lingua franca. In this new world, some people may even begin to ask themselves, Is this the fulfilment of an age-old dream, the end of Babel?

Epilogue: 'A Thoroughfare for All Thoughts'

The World's English

I never mastered Dari, the Persian dialect spoken by the Khan family, but several family members spoke English.

Asne Seierstad, The Bookseller of Kabul

1

Consider the powers of the earth and their languages, the working words of their daily transactions, and you open a door into a world of myth. In Genesis 11, we are told that 'the whole earth was of one language and one speech'. In the aftermath of Noah's flood, it came to pass that the survivors, settling in the 'land of Shinar', decided to celebrate their lucky escape in a time-honoured way – with triumphal architecture. 'Let us build us a city and a tower, whose top may reach even to heaven,' is how the Bible expresses this archetypal aspiration. The urge to unite and find human consequence is probably as primal as the urge to fight. 'Let us make us a name,' say the children of Noah, 'lest we be scattered abroad upon the face of the whole earth.'

Fat chance. According to the Bible, this impulse to find common purpose does not appeal to the Almighty, who believes in Divide and Rule. The idea that men should be like gods, with a tower that reaches 'even unto heaven', is insupportable. If mankind has one language, 'now nothing will be restrained from them, which they have imagined to do'. So the Lord intervenes in the project, like the most disruptive shop steward, to 'confound their language that they may not understand one another's speech'. Even more vengeful, in best Old Testament style, He 'scattered them abroad from thence upon the face of the earth: and they left off to build the city. Therefore is the name of it called Babel, because the Lord did there confound the language of all the earth.' This ancient tale is a timely reminder that the world remains a patchwork of some 5,000 separate and competing languages. As Steven Pinker reminds us in *The Language Instinct*, we are wise to concede Noam Chomsky's perception that, aside from mutually unintelligible vocabularies, 'Earthlings speak a single language'. Nonetheless, the conspicuous differences between English and some of its obvious rivals, like Russian or Japanese, only serve to emphasize the differences not the similarities. In this situation, the role of Globish in the twenty-first century can never be more than to provide a default position, a language for those who wish to communicate globally, regardless of good times or bad. And yet, what a priceless tool it turns out to be.

Estimates that about half the world's population have knowledge of, or acquaintance with, some kind of English point to an aspiration driven by the deepest, most ancient impulse for a global community. Radicals and dissenters who demonstrate to save the planet or against US military 'adventurism' will never take to the streets to promote a Globish agenda. They do not have to. Every time protestors parade English-language placards in front of television cameras they are advancing the cause of Globish. These changes at street level are mirrored in state policy: both Chile and Mongolia have recently declared their intention to become bilingual in English, as Singapore has already done, during the next two decades. In 2006 English was added to the Mexican primary school curriculum as a compulsory second language, a decision that automatically enrolled 200,000 Mexican schoolteachers in English-language training programmes. According to the British Council, this trend means that by 2020 'nearly a third of the world's population will all be trying to learn English at the same time'. The distinguished educationalist Sir Eric Anderson, formerly provost of Eton College, tells a story that illustrates the literally life-and-death significance of this fact. On the morning of the 7/7 bombings in London an overseas student from the Said Foundation tried to take the underground from Southfields in south-west London to his daily class in the City of London. When he found the station inexplicably closed, he boarded a bus. During his journey his mobile phone rang. It was a Greek friend from abroad who was watching the news of the bombings on CNN. His friend described the 'breaking news', and warned that London's buses had become terror targets. As a result of this conversation, the student disembarked from the bus. A minute later it was destroyed by a suicide bomber, with the loss of many lives. The student was badly shaken, but he survived.

Terror has its own grim logic. Generally, language brings culture, the sum of ordinary lives, expressing a taste for difference, and originality. Keats, in a famous letter, wrote of Shakespeare's 'negative capability'. He defined this as man's ability to be 'in uncertainties, Mysteries, doubts, without any irritable reaching after fact & reason'. This annihilation of self, says Keats, enables the poet to make his mind a 'thoroughfare for all thoughts'.

England, like its greatest writers, seems to have the same negative capability, the power to make its language and culture a 'thoroughfare' for all kinds of expression. But it has not been just passive. First a small family business, then a multinational, and finally a global brand, rarely has a language and its hegemony been more pervasive than Anglo-American culture. If one-third of mankind speaks some kind of English, millions more pay lip-service to an inheritance of Anglo-American cultural and political values. Or oppose it tooth and nail with bombs and propaganda. Those who want to characterize Globish as a kind of benign virus that has worked its way into every corner of daily life must also acknowledge its imperial and colonial past.

The enemies of English culture will criticize its guile and greed, but the outcome is beyond question. In the first decade of the twenty-first century English-speaking people and their culture are more widespread in numbers and influence than any civilization the world has ever seen. Globish, a world dialect, will be less a language and more a means to an end. It will continue to enfranchise millions who lack the benefits of a formal education into a global economy and provide a means of communication that will, for the most part, leave local languages unscathed. Globish might seem to have imperial roots, but it is not imperious. It derives its character from a language that has always been hospitable to change, from the roots up.

Walt Whitman, writing about the inspirational sources of the American way, identified a society that operated 'broad and low, close to the ground'. Those instincts have been magnified a million times in the era of the World Wide Web, the age of cyber-democracy. To a remarkable degree, the English-speaking world has now become a universal expression of global consciousness, an extraordinary weave of law, literature, advertising, film, gossip, sport, politics and tourism. Already, there are many indications of what a Globish world might look like.

2

Asne Seierstad is a Norwegian journalist, fluent in languages, and with a taste for foreign adventure. In the autumn of 2001 she spent six weeks with the commandos of Afghanistan's Northern Alliance in their offensive against the Taliban, living in the desert by the Tajikistan border, in the mountains of the Hindu Kush, and in the steppes north of Kabul. She slept on stone floors and in mud huts; she travelled in military vehicles, on horseback and on foot. When the Taliban were routed Seierstad headed for Kabul. Browsing one day in a city bookshop, she fell into conversation with the elegant grey-haired bookseller, Sultan Khan, and rapidly became friends with him and his family. Then she decided, as she put it to herself, that 'This is Afghanistan. How interesting it would be to write a book about this family.' The next day, as she tells the story, 'I called on Sultan in his bookshop and told him my idea.' 'Thank you', was his response. Seierstad explained that she would want to come and live with him and his family, go around with him, and live as he did, sharing the life of his wives, sisters and sons. 'You are welcome,' he repeated. A man of few words, Sultan Khan.

For a Norwegian journalist, alone in the capital of Afghanistan, writing about a Persian-speaking bookseller and his family must have seemed an unlikely subject for a book. When it was published, however, *The Bookseller of Kabul* was an instant success. Seierstad is frank about the limitations of her research. 'I never mastered Dari, the Persian dialect spoken by the Khan family, but several family members spoke English. Unusual? Yes.'

As she explains the Khan family's background, a contemporary snapshot of Globish begins to emerge: 'Sultan had picked up a colourful and verbose form of English while teaching a diplomat his own Dari dialect. His younger sister Leila spoke excellent English, having attended Pakistani schools when she was a refugee.' Other members of the Khan family enjoyed various levels of English-language competence, including Sultan's oldest son, who included Seierstad in all his business and shopping trips, wedding preparations, and visits to school, police station, government ministry and prison.

It is a fair bet that, apart from Norwegian diplomats, few, if any, in Kabul speak Norwegian. Seierstad communicated with the wider world in Globish, 'the worldwide dialect of the third millennium'. Today, in every country struggling to participate in capitalist democracy, it is Globish that provides the main avenue of advancement. As Chris Patten puts it in his monograph *What Next?*, 'There are more people living in what in less free days we called "the free world" than ever before. Many more are desperate to join us. For every failed state there are numerous liberalising others quietly getting on with the business of building free and secure institutions in prosperous, plural societies.' For these aspiring millions, it will be Globish that offers a way forward.

As we enter the second decade of the new century, we are witnessing, in Globish, a contemporary phenomenon of extraordinary range and complexity, expressing a new world of global interconnections. When I was completing the first draft of this book in October 2008 I would break off from the day's work to watch the television news. These were momentous hours, as the 'credit crunch' swiftly became the 'global financial crisis'. Hour after hour, there were reports of falling markets in Japan, Hong Kong, Singapore, Frankfurt, Paris, Milan, London and New York. Across a dozen different time zones, financial journalists in each of these cities filed reports for their national desks, but the language of the crisis was unvaryingly Globish. European finance ministers held urgent press conferences, addressing the world's media in Globish. The doomed prime minister of Iceland, Geir Haarde, watching his country slide into bankruptcy, stoically maintained an even flow of Globish sentiment to calm the nerves of his people while appealing to an international television audience.

The crisis of Meltdown Monday (and its successive aftershocks) emphasized that Globish is a cultural and media phenomenon, one whose infrastructure is economic. Boom or bust, it is a story of 'Follow the money'. Globish remains based on trade, advertising and the global market. Traders in Singapore inevitably communicate in local languages at home; internationally they default to Globish. Now the global equation ran as follows: Microsoft plus Dow Jones = Globish. So viral is its ceaseless expression round the world that to separate cause and effect is virtually impossible. With its supranational momentum, above and beyond American and British influence, Globish sustains itself as both chicken and egg. To a world community in economic turmoil, at least it offers a means of sharing remedies and counter-measures.

In the midst of this financial maelstrom, the 2008 Man Booker Prize was awarded in London's Guildhall to Aravind Adiga, the Indian author of *The White Tiger*. Some of the press commentary about this prize focused on the fact that this was the fourth 'Indian novel' to win this important prize, joining a list that includes *Midnight's Children* by Salman Rushdie and *The God of Small Things* by Arundhati Roy. But that is rather to miss the point: the Man Booker is now a global phenomenon, with a powerful website and an international audience. The prize that was dreamed up in 1968, after a game of golf, to reward novelists from 'Britain and the Commonwealth', has become progressively more Globish.

Take, for instance, the roll-call of Booker winners. In its first decade the prize went to a British writer seven times, in 1969, 1970, 1972, 1973, 1976, 1977 and 1978, and excited virtually no international comment. From 1991, however, the catalogue of winners has been significantly more diverse: Nigerian (1991), Canadian/Sri Lankan (1992), Irish (1993, 2005 and 2007), Scottish (1994), English (1995, 1996, 1998, 2004 and 2009), Indian (1997, 2006 and 2008), South African (1999), Canadian (2000 and 2002), and Australian (2001 and 2003). Sheerin Aswat, who runs the Man Booker website in London, is a Globish citizen: a British Indian educated at London University whose family runs an Anglo-Indian business and commutes between Bangalore and London's East End.

In 2002 the sponsorship of the Booker prize passed to the Man Group plc, which describes itself as 'a leading global provider of alternative investment products' employing some 1,600 people in thirteen countries, with offices in Chicago, Dubai, Hong Kong, Montevideo, Nassau, New York, Singapore, Sydney, Tokyo and Toronto. Global sponsorship means global audiences. If the readers of the Man Booker winners were confined to Britain and the Commonwealth, then the prize, which excludes American writers, would qualify as a colonial trophy from Churchill's 'English-speaking world'. What is impressive is the remarkable global reach of the Man Booker. In the run-up to the recent award of this English-language prize, its website recorded visits from all over mainland China, from Kowloon, Beijing and Guangzhou to Shanghai and Nanjing. Sheerin Aswat, and the administrators for both the Man Booker and the Orange Prize for fiction, note a new phenomenon. Year on year, they say, the publicity generated by these awards inspires a new generation of writers as far apart as Saudi Arabia and the Balkans to undertake the hitherto unimaginable step of writing their first novels, not in their mother tongue, but in English.

Surrounding every one of these English-language fictions, in publicity, marketing, sales and media activity, there will be a local fever of Globish communication. The more that Globish gathers momentum, the greater will be the pressure for a more universal adoption, but already there are signs. In 2007, Leonard Orban, the European Commissioner responsible for multilingualism, launched a Year of Intercultural Dialogue. Orban called together a group of well-known European commentators, writers, philosophers and sociologists to reflect on how language could promote 'intercultural dialogue and mutual understanding within the EU'. The result was to provoke a furious backlash in favour of Globish. Basil Venitis, an Athenian Greek, declared that 'multilingualism is a euphemism for anglophobia. For the European Union to work as one *it only needs English*. Multilingualism brings eurobabble, Babelism, nonsense and the loss of millions of euros.' As the European project develops, the battle between the Anglophobes and the Anglophiles will only intensify, with Globish as the lightning rod for every socio-cultural thunderstorm.

3

To be realistic: Globish has become an extraordinary phenomenon, but it has not replaced Babel. Language evolves like the species, slowly. The extraordinary process described here may be at least a thousand years old, but it is still in its infancy, linguistically speaking. The world, flatter and smaller than ever before, is still distinctive as much for its approximately 5,000 different languages as for its emerging Globish. The big picture is infinitely more complex, with native speakers clinging fiercely to their ancient languages. Jacques Chirac, former president of France, once said that nothing would be more damaging for humanity than for several thousand languages to be reduced to one. He was referring to English, of course, but perhaps he had forgotten the Celts. Towards the end of 2005 a fine old row broke out in England's West Country among the speakers of Cornish about the correct form of their language, a Gaelic language-fossil dating back to the Dark Ages. As many newspapers observed, this was a debate conducted between some 200 participants – in English. The *Sunday Times* commented that 'to be born an English-speaker is to win one of the top prizes in life's lottery. And this can be said without a hint of triumphalism, sexism, or racism, without annoying anybody much except the French.'

Is this anglophone future really secure? And, if so, what might Globish achieve? When it comes to the future of any language, the cultural commentator is advised to proceed with caution. The highway of English is littered with the debris of burned-out predictions. I recall, with affection, the former chief editor of the *Oxford English Dictionary*, Robert Burchfield, a distinguished lexicographer who was always a sparkling refutation of Dr Johnson's celebrated definition. Burchfield was never 'a harmless drudge'. In fact, he made the language news. More accurately, he recognized that what was happening to the mother tongue in the late twentieth century was unprecedented, and he used his position at Oxford to publicize the fact. Before Burchfield the state of the language was an unreported story; after him, it was always a source of debate, and often a headline.

Burchfield's first foray into linguistic controversy occurred in the late 1970s, a world almost as unimaginably remote as the Regency. His thrilling and controversial thesis was simple enough, and linked to Britain's post-imperial twilight. According to Burchfield, English was like Latin. Just as Latin broke up into mutually unintelligible languages like French, Spanish and Italian, so would global English similarly disintegrate into separate, mutually distinctive tongues. Burchfield made his point by noting the impossibility of a conversation between a Jamaican, a Glaswegian and a Nigerian. To the delight of leader-writers from Sydney to Saskatchewan, he pointed out that, historically speaking, languages have always had a tendency to break up, or to evolve. There were, he argued, some 'powerful models of the severance of a language into two or more constituent parts, especially the emergence of the great Germanic languages of Western Europe – English, German, Dutch, Norwegian, Swedish and so on – from the mutually intelligible dialects of the fifth century AD'.

The obvious objection to this model, which his critics were swift to deploy, was the contemporary vigour and interconnectedness of global English. In the age of mass media, the future of world English, said Burchfield's opponents, would never follow the Latin model. To which he replied that such objections overlooked one vital fact: 'English, as the *second* language of many speakers in countries throughout the world, is no more likely to survive the inevitable political changes of the future than did Latin, once the second language of the governing classes or regions within the Roman Empire.' At the moment when Burchfield made this pronouncement the global reach of English was inextricably bound up with American power, on the Roman model. These were the Reagan years. In this new imperium, the local varieties, for example Asian, Indian and Caribbean English, did seem to illustrate the argument for centrifugal change. These were sometimes described as 'the new Englishes', second languages in countries like India, Sierra Leone, Singapore and Nigeria.

Once the Cold War ended, the nature of American power became transformed. Today, with the emergence of Globish, the evolution of the 'new Englishes' into separate languages seems increasingly unlikely. The broad river of Globish becomes the beneficiary of these sparkling tributaries. Moreover, the colossal financial underpinning of Globish (many trillions of dollars) must ensure its viability, at least for now. At this point it is fashionable to refer to China, a giant economic and cultural force that may, in the words of Napoleon, 'shake the world'. But the Chinese language, like Chinese civilization, is self-contained and difficult to penetrate, ill-suited to an international role, especially in the industrialized West. Globish, not Mandarin, is better equipped to enjoy international influence. Does China want to extend its influence across Asia in countries like Korea, Singapore and the Philippines? It would achieve this most effectively through Globish. Might China want to offer an alternative to American cultural imperialism? Globish is the obvious means of communicating an international message. When, in April 2006, the Nigerian president Olusegun Obasanjo told President Hu Jintao, 'when you are leading the world, we want to be close behind you', he spoke in English. More broadly, does China favour the exploitation of 'soft power' – movies, books and advertising? Globish is available for instant mobilization. For China, Globish has the virtue of an immediate worldwide audience. This raises some interesting issues. Much gloomy American thinking about the future of its language and culture revolves around the assumption that it will inevitably become challenged by Mandarin Chinese or Spanish or even Arabic. What if the real threat – actually, no more than a challenge – is closer to home, and lies with this Globish supranational lingua franca, one that all Americans can identify with?

Culture is about identity. For as long as the peoples of the world wish to express themselves in terms of ideas like 'freedom', 'individuality' and 'originality', and for as long as there are generations of the world's schoolchildren versed in Shakespeare, The Simpsons, the Declaration of Independence and the Bible, Globish will remain the means by which an educated minority of the planet communicates. This will be so because of its robust constitution. Consider, in contrast, the globalizing skills of France. In public utililties like water and electricity, in aerospace, luxury goods and wine, the French have been immensely successful around the world. As a mass-market superstore, Carrefour runs Wal-Mart a very close second. Sometimes it can seem as if croissants have become almost as universal as burgers. For all that, the French see the chaos and imprecision of the non-French world as a threat, not an opportunity. The French state and its culture feel challenged by the irreverence and ebullience of the Anglo-American tradition and its values, and make periodic attempts to keep 'airport English' at bay. This is a far cry from the days of the Enlightenment, a formidably French movement which once gave western society's quest for happiness, welfare, prosperity and good government a powerful sense of purpose, inspiring America's Founding Fathers. France still identifies with progress, but it has grown out of sympathy with the medium in which that progress is expressed. This is not to say that Globish is intrinsically American, though there is no doubt that, in this latest phase, it is heavily influenced by linguistic and cultural developments in the United States, and the so-called 'Anglosphere'.

In 2009 both Britain and the United States remained net importers of intelligence, from the Far East, the Indian subcontinent and from the accession states of the enlarged EU. Even in a severe recession, that single fact will guarantee the flourishing of Globish. The IT revolution (an expansion of communications combined with a centrifugal dispersal of information) ensures that the global community now operates quite differently from the way it did in the past. Before the twenty-first century most of the world enjoyed an adequate, but limited, supply of data. Individual nations disseminated a commonality of information through centralized distribution networks, like state media and a unified print culture. No longer. In a Globish world, everyone has access to an unlimited supply of data which floats, detached from all cultural anchors, in the infinite reservoir of cyberspace. These are early days, but Globish is beginning to sponsor a new approach to intellectual property. A new belief system is emerging to validate the rights of this public domain, the so-called Free Culture Movement. The rhetoric of this largely American school derives from the English libertarian tradition and the masters of puritan radicalism. The Free Culture Movement is an almost wholly Globish phenomenon. As in the past, language and social change will go hand in hand. Globish will be used to argue for a 'free commons' of the mind. All this will happen in the cloisters of the law, and in the academy. Simultaneously, in the wider world, there will be Globish events like the famous final of the Iraqi cup tie in 2007.

Iraq's national football players are known as the 'Lions of Mesopotamia'. Immensely popular, the team is drawn from all sections of Iraqi society, including Kurds, Sunnis, Shias and Turkomans. The 'Lions' are brave men: to represent their country, these footballers have to overcome kidnap threats, the murder of family members and the constant disruption of training schedules. In a bizarre tribute to the redemptive power of football, the 'Lions of Mesopotamia' are also symbolic of national unity, an elusive concept in contemporary Iraq. In the summer of 2007 this team found itself competing for the Asia Cup, eventually playing against the favourites, Saudi Arabia, on neutral ground. The suspicion and hatred between these two countries persuaded many Iraqis to accuse Saudi Arabia of fomenting violence, arming suicide bombers and generally working to destabilize Iraq's fragile post-Saddam society.

But, as the final unfolded in Jakarta, an eerie calm descended on the centres of Iraq's main cities. Fans of all ages congregated around their television sets to watch the game. When the Iraq team went one goal up against the Saudis and held the lead to snatch a surprise victory, hundreds of thousands poured onto the streets of Iraq in scenes of rare jubilation. Waving flags, dancing to protest songs and firing into the air, the crowds regained the streets of Bagdad for a celebration of the unthinkable, an unlikely explosion of hope. On this occasion, Taha Mahmoud, a twenty-five-year-old computer programmer, was reported to have expressed a perfect Globish comment: 'In 90 minutes, eleven men on a soccer pitch thousands of miles away have made millions of Iraqis happy, while 250 MPs, our government, the mullahs, imams, and warlords can't provide us with a single smile. I hope', he concluded, 'that this is a turning-point for our country.'

Notes

Prologue: 'Crazy English'

page 2 *Mandarin . . . outnumbers*: Martin Jacques, *When China Rules the World* (London, 2009), pp. 115–18. I am indebted to Dr Jacques for his help with my research in China.

page 3 *the cultural revolution of my generation*: from the vast literature of 'globalization', I recommend *A Brief History of Globalization* by Alex MacGillivray (London, 2006), *Globalisation and its Discontents* by Joseph Stiglitz (London, 2004) and *Why Globalization Works* by Martin Wolf (New Haven, 2004).

page 3 *expressed by America's Founding Fathers*: these words are found in the preamble to the Declaration of Independence, and they reflect values expressed by Labour Prime Minister Gordon Brown. 'When, at my meeting with President Bush,' said Brown, 'I talk of a joint inheritance – not just of shared history but shared values founded on a shared destiny – I mean the idea that everyone is created equal, that there should be freedom of expression for all faiths, that arts and culture should celebrate diversity, that government should be open and accountable, that there should be opportunity for all – for all men and women – and a belief in free trade.' *The Times*, 30 July 2007.

page 4 *the angry banlieues of Paris*: Andrew Hussey, 'The Paris Intifada', *Granta*, 101 (2008), p. 47.

page 4 *the lyrics of hip-hop songs*: cf. Mark Abley, *The Prodigal Tongue: Dispatches from the Future of English* (London, 2008), pp. 74–6.

page 4 *'as the business language of Asia'*: Nury Vittachi, 'Travellers' Tales', *Far Eastern Economic Review*, April 2003. See also Nury Vittachi, *Mr Wong Goes West* (Crows Nest, NSW, 2008).

page 5 *'a kind of global-hegemonic post-clerical Latin'*: Benedict Anderson, *Imagined Communities* (London, 1983), p. 207.

page 5 *Microsoft at their Bangalore headquarters*: Evan Osnos, 'Letter from China', *New Yorker*, 28 April 2008.

page 6 *'gives all its members a chance to speak'*: Abley, *The Prodigal Tongue*, p. 2.

page 7 *debates surrounding Magna Carta*: I thank Philippe Sands for this important insight into the law lords' deliberations.

page 7 *Bollywood English*: Dominic Rushe, *Sunday Times Magazine*, 15 June 2008.

page 8 *'I was recently waiting'*: Ben MacIntyre, *The Last Word: Tales from the Tip of the Mother Tongue* (London, 2009), p. 239.

page 10 *'the worldwide dialect of the third millennium'*: Robert McCrum, 'The Globish Revolution', *Observer*, Review, 3 December 2006.

page 10 *the linguistic default position*: see Thomas L. Friedman, *The World is Flat: The Globalised World in the Twenty-First Century* (London, 2005).

page 10 *Alan Rusbridger recently codified*: the full list is as follows:

1. There is no such thing as Abroad.
2. Most of our readers are 'foreign'.
3. They expect us to inform them about their own countries.
4. Their decisions will affect us.
5. No economy is an island.
6. 'They' will want to come here.
7. It matters in London what they teach in Lahore.
8. The environment is global.
9. Technology is global.
10. Their own media won't do this: but we will!

I am grateful to Alan Rusbridger, editor-in-chief of the *Guardian*, for permission to quote this internal company document.

page 11 *the breakaway republic of South Ossetia*: see 'Russia Prevailed on the Ground, but Not in the Media', *New York Times*, 22 August 2008.

page 11 *'the unipolar, American-dominated world'*: Roger Cohen, 'The Intelligencer', *New York Times*, 7 September 2008.

page 13 *'American English has a global role'*: Tom MacArthur (ed.), *Oxford Guide to World English* (Oxford, 2002), p. 165.

page 13 *'English admiration for business acumen'*: Nicholas Ostler, *Empires of the Word* (London, 2005), p. 557.

page 13 *'English . . . a place of strange meetings'*: Henry Hitchings, *The Secret Life of Words* (London, 2008), p. 5.

page 16 *'a museum inside our heads'*: Penelope Lively, *Moon Tiger* (London, 1987).

Chapter 1. In the Beginning

page 19 *epigraph*: quoted in Humphrey Carpenter, *J. R. R. Tolkien: A Biography* (London, 1977), p. 64.

page 19 *the Roman historian Tacitus*: Tacitus, *The Agricola and the Germania*, trans. H. Mattingly (London, 1970).

page 19 *astonishingly well preserved*: P. V. Glob, *The Bog People* (London, 1969), pp. 18–19.

page 20 *a hard day's ride from the sea*: John Kerrigan, *Archipelagic English* (Oxford, 2008).

pages 21–2 *watching from the white cliffs*: David Miles, *The Tribes of Britain* (London, 2005), p. 87, cf. Robin McKie, *The Face of Britain* (London, 2006), p. 28.

page 22 *Caesar's legions finally struggled ashore*: Caesar, *Gallic War*, trans. H. J. Edwards (Loeb Classical Library, Cambridge, Mass., 1917).

page 22 *knights of the Round Table*: see N. J. Higham, *King Arthur: Myth-Making and History* (London, 2002).

page 23 *'concept of unspecified yearning'*: Jan Morris, *Hav* (London, 2005).

page 24 *Their love of innuendo*: Seth Lerer, *Inventing English: A Portable History of the Language* (New York, 2007), p. 21.

page 25 *pleasure they took in punning ambiguity*: Michael Alexander (trans.), *The Earliest English Poems* (London, 1966), and Kevin Crossley-Holland (trans.), *The Exeter Book of Riddles* (London, 1978).

page 25 *the global communion of the Anglican Church*: compared to the 25 million adherents in the Church of England, the African, Commonwealth and US figures are, approximately, as follows: 15 million (Nigeria); 4 million (Australia); 2.5 million (Kenya); 2.5 million (USA); 2.4 million (Southern Africa); 2 million (Sudan); 1.27 million (Rwanda).

page 25 *'Alleluia, the praise of God the Creator must be sung in those parts'*: Bede, *History of the English Church and People*, trans. with an introduction by Leo Sherley-Price (London, 1968).

page 26 *Augustine's mission went ahead unimpeded*: ibid.

page 27 *First there was Miriwu*: Barack Obama, *Dreams from My Father* (New York, 2004), p. 394.

page 27 *a farmer's son in Co. Derry*: author interview with Seamus Heaney, September 2006.

page 27 *from Milton to the present*: cf. Peter Ackroyd, *Albion: The Origins of the English Imagination* (London, 2002), p. 94.

page 28 *'Mixture is a secret of the English island'*: R. W. Emerson, ed. D. Emory Wilson, *English Traits* (Cambridge, Mass., 1994), p. 132.

page 29 *'a moment in history that probably never happened'*: David Horspool, *Why Alfred Burned the Cakes* (London, 2006), p. 1.

page 29 *'thinking deeply of his poor unhappy subjects'*: ibid., p. 2.

page 29 *A fugitive king, lost among his own people*: see 1 Samuel 16 and 2 Samuel 15.

page 30 *a sense of national identity*: see Alfred's Preface to St Gregory's *Pastoral Care*, in Michael Swanton (ed.), *Anglo-Saxon Prose* (London and Toronto, 1975).

page 31 *'South of the Thames . . . able to read English writing'*: ibid.

page 31 *'if I live long enough'*: quoted in David Reynolds, *In Command of History: Churchill Fighting and Writing the Second World War* (London, 2005), p. 38.

page 31 *radical Chartists liked to equate*: Edward Vallance, *A Radical History of England* (London, 2009), p. 10.

page 32 *Demobilized and unemployed*: Peter Gilliver, Jeremy Marshall and Edmund Weiner, *Tolkien and the Oxford English Dictionary* (Oxford, 2006), pp. 3–41.

page 32 *'remote and strange and beautiful'*: quoted ibid., p. 5.

page 33 *the* witan *that chose a new king*: Frank Barlow, *Edward the Confessor* (New Haven, 1997).

page 34 *Harold might even have won*: there are many excellent accounts of the Norman Conquest. I have relied on H. R. Loyn, *The Norman Conquest* (London, 1982); P. F. McLynn, *1066: The Year of the Three Battles* (London, 1999); and David Douglas, *William the Conqueror* (New Haven, 1999).

Chapter 2: Defeat into Victory

page 36 *admired by the Nazis*: this paragraph relies on the account published in Carola Hicks, *The Bayeux Tapestry: The Life Story of a Masterpiece* (London, 2006).

page 36 *an example of Aryan art*: ibid., p. 211.

page 37 *'most English boast of their Norman heritage'*: ibid., p. 227.

page 37 *a wholesale foreign occupation*: see M. F. Wakelin, *English Dialects* (London, 1963).

page 37 *'With only a little strength'*: J. H. W. Atkins (ed.), *The Owl and the Nightingale* (Cambridge, 1922).

page 38 *'Foreigners grew wealthy with the spoils of England'*: Orderic Vitalis, quoted in Albert C. Baugh and Thomas Cable, *A History of the English Language* (London, 1959), pp. 112–19.

page 39 *living among a hostile English population*: Michael Clanchy, *From Memory to Written Record* (London, 1979).

page 40 *little or no Latin, and no French*: R. W. Chambers, 'On the Continuity of English Prose', Introduction to *The Life of Sir Thomas More* (London, 1932).

page 40 *Old French sources*: see Seth Lerer, *Inventing English: A Portable History of the Language* (New York, 2007), p. 54.

page 41 *The Winter's Tale*: Act 4, scene 4, lines 835–42.

page 42 *'Look out! Lithulf has drawn his sword!'*: Peter Ackroyd, *Albion: The Origins of the English Imagination* (London, 2002), p. 104.

page 42 *'deceitful and transitory'*: in *The Anglo-Saxon Chronicle*, trans. G. N. Garmonsway (London, 1953).

page 43 *prophesied by the Welsh wizard*: Geoffrey of Monmouth, *The History of the Kings of Britain*, trans. Lewis Thorpe (London, 1976).

page 43 *'the national linguistic enterprise'*: Ackroyd, *Albion*, p. 118.

page 44 *Malory's book was an immediate hit*: see Christina Hardyment, *Malory: The Life and Times of King Arthur's Chronicler* (London, 2005).

page 44 *a showdown with his barons at home*: Ralph V. Turner, *King John* (London, 1994).

page 45 *The principle of habeas corpus*: Danny Danziger and John Gillingham, *1215: The Year of Magna Carta* (London, 2004), p. 278.

page 45 *the history of English freedoms*: ibid., pp. 255–76. I am indebted to Philippe Sands for this insight.

page 45 *The surviving French in government*: see George Clark, *English History: A Survey* (Oxford, 1971), p. 118.

page 48 *'the worst enemies of England'*: for Bishop Grosseteste, see Baugh and Cable, *History*, pp. 131–2.

page 46 *'the closest that England'*: Simon Schama, *A History of Britain: At the Edge of the World? 3000 BC–AD 1603* (London, 2000), p. 180.

page 47 *'the affairs that concern him'*: quoted ibid., p. 221.

page 47 *'the only sovereign between Canute and George III'*: Clark, *English History*, p. 168.

page 47 *a contemporary poet*: in *The Romance of Richard the Lion-hearted*, Baugh and Cable, *History*, p. 124.

page 48 *'is translated into English'*: from *Cursor Mundi*, Baugh and Cable, *History*, p. 137.

page 48 *deeply coded instincts of self-expression*: Ian Buruma, *Voltaire's Coconuts, or Anglomania in Europe* (London, 1999), pp. 15–19.

page 48 *the Order of the Garter*: the brotherhood of the Garter boasted just twenty-six members, who sported the luxurious blue-and-gold badge of the Order.

page 48 *'The pestilence grew so strong'*: quoted in Schama, *History of Britain*, p. 230.

page 48 *One Irish Franciscan*: ibid., p. 231.

page 50 *'Welcome to our lord'*: quoted in Miri Rubin, *The Hollow Crown* (London, 2005), p. 126.

page 51 *'only the King and Commons'*: ibid., p. 125.

page 52 *Geoffrey Chaucer's decision*: the fullest account of Chaucer's life and career is by Derek Brewer, *Geoffrey Chaucer* (London, 1953).

page 52 *'Simple or learned, old or young'*: William of Nassyngton, in Baugh and Cable, *History*, p. 144.

page 53 *'He must have been a man'*: Dryden, 'Preface' to *Fables Ancient and Modern* (1700).

page 53 *'relies upon borrowings and adaptations'*: Ackroyd, *Albion*, p. 160.

page 53 *'translate any text of holy scripture into the English tongue'*: see Rubin, *The Hollow Crown*, pp. 194–5.

Chapter 3: 'Lighte Englisshe'

page 54 *epigraph*: George Orwell, *Nineteen Eighty-Four* (London, 2003), chapter III, p. 36.

page 55 *the words of William Caxton*: my account of Caxton relies on George D. Painter, *William Caxton* (London, 1976).

page 55 *ten years before Caxton was born*: according to Painter, *Caxton*, p. 9, 'we can be sure of no more than that Caxton was born between the extremes of 1415 and 1424'.

page 55 *hard to please every man*: see W. F. Bolton (ed.), *The English Language*, 2 vols. (Cambridge, 1966 and 1969), vol. 1, pp. 1–4.

page 56 *'first foundeur and embellissher'*: Painter, *Caxton*, p. 134.

page 57 *'What subject can give sentence on his king?'*: *Richard II*, Act 4, scene 1, line 112.

page 57 *he surrounded himself with 'new men'*: see Miri Rubin, *The Hollow Crown* (London, 2005), p. 175.

page 57 *declare war on France*: Robert and Isabelle Tombs, *That Sweet Enemy: The French and the British from the Sun King to the Present* (London, 2006), *passim*.

page 57 *'Then shall our names'*: *Henry V*, Act 4, scene 3, lines 51–3.

page 58 *An anonymous chronicler noted*: see John Lewis-Stempel (ed.), *England, the Autobiography* (London, 2005), pp. 98–101.

page 59 *the London Company of Brewers noted*: Albert C. Baugh and Thomas Cable, *A History of the English Language* (London, 1959), pp. 153–4.

page 60 *'more than ever did king in England'*: quoted in Christina Hardyment, *Malory: The Life and Times of King Arthur's Chronicler* (London, 2005), p. 270.

page 60 *'let's kill all the lawyers'*: *2 Henry VI*, Act 4, scene 2, line 68.

page 60 *'the youth of the realm . . . no Christian ear can endure'*: ibid., Act 4, scene 7, lines 27–34.

page 61 *Otto Jespersen*: in *The Growth and Structure of the English Language* (Chicago, 1982).

page 61 *Townspeople and country gentry*: R. Virgne (ed.), *The Illustrated Letters of the Paston Family* (London, 1989). See also Colin Richmond, *The Paston Family* (Cambridge, 1996).

page 62 *took two scribes five years . . . to complete*: see John Man, *The Gutenberg Revolution* (London, 2002), p. 90.

page 62 *'all Europe's printed books could have been carried'*: ibid., p. 4.

page 62 *William Caxton, a former diplomat*: see Painter, *Caxton*.

page 63 *abandoned his task and laid it aside*: ibid., pp. 60–63.

page 63 *appeared not in London but in Bruges*: ibid., pp. 62–3.

page 64 *several other Caxtons were living thereabouts*: ibid., pp. 82–3.

page 64 *an attractive, original and thoroughly English character*: ibid., *passim*.

page 65 *the new clarity and directness of the written word*: this discussion of Chancery English is indebted to John Hurt Fisher, *The Emergence of Standard English* (Lexington, Ky., 1996).

page 65 *a strand of English prose*: George Orwell, 'Why I Write', *Shooting an Elephant and Other Essays* (London, 2003), p. 10.

Chapter 4: Eating Paper, Drinking Ink

page 66 *epigraph*: Thomas Heywood, *An Apology for Actors*, quoted in Stanley Wells, *Shakespeare & Co.* (London, 2006), p. 59.

page 66 *The Sarum liturgy*: Miri Rubin, *The Hollow Crown* (London, 2005), p. 302.

page 67 *'owners of suspicious books in the English tongue'*: ibid., p. 195.

page 67 *throw their books into the fire with him*: Susan Brigden, *New Worlds, Lost Worlds: The Rule of the Tudors, 1485–1603* (London, 2000), p. 87.

page 68 *'poor men and idiots have the truth'*: ibid., p. 89.

page 70 *'There was never anything by men so well devised'*: see Diarmaid MacCulloch, *Thomas Cranmer* (New Haven, 1996), pp. 225–6.

page 71 *'for all manner of persons'*: Brigden, *New Worlds*, p. 128.

page 72 *the Pilgrimage of Grace*: Simon Schama, *A History of Britain: At the Edge of the World? 3000 BC–AD 1603* (London, 2000), p. 316.

page 73 *'Without the great English translation'*: Stephen Greenblatt, *Will in the World* (London, 2004), p. 91.

page 73 *'the diction of common life from Shakespeare'*: see W. F. Bolton (ed.), *The English Language*, 2 vols. (Cambridge, 1966 and 1969), vol. 1, pp. 5–45.

page 73 *Between 1558 and 1579*: see Michael Hattaway, *The Cambridge Companion to English Renaissance Literature and Culture* (Cambridge, 1990).

page 73 *in a population of about 4 million*: John Guy, *Tudor England* (Oxford, 1988), p. 416.

page 74 *writing for an audience that was insatiably hungry for the printed word*: Shakespeare's audiences liked to read, as well as watch, his plays. An edition of *Henry the Fourth* sold out two editions in 1598; copies of *Richard the Second* and *Hamlet* always sold well.

page 74 *going to the theatre approximately once a month*: see James Schapiro, *1599: A Year in the Life of William Shakespeare* (London, 2005), p. 10.

page 74 *'many of the leading writers drinking and eating together'*: see Greenblatt, *Will in the World*, p. 200. See also Wells, *Shakespeare & Co.*

page 75 *'serche out of some rotten Pamphlet'*: quoted in Albert C. Baugh and Thomas Cable, *A History of the English Language* (London, 1959), p. 217.

page 75 *Shakespeare himself wittily alludes*: *Love's Labour's Lost*, Act 5, scene 2, lines 407–14.

page 75 *'Grace me no grace'*: *Richard II*, Act 2, scene 3, line 86.

page 75 *'His mind and hand went together'*: see *William Shakespeare: The Complete Works*, ed. Jonathan Bate and Eric Rasmussen (London, 2007), p. 61.

page 75 *Recent scholarship*: in addition to the Stephen Greenblatt and James Schapiro volumes already cited, see also A. Holden, *William Shakespeare* (London, 1999), Park Honan, *Shakespeare: A Life* (London, 1998) and the indispensable S. Schoenbaum, *Shakespeare's Lives* (Oxford, 1991).

page 75 *'Others abide our question'*: Matthew Arnold, 'Shakespeare'.

pages 75–6 *He never completely forgot his origins*: this paragraph relies on C. T. Onions, *A Shakespeare Glossary* (New York, 1919).

page 76 *'Is not parchment made of sheepskins?'*: *Hamlet*, Act 5, scene 1, lines 104–5.

page 76 *'A sentence is but a cheverel glove'*: *Twelfth Night*, Act 3, scene 1, lines 10–12.

page 76 *draws on his countryside experience*: *A Midsummer Night's Dream*, Act 3, scene 2, lines 20–23.

pages 76–7 *'the only Shake-scene'*: Robert Greene, *Greenes Groats-worth of Witte, Bought with a Million of Repentance* (1592).

page 77 *'to enclose in poetic speech'*: George Steiner, *Language and Silence* (London, 1968), pp. 205–6.

page 77 *Macbeth's lament after the murder of Duncan*: *Macbeth*, Act 2, scene 2, lines 59–62.

page 78 *a memorable riff on the clown Feste's bitter comment to Malvolio*: Philip Roth, *I Married a Communist* (London, 1998), p. 302.

page 79 *never so memorably as in Mark Twain's Adventures of Huckleberry Finn*: chapter 20.

page 80 *'one uniforme translation'*: see Ward Allen (ed.), *Translating for King James* (London, 1970). A richer account is Adam Nicolson, *Power and Glory*: *Jacobean England, and the Making of the King James Bible*, (London 2003).

page 80 *'another no less fit, as commodiously'*: Allen, *Translating for King James*, p. 12.

page 80 *In the beginning was the Word*: John 1: 1–5.

page 80 *To every thing there is a season*: Ecclesiastes 3: 1–3.

page 81 *'England's equivalent of the great baroque cathedral'*: Nicolson, *Power and Glory*, p. 70.

page 81 *'treasured as much by Americans as by the British'*: ibid., p. 230.

Chapter 5: 'A Whole Country of English'

page 85 *epigraph*: Philip Roth, *The Dying Animal* (London, 2001), pp. 81–2.

page 85 *I sat down at a good fire to dry*: a longer version of this letter is quoted in David McCullough, *John Adams* (New York, 2001), p. 74.

page 86 *One of John Donne's most celebrated poems*: 'To his Mistress, on Going to Bed', *Songs and Sonnets of John Donne* (Oxford, 1965).

page 87 *'You shall live freely there'*: Ben Jonson, John Marston, George Chapman, *Eastward Ho!*, Act 3, scene 3.

page 87 *Smith helped to sustain the romantic ideal of an American exile*: see 'American Chronicle', *New Yorker*, 2 April 2007, pp. 40–45.

page 88 *wittily characterized the Virginians*: see Philip Rahv, *Essays on Literature and Politics, 1932–72* (Boston, 1978). See also Philip Roth, *Reading Myself and Others* (London, 2007), p. 72.

page 88 *'Being thus passed the vast ocean'*: William Bradford, *History of Plymouth Plantation* (Boston, 1901). See also Jay Parini, *Promised Land* (New York, 2009), pp. 7–28.

page 89 *'Engis mon got two hed . . .'*: see J. L. Dillard, *American Talk* (New York, 1976).

page 89 *'I know not a language'*: Bonamy Dobrée, *William Penn: Quaker and Pioneer* (Boston, 1932).

page 89 *Thomas Jefferson would write later*: Christopher Hitchens, *Thomas Jefferson: Author of America* (London, 2007).

page 91 *the Putney Debates*: Jack Emery (ed.), *The Putney Debates* (Cambridge, 1983).

page 92 *the best wisdom on constitutional reform*: see John Dunn, *Locke* (Oxford, 1984).

page 94 *'Who is the author of Common Sense?'*: see McCullough, *John Adams*, p. 96.

page 94 *'The sun never shined on a cause of greater north . . .'*: ibid., pp. 96–7.

page 95 *Jefferson . . . intended his words*: ibid., p. 121. I gratefully acknowledge McCullough for the narrative of these momentous events.

page 95 *the Declaration was celebrated*: see Peter de Bolla, *The Fourth of July and the Founding of America* (London, 2007), pp. 10–46.

page 96 *Some of the defeated British officers wept*: Piers Brendon, *The Decline and Fall of the British Empire, 1781–1997* (London, 2007), pp. 1–2.

page 97 *'English is destined'*: Albert C. Baugh and Thomas Cable, *A History of the English Language* (London, 1959), pp. 356–8.

page 97 *'American population will produce'*: ibid.

page 97 *'it would be more convenient'*: ibid.

page 98 *The words are Noah Webster's*: see ibid., pp. 350–51.

page 98 *'The master gave the signal'*: Robert McCrum, William Cran and Robert MacNeil, *The Story of English* (London, 1986), p. 257.

page 99 *a ceaseless quest for originality*: Ralph Waldo Emerson, 'The American Scholar', 31 August 1837, quoted in William Safire (ed.), *Lend Me Your Ears: Great Speeches in History* (New York, 2004), pp. 591–4.

page 99 *one Massachusetts father*: quoted in Alistair Cooke, *America* (London, 1973), p. 156.

page 101 *'We really have everything in common with America'*: a paradox he later put into a story: *The Canterville Ghost* (London, 1887).

Chapter 6: 'Common Hopes and Common Dreams'

page 103 *'It is an absorbing thing to watch'*: Harriet Martineau, *Society in America* (New York, 1837), vol. 1, p. 156.

page 103 *'These people think so loftily'*: Nathaniel Hawthorne, *Our Old Home* (Boston, 1907), pp. xi–xii.

page 103 *an early word-of-mouth Anglo-American publishing sensation*: see

Fanny Trollope, *Domestic Manners of the Americans*, ed. Pamela Neville-Sington (London, 1997), p. vii.

page 103 *a new literary market to conquer*: quoted in Kathleen Burk, *Old World, New World: The Story of Britain and America* (London, 2007), p. 295.

page 104 *'Mind and matter'*: Charles Dickens, *Martin Chuzzlewit*, chapter 34.

page 104 *'we still have an unspeakable yearning towards England'*: quoted in Burk, *Old World, New World*, p. 303.

page 105 *'All classes of our citizens'*: J. S. Holliday, *The World Rushed In* (New York, 1981), p. 48.

page 105 *"You've seen the elephant"*: *New York Times*, 30 September 2008.

page 105 *One doctor wrote to his wife*: Robert McCrum, William Cran and Robert MacNeil, *The Story of English* (London, 1986), p. 273.

page 106 *the Californian madness in '49*: Holliday, *World Rushed In*, p. 45–79.

page 106 *'a bold, reckless, daredevil kind of a woman'*: quoted in Thomas Keneally, *Lincoln* (London, 2003), p. 1.

page 106 *'My politics . . . is short and sweet'*: ibid., p. 18. See also, for the life of Lincoln, Carl Sandburg, *Lincoln* (New York, 1974).

page 107 *'Here he would pore over Blackstone'*: William Dean Howell, *The Life of Abraham Lincoln* (New York, 1860).

page 107 *'common hopes and common dreams'*: *Washington Post*, 10 February 2007.

page 108 *'I believe this government cannot endure permanently half slave and half free'*: Sandburg, *Lincoln*, p. 179.

page 108 *'Any people,' said Lincoln*: see Alistair Cooke, *America* (London, 1973), p. 234.

page 109 *but each refused*: I gratefully acknowledge Garry Wills, *Lincoln at Gettysburg* (New York, 1992), for the details of this account.

page 110 *Lincoln knew exactly what he was doing*: ibid., p. 28.

page 111 *'grapple naked in an airy battle of the mind'*: ibid., p. 37.

page 112 *neither parody nor caricature*: see Ron Powers, *Mark Twain: A Life* (London, 2005).

page 113 *'into the vapour of national fame'*: ibid., p. 154.

page 114 *'All modern American literature comes'*: Ernest Hemingway, *The Green Hills of Africa* (New York, 1935).

Chapter 7: 'The Audacity Of Hope'

page 115 *the worst possible circumstances*: Randall Kennedy, *Nigger: The Strange Career of a Troublesome Word* (New York, 2003), p. 3.

page 115 *'I couldn't have the assumptions'*: V.S. Naipaul, *Reading and Writing: A Personal Account* (New York, 2000), p. 37.

page 116 *out of this horrifying traffic*: see J. L. Dillard, *Black English* (New York, 1973).

page 117 *Hawkins enjoyed the approval of the queen*: Hugh Thomas, *The Slave Trade: The History of the Atlantic Slave Trade, 1440–1850* (London, 1997), p. 156.

page 118 *Caliban, the demonic slave*: *The Tempest*, Act 2, scene 2, lines 183–4, and Act 1, scene 2, lines 366–8.

page 118 *'by having some of every Sort on board'*: Dillard, *Black English*, pp. 73–93. See also Dwight Bolinger, *Language: The Loaded Weapon* (London, 1980).

page 119 *'not a house in Boston'*: Thomas, *Slave Trade*, p. 207.

page 119 *a sought-after prize, the Asiento*: ibid., p. 237.

page 119 *Defoe had been imprisoned for debt*: ibid., p. 236.

page 120 *the conventions of pidgin and creole*: Dillard, *Black English*, p. 125.

page 120 *Pope asked the essential question*: Thomas, *Slave Trade*, p. 452.

page 120 *'She helped prepare literary people's minds'*: ibid., pp. 452–3.

page 120 *'compass the earth and seas'*: Linda Colley, *The Ordeal of Elizabeth Marsh* (London, 2007), pp. 134–6.

page 121 *used to read prayers twice a day*: Thomas, *Slave Trade*, p. 307.

page 121 *was taken up by the king*: ibid., p. 465.

page 121 *years of legal wrangling*: Simon Schama, *Rough Crossings: Britain, the Slaves and the American Revolution* (London, 2005), p. 46.

pages 121–2 *200 people at a London tavern*: ibid., p. 63.

page 122 *Until 1807, when the slave trade was abolished*: Thomas, *Slave Trade*, p. 488.

page 122 *Benjamin Franklin attempted a version*: Dillard, *Black English*, pp. 86–9.

page 123 *the true liberators*: Schama, *Rough Crossings*, p. 65.

page 123 *'have a wonderful art of communicating intelligence among themselves'*: quoted ibid., p. 74.

page 123 *Black preachers were already telling their congregations*: ibid., p. 95.

page 123 *'the greatest exodus from bondage'*: ibid., p. 108.

page 124 *'we should beware how we forfeited'*: quoted in Linda Colley, *Britons: Forging the Nation 1707–1837* (London, 2005), p. 353.

page 124 *'a negro becomes a freeman'*: ibid., p. 354.

page 125 *'What to the slave is the Fourth of July?'*: Schama, *Rough Crossings*, p. 17.

page 125 *'When you have succeeded in dehumanising'*: see Thomas Keneally, *Lincoln* (London, 2003).

page 126 *'If the language of Uncle Remus'*: Joel Chandler Harris, 'Plantation Music', *Critic*, 3/5 (December 1883).

page 127 *'The word jazz'*: F. Scott Fitzgerald, *The Crack-Up* (New York, 1931), p. 16.

page 128 *As the story goes*: Edward Jablonski, *Gershwin: A Biography* (New York, 1998).

page 129 *'the near burned-out, throttled, hate-filled dying affair'*: Norman Mailer, 'Huckleberry Finn – Alive at 100', *New York Times Book Review*, 9 December 1984.

page 130 *He lists the Hip words*: Norman Mailer, *Advertisements for Myself* (New York, 1959).

page 130 *Let freedom ring from the mighty mountains*: quoted in William Safire (ed.), *Lend Me Your Ears: Great Speeches in History* (New York, 2004), pp. 560–66.

page 131 *Obama himself*: Barack Obama, *Dreams from My Father* (New York, 2004), p. 437.

page 132 *'No attempt needed. We go on our own'*: *Indian Express*, 29 October 2008.

page 132 *'the absolute clarity and simplicity'*: Mark Danner, 'Obama and Sweet Potato Pie', *New York Review of Books*, 20 November 2008, p. 12.

page 132 *'I learned to slip back and forth'*: Obama, *Dreams from My Father*, p. 392.

page 132 *'the right man for a new and globalised age'*: Jonathan Freedland, 'The Improbable Journey', *Guardian*, 6 November 2008.

page 133 *Timothy Garton Ash*: 'The USA Doesn't Look to Europe as it Used to', *Guardian*, 11 October 2009.

Chapter 8: Rule, Britannia!

page 137 *epigraph*: quoted in Robert and Isabelle Tombs, *That Sweet Enemy: The French and the British from the Sun King to the Present* (London, 2006),

p. 151. This volume is an engaging cornucopia of Anglo-French anecdote.

page 138 *'Ignorance, madam, pure ignorance'*: Boswell, *Life of Johnson* (1791), vol. 1, p. 293 (for 1755).

pages 138–9 *'I have protracted my work'*: ibid., p. 297 (for 1755).

page 142 *John Locke, who had gone into exile*: Julian Hoppit, *A Land of Liberty? England 1689–1727* (Oxford, 2000), p. 33.

page 143 *By 1707, the year England and Scotland signed the Act of Union*: the essential clause in the negotiations before the Act of Union was explicit about the new kingdom's identity. 'That the two kingdoms of England and Scotland be for ever United into one kingdom by the name of Great Britain. That the United Kingdom of Great Britain be represented by one and the same parliament…'

page 145 *For Swift, things had hardly improved with Charles II*: see W. F. Bolton (ed.), *The English Language*, 2 vols. (Cambridge, 1966 and 1969), vol. 1, pp. 107–23.

page 146 *England, he decided*: see Ian Buruma, *Voltaire's Coconuts, or Anglomania in Europe* (London, 1999), pp. 20–52.

page 146 *Shakespeare was playing to full houses in Paris*: Tombs and Tombs, *That Sweet Enemy*, p. 110.

page 147 *There was also a frisson*: ibid., p. 151.

page 147 *Enter Dr Johnson*: for the life of Dr Johnson there are many lives, from Boswell forwards. See, in particular, Walter Jackson Bate, *Samuel Johnson* (New York, 1977).

page 148 *he would correct himself*: Peter Ackroyd, *Albion: The Origins of the English Imagination* (London, 2002), p. 367.

page 148 *He told Boswell that Robert Burton's*: Boswell, *Life of Johnson*, vol. 1, p. 121 (for 1770).

page 149 *'the entire history of the world'*: Frank McLynn, *1759: The Year Britain Became Master of the World* (London, 2004), p. 1.

page 150 *'Ministers in this country'*: John Brewer, *Sinews of Power* (New York, 1989), p. 181.

page 150 *the French siege of Madras*: ibid., pp. 158 ff.

page 151 *the strange and reckless figure of James Wolfe*: McLynn, *1759*, p. 201.

page 151 *Wolfe rebuked them*: ibid., p. 286.

page 152 *the nation's exuberant jingoism*: ibid., pp. 312–13.

page 153 *a sharp new consciousness of global connections*: see Linda Colley, *The Ordeal of Elizabeth Marsh* (London, 2007), p. xxv.

page 153 *Anticipating Thomas Friedman's characterization*: ibid. See also *The Correspondence of Edmund Burke* (Cambridge, 1958–78), vol. 3, pp. 350–51.

page 153 *The two-hundredth anniversary of Shakespeare's birth*: This account of the Shakespeare Jubilee relies on S. Schoenbaum, *Shakespeare Lives* (Oxford, 1993), pp. 104–10.

page 154 *'Let me search for the clue'*: David McCullough, *John Adams* (New York, 2001), pp. 48–9.

page 154 *'There is nothing preserved of this great genius'*: ibid., p. 359.

page 155 *Abraham Lincoln used to derive special pleasure from reading Shakespeare*: Doris Kearns Goodwin, *Team of Rivals* (London, 2009), p. 546.

page 155 *The discovery of America*: Adam Smith, *The Wealth of Nations* (1776).

page 156 *The surge in Britain's fortunes was palpable*: Piers Brendon, *The Decline and Fall of the British Empire, 1781–1997* (London, 2007), p. 28.

page 157 *Closer to home, in Egypt*: Maya Jasonoff, *Edge of Empire: Conquest and Collecting in the East, 1750–1850* (London, 2005), p. 243.

page 157 *'oak planted in a flower pot'*: Brendon, *Decline and Fall*, p. 28.

page 158 *The British media was playing its part too*: Tombs and Tombs, *That Sweet Enemy*, pp. 188–9.

page 158 *'The greatest revolution'*: quoted ibid., p. 189.

page 158 *So the French Revolution was denied*: this account of the duke of Dorset's abortive game relies on 'Carry on Cricket: The Duke of Dorset's 1789 Tour', *History Today*, 39 (August 1989).

Chapter 9: East, in a Western Voice

page 160 *Work ... came to a halt*: Peter Ackroyd, *Dickens* (London, 1990), pp. 615–16.

page 161 *'England has rather lost ground'*: quoted ibid., p. 421.

page 161 *Just over 1,000 people*: Robert Hughes, *The Fatal Shore* (London, 1987).

page 163 *'The history of empires'*: quoted in Piers Brendon, *The Decline and Fall of the British Empire, 1781–1997* (London, 2007), p. xix.

page 163 *This strange clash of English tradition*: ibid., p. 227.

page 164 *the first governor of the New South Wales penal colony*: Hughes, *Fatal Shore*.

page 164 *sometimes hunted for sport*: Brendon, *Decline and Fall*, p. 69.

page 165 *'Called by the natives Kangooroo'*: Hughes, *Fatal Shore*, p. 5.

page 165 *'a scene too rich for the pencil to portray'*: quoted in Robert McCrum, William Cran and Robert MacNeil, *The Story of English* (London, 1986), p. 312.

page 166 *an atmosphere of forlorn desperation*: Hughes, *Fatal Shore*.

page 166 *the convicts of New South Wales*: Brendon, *Decline and Fall*, pp. 69–72.

page 167 *for Londoners, the spoils of empire*: Maya Jasanoff, *Edge of Empire: Conquest and Collecting in the East, 1750–1850* (London, 2005), p. 154.

page 167 *the first British detective novel*: ibid., p. 175.

page 167 *Today more than half the cricket*: John Major, *More than a Game* (London, 2007), p. 194.

page 168 *The first match there was played*: ibid., p. 195.

page 168 *'Our generals entered into it'*: quoted ibid., p. 200.

page 168 *it was the Parsees*: Ramachandra Guha, *A Corner of a Foreign Field: The Indian History of a British Sport* (London, 2002).

page 168 *So the Parsees played*: ibid., p. 272.

page 169 *There is no doubt that western ideas*: Braj Kachru, *The Indianization of English* (Oxford, 1983), pp. 59–60.

page 169 *The real beginnings of bilingualism*: ibid., pp. 62–5.

page 169 *In this scenario, Macaulay*: Brendon, *Decline and Fall*, pp. 127–8.

page 170 *Under Gandhi and Nehru*: ibid., p. 128.

page 170 *Military whiskers of Indian inspiration*: ibid., p. 124.

page 171 *In 1881 the Cambridge historian J. R. Seeley*: ibid., p. 145.

page 172 *'the Niger will become as romantic as the Rhine'*: quoted ibid., p. 148.

page 172 *After an epic march*: ibid., p. 158.

page 173 *'his death has bequeathed the work'*: quoted ibid., p. 160.

page 174 *Owing to the recent development*: Lockwood Kipling to Edith Plowden, undated, 1890, quoted in Charles Allen, *Kipling Sahib: India and the Making of Rudyard Kipling* (London, 2007), p. 301.

Chapter 10: 'At the Top of the World'

page 175 *epigraph*: in *Henry James Letters*, ed. Leon Edel (London, 1975), vol. 2, p. 145.

page 175 *The Jubilee of 1897 was a worldwide festival*: James Morris, *Pax Britannica* (London, 1979), *passim*.

page 176 *'We are a part, and a great part'*: Fareed Zakaria, *The Post-American World* (London, 2008), p. 171.

page 176 *To the historian Sir Alfred Lyall*: Piers Brendon, *The Decline and Fall of the British Empire, 1781–1997* (London, 2007), p. 207.

page 176 *the oppressors' lives were no less scarred*: see Elizabeth Buettner, *Empire Families* (Oxford, 2004).

page 179 *'mobilized the English language'*: the words are John F. Kennedy's.

page 179 *'I have always earned my living by my pen'*: Winston Churchill, speech given to both Houses of Parliament, 30 November 1954, 'the most memorable public occasion of my life'.

page 180 *the Morning Post's fearless correspondent*: Winston Churchill, *My Early Life* (London, 1930), pp. 239–97.

page 180 *'Youth seeks Adventure'*: ibid., p. 298.

page 182 *a loose affiliation with the fatherland*: Norman Stone, *World War One: A Short History* (London, 2007).

page 182 *'This is a war of kings'*: quoted in David Nasaw, *Hearst* (London, 2002), p. 241.

page 183 *'France is really a first class power no longer'*: in *Letters of Aldous Huxley*, ed. Grover Smith (New York, 1969), p. 124.

page 183 *'The Americanization of Europe'*: Paul Fussell, *The Great War and Modern Memory* (Oxford, 1975), p. 12.

page 184 *'a willingness of the heart'*: F. Scott Fitzgerald, *The Crack-Up* (New York, 1931), p. 197.

page 184 *'Once that is a fait accompli'*: quoted in Charles Seymour, *The Intimate Papers of Colonel House*, 4 vols. (London, 1928), vol. 4, p. 263.

page 184 *'give him the League of Nations'*: Kathleen Burk, *Old World, New World: The Story of Britain and America* (London, 2007), p. 458.

Chapter 11: *'A Willingness of the Heart'*

page 187 *'the two great English-speaking commonwealths'*: quoted in Margaret Macmillan, *Peacemakers* (London, 2001), p. 48.

page 187 *'You must not speak of us who come over here as cousins'*: quoted ibid., p. 21.

pages 190–91 *'trying to deliver a lecture on the influence of American literature'*: Cyril Connolly, *Selected Works*, ed. Matthew Connolly, 2 vols. (London, 2002), vol. 1, p. 160.

page 191 *'a gold-mine of judgement and culture'*: F. Scott Fitzgerald, *The Crack-Up* (New York, 1931), p. 21.

page 192 *'the greatest power on earth'*: Piers Brendon, *The Decline and Fall of the British Empire, 1781–1997* (London, 2007), p. 329.

page 193 *'Britain's greatness and our vast possessions'*: ibid., p. 329.

page 193 *'no business with America at all'*: quoted in Kathleen Burk, *Old World, New World: The Story of Britain and America* (London, 2007), p. 461.

page 193 *'chose to put all their resources'*: ibid., pp. 464–71.

page 193 *'one continent, a hundred peninsulas'*: Brendon, *Decline and Fall*, p. 328.

page 194 *'I wished to be a writer'*: V. S. Naipaul, *Literary Occasions* (London, 2003), pp. 5–6.

page 194 *'The broadcasting of aural language'*: see Howard Davis and Paul Walton (eds.), *Language, Image, Media* (Oxford, 1983).

Chapter 12: 'The Unity of the English-Speaking Peoples'

page 196 *epigraph*: quoted in Angus Calder, *The People's War: Britain 1939–1945* (London, 1969), p. 77.

page 196 *This was an overdue volume*: Roy Jenkins, *Churchill* (London, 2001), p. 560.

page 197 *'It was the nation that had the lion's heart'*: Winston Churchill, in a speech given to both Houses of Parliament, 30 November 1954.

page 197 *'Never have I admired a people more'*: Cordell Hull, *Memoirs* (London, 1948), p. 855.

page 197 *'Churchill brought himself nearer the post of Prime Minister'*: Harold Nicolson, quoted in Jenkins, *Churchill*, p. 557.

page 197 *a patriotic defiance to Nazism*: ibid.

page 197 *'You may take it absolutely for certain'*: ibid., p. 558.

page 198 *Churchill agreed to supply*: David Reynolds, *In Command of History: Churchill Fighting and Writing the Second World War* (London, 2004), p. 15.

page 198 *'The day will come when the joy-bells will ring'*: Jenkins, *Churchill*, p. 568.

page 198 *'made himself the orator of the government'*: ibid.

page 199 *a volume that sold well on both sides of the Atlantic*: Reynolds, *In Command of History*, p. 15.

pages 199–200 *the burden of fighting alone against Germany 'may be more than we can bear'*: Jenkins, *Churchill*, pp. 614–15.

page 200 *'if American assistance is to play any part'*: ibid.

page 200 *'There was still a distance between their minds'*: John Lukacs, *Five Days in London: May 1940* (New Haven, 1999), p. 74.

page 200 *'if we go down, the responsibility will be America's'*: Kathleen Burk, *Old World, New World: The Story of Britain and America* (London, 2007), p. 494.

page 201 *'Great Britain virtually ceased to be an exporting country'*: A. J. P. Taylor, *English History 1914–1945* (Oxford, 1965), p. 513.

page 201 *With Britain and America in alliance*: Burk, *Old World, New World*, p. 497.

page 201 *'I wanted – I wanted to do the Peace too'*: Reynolds, *In Command of History*, p. 38.

page 202 *'Congress will ask me to address them'*: ibid., p. 41.

page 202 *'This is a wonderful school in my home state'*: ibid., p. 42.

page 202 *a critical reaction to the old war leader's ferocious drum-beating*: ibid., pp. 42–3.

page 203 *Churchill angrily pulled out of a serialization deal*: Jenkins, *Churchill*, p. 811.

page 203 *'There were concerted efforts'*: see Frances Stonor Saunders, *Who Paid the Piper? The CIA and the Cultural Cold War* (London, 1999), p. 24.

page 204 *'Not since Rome and Carthage'*: ibid., p. 25.

page 204 *Shortly after Orwell's death*: ibid., p. 293.

page 204 *Cecil B. De Mille*: ibid., p. 24.

page 205 *After dinner one evening*: ibid., pp. 284–5.

page 205 *'I want to show our people their country'*: ibid., pp. 286–7.

page 205 *'our flag shall fly high'*: Piers Brendon, *The Decline and Fall of the British Empire, 1781–1997* (London, 2007), p. 206.

page 206 *He told Anthony Eden*: Burk, *Old World, New World*, pp. 515–17.

page 206 *'lock the United States into a rule-based post-war financial order'*: quoted ibid., p. 524.

page 207 *his history might 'play some small part'*: Winston Churchill, *A History of the English-Speaking Peoples,* vol. 1, (London, 1956), p. xvii.

page 207 *'at the height of the Cold War'*: Tony Judt, *Postwar: A History of Europe Since 1945* (London, 2007), p. 223.

page 208 *the preferred choice of Austrian secondary students*: ibid., p. 224.

page 209 *By the late 1970s*: ibid., p. 482.

Chapter 13: 'The World At Your Fingertips'

page 210 *'the process whereby American girls turn into American women'*: Christopher Hampton, *Savages* (London, 1974), scene 16, p. 75.

page 210 *In 1959 Alistair Cooke complained*: Alistair Cooke, *America Observed* (New York, 1988), p. 120.

page 211 *Many legislators were alarmed*: Jean-Benoît Nadeau and Julie Barlow, *The Story of French* (Toronto, 2007), p. 409.

page 212 *'Les angleglottes', declared the petitioners*: Tony Judt, *Postwar: A History of Europe Since 1945* (London, 2007), p. 761.

page 212 *'a miserable time in Brussels'*: author interview with MEP Charles Tannock.

page 212 *'British interpreters are now so rare in Brussels'*: The Times, 15 February 2009.

page 213 *a complex adolescent mixture*: Judt, *Postwar*, p. 758.

page 214 *farcical interludes, like the Parsley Crisis*: Fareed Zakaria, *The Post-American World* (London, 2008), p. 215.

page 214 *'Our souls and our blood are sacrifices'*: ibid., p. 216.

page 215 *The Berlin Wall began to crumble*: Judt, *Postwar*, p. 614.

page 215 *'If I celebrate the fall of the Wall'*: quoted in Thomas L. Friedman, *The World is Flat: The Globalized World in the Twenty-First Century* (London, 2005), p. 53.

page 216 *In the next two decades*: Zakaria, *The Post-American World*, p. 20.

page 217 *'the Internet boom triggered'*: Michael Lewis, *The New New Thing* (New York, 1999), p. 2.

page 218 *Tim Berners-Lee*: quoted in Friedman, *The World is Flat*, p. 60.

page 218 *Two weeks after Netscape*: see Lewis, *The New New Thing*.

page 218 *the next Californian Gold Rush*: see John Naughton, *A Brief History of the Future: The Origins of the Internet* (London, 1999).

page 218 *'a whole new global platform for collaboration'*: Friedman, *The World is Flat*, p. 91.

page 220 *Anglophile Latin Americans*: Allen Guttmann, *Sports: The First Five Millennia* (Amherst, Mass., 2004).

page 220 *the Superbowl and the World Cup*: Franklin Foer, *How Soccer Explains the World* (London, 2004).

page 220 *The international dimension is comparatively new*: David Goldblatt, *The Ball is Round: A Global History of Football* (London, 2006), p. 681

page 221 *a dreadful anthem*: ibid., p. 840.

page 222 *'You like muffin?'*: Peter Carey, *Wrong about Japan* (London, 2005), pp. 121–2.

page 222 *'has always tried to make his characters as standard and as universal as possible*: ibid., p. 98.

page 223 *'The hybrid speech that many young people now favour in Japan'*: Mark Abley, *The Prodigal Tongue: Dispatches from the Future of English* (London, 2008), p. 103.

page 223 *Friedman's 'Eureka moment'*: Friedman, *The World is Flat*, p. 7.

page 224 *'flattening of the world'*: ibid., p. 205.

page 225 *In the words of the German publisher*: ibid., p. 411.

page 226 *'a few ripples on the surface of the sea of language'*: David Crystal, *Texting: The Gr8 Db8* (Oxford, 2008).

page 226 *'Write the character you want'*: interview with Rob Gifford, August 2008.

page 227 *'the culture of electronic communication'*: Sven Birkerts, *The Gutenberg Elegies* (New York, 1994).

Chapter 14: One World, One Dream

page 231 *epigraph*: Martin Jacques, *When China Rules the World* (London, 2009), p. 429.

page 234 *'the world's only language teacher known to bring students to tears of excitement'*: Evan Osnos, 'Letter from China', *New Yorker*, 28 April 2008.

page 236 *'the unassailable fortress of the written Chinese character'*: Rob Gifford, *China Road* (London, 2007), p. 251.

page 236 *'This is not the 17th century'*: 'Four Keys to China's Peaceful Rise', *Guardian*, 18 December 2008.

pages 236–7 *'the Chinese enthusiasm for English'*: Jacques, *When China Rules the World*, p. 117.

page 237 *'a hidden world of intellectuals'*: Mark Leonard, 'China's New Intelligentsia', *Prospect*, March 2008, p. 26.

page 237 *According to Leonard, some Chinese intellectuals*: ibid. See also Mark Leonard, *What Does China Think?* (London, 2008).

page 238 *'for all China's success to date'*: Will Hutton, *The Writing on the Wall* (London, 2007), pp. 8–9. See also Gifford, *China Road*, pp. 249–61.

page 238 *'the balance of power in Beijing'*: Leonard, 'China's New Intelligentsia', p. 28.

page 239 *China's interaction with English*: see Serge Michel and Michel Beuret, *China Safari: On the Trail of Beijing's Expansion in Africa* (New York, 2009).

page 239 *Ethiopia's prime minister Meles Zenawi declared*: Ernest Harsch, 'Big Leap in China-Africa Ties', *Africa Renewal* (January 2007).

page 239 *The inevitable reckoning*: Michel and Beuret, *China Safari*, pp. 61–70.

page 240 *'The goal for China is not conflict'*: Joshua Cooper Ramo, 'The Beijing Consensus', Foreign Policy Centre, London, 2004, quoted in Fareed Zakaria, *The Post-American World* (London, 2008), p. 127.

Chapter 15: 'Virtually Running America'

page 241 *epigraph*: Aravind Adiga, *The White Tiger* (London, 2008), p. 8.

page 243 *'speak globalization fluently'*: Fareed Zakaria, *The Post-American World* (London, 2008), p. 135.

page 246 *a symbolic figure from this transitional decade*: ibid., p. 133.

page 247 *Bhagat's latest novel*: *Guardian*, 10 October 2008.

page 247 *'In China it was bloody, but India needs to learn'*: ibid.

page 248 *'India's entertainment industry is growing rapidly'*: *Observer*, 5 July 2009.

page 250 *Glenny's catchy title*: author interview, 7 October 2008.

pages 250–51 *'English has emerged as a backbone for growth and development'*: 'Rwanda's decision to ditch French for English is yet another blow for the most wonderful language', *Guardian*, 15 October 2008.

page 251 *When the world's press arrived in Nuuk*: see *New York Times*, 22 June 2009.

page 252 *'There is this naive belief'*: interview with Lee Kuan Yew, in Robert McCrum, William Cran and Robert MacNeil, *The Story of English* (London, 1986).

page 253 *'Speaking good English does not mean'*: Mark Abley, *The Prodigal Tongue: Dispatches from the Future of English* (London, 2008), p. 66.

Epilogue: 'A Thoroughfare for All Thoughts'

page 255 *Consider the powers of the earth*: see Stephen Pinker, *The Language Instinct* (London, 2004).

page 255 *'the whole earth was of one language'*: Genesis 11: 1–9.

page 256 *As Steven Pinker reminds us*: Steven Pinker, *The Language Instinct* (London, 2004).

page 256 *According to the British Council*: reported in *The Economist*, 16 December 2006.

page 257 *'a thoroughfare for all thoughts'*: in *The Letters of John Keats 1814–1821*, ed. Hyder Edward Rollins (Cambridge, Mass., 1958), vol. 1, p. 193.

page 259 *'There are more people'*: Chris Patten, *What Next? Surviving the Twenty-First Century* (London, 2008), p. 427.

page 262 *'to be born an English-speaker'*: *Sunday Times*, 5 October 2008.

page 264 *'when you are leading the world'*: Serge Michel and Michel Beuret, *China Safari: On the Trail of Beijing's Expansion in Africa* (New York, 2009), p. 11.

page 265 *A new belief system is emerging*: see James Boyle, *The Public Domain* (New Haven, 2009).

page 266 *Taha Mahmoud, a twenty-five-year-old computer programmer*: reported in the *Guardian*, 30 July 2007.

Select Bibliography

Mark Abley, *The Prodigal Tongue: Dispatches from the Future of English* (London, 2008).

Peter Ackroyd, *T. S. Eliot* (London, 1984).

—— *Albion: The Origins of the English Imagination* (London, 2002).

Aravind Adiga, *The White Tiger* (London, 2008).

Charles Allen, *Kipling Sahib: India and the Making of Rudyard Kipling* (London 2007).

Albert C. Baugh and Thomas Cable, *A History of the English Language* (London, 1959).

David J. Becuson and Holger H. Herwig, *One Christmas in Washington: Churchill and Roosevelt Forge the Grand Alliance* (London, 2005).

W. F. Bolton (ed.), *The English Language*, 2 vols. (Cambridge, 1966 and 1969).

Piers Brendon, *The Decline and Fall of the British Empire, 1781–1997* (London, 2007).

Susan Brigden, *New Worlds, Lost Worlds: The Rule of the Tudors, 1485–1603* (London, 2000).

Elizabeth Buettner, *Empire Families* (Oxford, 2004).

Kathleen Burk, *Old World, New World: The Story of Britain and America* (London, 2007).

Ian Buruma, *Voltaire's Coconuts, or Anglomania in Europe* (London, 1999).

Angus Calder, *The People's War: Britain 1939–1945* (London, 1969).

David Cannadine, *Ornamentalism: How the British Saw their Empire* (London, 2001).

Peter Carey, *Wrong about Japan* (London, 2005).

George Clark, *English History: A Survey* (Oxford, 1971).

Peter Clarke, *The Last Thousand Days of the British Empire* (London, 2007).

Sue Clifford and Angela King, *England in Particular* (London, 2006).

Linda Colley, *The Ordeal of Elizabeth Marsh* (London, 2007).

—— *Britons: Forging the Nation, 1707–1837* (London, 2005).

Cyril Connolly, *Selected Works*, ed. Matthew Connolly (London, 2002).

Alistair Cooke, *America* (London, 1973).

David Crystal, *Language and the Internet* (Cambridge, 2006).

Danny Danziger and John Gillingham, *1215: The Year of Magna Carta* (London, 2004).

John Darwin, *After Tamerlane: The Global History of Empire since 1405* (London, 2007).

Peter de Bolla, *The Fourth of July and the Founding of America* (London, 2007).

J. L. Dillard, *Black English* (New York, 1973).

J. H. Elliott, *Empires of the Atlantic World* (New Haven, 2006).

Stuart Berg Flexner, *I Hear America Talking* (New York, 1976).

Graham Fraser, *Sorry, I Don't Speak French: Confronting the Canadian Crisis that Won't Go Away* (Toronto, 2006).

Thomas L. Friedman, *The World is Flat: The Globalised World in the Twenty-First Century* (London, 2005).

Peter Fryer, *Staying Power: The History of Black People in Britain* (London, 1984).

Paul Fussell, *The Great War and Modern Memory* (Oxford, 1975).

John Lewis Gaddis, *The Cold War* (London, 2005).

Rob Gifford, *China Road* (London, 2007).

Peter Gilliver, Jeremy Marshall and Edmund Weiner, *Tolkien and the Oxford English Dictionary* (Oxford, 2006).

David Goldblatt, *The Ball is Round: A Global History of Football* (London, 2006).

Doris Kearns Goodwin, *Team of Rivals* (London, 2009).

Stephen Greenblatt, *Will in the World* (London, 2004).

Ramachandra Guha, *A Corner of a Foreign Field: The Indian History of a British Sport* (London, 2002).

Christina Hardyment, *Malory: The Life and Times of King Arthur's Chronicler* (London, 2005).

Carola Hicks, *The Bayeux Tapestry: The Life Story of a Masterpiece* (London, 2006).

Christopher Hitchens, *Thomas Jefferson: Author of America* (London, 2007).

Henry Hitchings, *The Secret Life of Words* (London, 2008).

David Horspool, *Why Alfred Burned the Cakes* (London, 2006).

Robert Hughes, *The Fatal Shore* (London, 1987).

Will Hutton, *The Writing on the Wall* (London, 2007).

Martin Jacques, *When China Rules the World* (London, 2009).

Maya Jasanoff, *Edge of Empire: Conquest and Collecting in the East, 1750–1850* (London, 2005).

Roy Jenkins, *Churchill* (London, 2001).

Samuel Johnson, *Rasselas* (London, 1976).

Tony Judt, *Postwar: A History of Europe Since 1945* (London, 2007).

——*Reappraisals: Reflections on the Forgotten Twentieth Century* (London, 2008).

Fred Kaplan, *Lincoln: The Biography of a Writer* (New York, 2008).

Thomas Keneally, *Lincoln* (London, 2003).

Frank Kermode, *The Age of Shakespeare* (London, 2004).

Parag Khanna, *The Second World: Empires and Influence in the New Global Order* (London, 2008).

Mark Kishlansky, *A Monarchy Transformed: Britain 1603–1714* (London, 1996).

Naomi Klein, *The Shock Doctrine: The Rise of Disaster Capitalism* (London, 2007).

James Kynge, *China Shakes the World* (London, 2006).

Mark Leonard, *What Does China Think?* (London, 2008).

Seth Lerer, *Inventing English: A Portable History of the Language* (New York, 2007).

John Lukacs, *Five Days in London: May 1940* (New Haven, 2001).

Robert McCrum, William Cran and Robert MacNeil, *The Story of English* (London, 1986).

Alex MacGillivray, *A Brief History of Globalization* (London, 2006).

Robin McKie, *The Face of Britain* (London, 2006).

Frank McLynn, *1759: The Year Britain Became Master of the World* (London, 2004).

Robert MacNeil and William Cran, *Do You Speak American?* (New York, 2005).

Kenan Malik, *From Fatwa to Jihad: The Rushdie Affair and its Legacy* (London, 2009).

John Man, *The Gutenberg Revolution* (London, 2002).

Walter Russell Mead, *God and Gold: Britain, America and the Making of the Modern World* (London, 2007).

Jean-Benoît Nadeau and Julie Barlow, *The Story of French* (Toronto, 2007).

V. S. Naipaul, *Reading and Writing: A Personal Account* (New York, 2000).

——*Literary Occasions* (London, 2003).

John Naughton, *A Brief History of the Future: The Origins of the Internet* (London, 1999).

Jean-Paul Nerrière, *Parlez Globish* (Paris, 2004).

—— and David Hon, *Globish the World Over*, ebook (2009).

Adam Nicolson, *Earls of Paradise: England and the Dream of Perfection* (London, 2008).

—— *Power and Glory: Jacobean England, and the Making of the King James Bible* (London, 2003).

Barack Obama, *Dreams from My Father* (New York, 2004).

George Orwell, *The Collected Works*, 20 vols., ed. Peter Davidson (London, 1998).

—— *Nineteen Eighty-Four* (London, 1949).

George D. Painter, *William Caxton* (London, 1976).

Patrick Parrinder, *Nation and Novel: The English Novel from its Origins to the Present Day* (Oxford, 2006).

Chris Patten, *What Next? Surviving the Twenty-First Century* (London, 2008).

Stephen Pinker, *The Language Instinct* (London, 2004).

David Reynolds, *In Command of History: Churchill Fighting and Writing the Second World War* (London, 2004).

Mordechai Richler, *Oh Canada! Oh Quebec!* (London, 1992).

Miri Rubin, *The Hollow Crown* (London, 2005).

Donald Sassoon, *The Culture of the Europeans: From 1800 to the Present* (London, 2006).

Frances Stonor Saunders, *Who Paid the Piper? The CIA and the Cultural Cold War* (London, 1999).

Simon Schama, *Rough Crossings: Britain, the Slaves and the American Revolution* (London, 2005).

James Schapiro, *1599: A Year in the Life of William Shakespeare* (London, 2005).

S. Schoenbaum, *Shakespeare's Lives* (Oxford, 1993).

Tom Shippey, *The Road to Middle-Earth* (London, 2005).

Jonathan Spence, *Mao Zedong* (New York, 1999).

George Steiner, *Language and Silence* (London, 1968).

Norman Stone, *World War One: A Short History* (London, 2007).

A. J. P. Taylor, *English History 1914–1945* (Oxford, 1965).

—— *The Origins of the Second World War* (New York, 1961).

Hugh Thomas, *The Slave Trade: The History of the Atlantic Slave Trade, 1440–1870* (London, 1997).

Robert and Isabelle Tombs, *That Sweet Enemy: The French and the British from the Sun King to the Present* (London, 2006).

Barbara Tuchman, *The Proud Tower* (New York, 1965).

—— *A Distant Mirror* (New York, 1978).

Edward Vallance, *A Radical History of England* (London, 2009).

Nury Vittachi, *Mr Wong Goes West* (Crows Nest, NSW, 2008).

James Walvin, *A Short History of Slavery* (London, 2007).

Jacob Weisberg, *The Bush Tragedy* (New York, 2008).

Stanley Wells, *Shakespeare & Co.* (London, 2006).

Garry Wills, *Lincoln at Gettysburg* (New York, 1992).

Fareed Zakaria, *The Post-American World* (London, 2008).

PERMISSIONS

Acknowledgements

Globish has grown out of half a lifetime of watching the English language at work in various international media, starting with my involvement in *The Story of English*, and my collaboration with the director William Cran and the broadcaster Robert MacNeil. Thank you, Bill and Robin. And deepest thanks, too, to the late Brian Wenham, an intellectual godfather in all senses.

Some of the ideas in this book had their first exposure at the *Observer*, my second home for the past fifteen years. Many colleagues at Kings Place (an address that delights in resisting the apostrophe) have been fantastically supportive and generous in their support. My former editor, Roger Alton, a true patron of ambitious ideas, kindly agreed to give me the time off to write the main draft. John Mulholland, his successor, generously sustained Roger's initial commitment. Thanks to them, and also to Paul Webster, Jane Ferguson, Allan Jenkins, Ursula Kenny and managing editor Jan Thompson. In the newsroom, my fellow pod-mates, a constellation of extraordinary talent, David Smith, Vanessa Thorpe, Caroline Davies and Ed Vulliamy, have all contributed in ways I have greatly appreciated. Rafael Behr, Jacob Weisberg, Olivia Laing, Roland Manthorpe and Jonathan Bouquet all contributed invaluable first readings. For two summers, Hilary Newiss and Peter Bazalgette provided a wonderful base in which to read at leisure and to begin thinking out some of the narrative.

Much of my overseas research was made possible through the British Council, especially Susanna Nicklin. Further afield, *Condé Nast Traveller*'s Sarah Spankie has been a generous supporter, and I gratefully acknowledge her help. Becky Swift opened several doors. For the Indian sections, I thank Ramachandra Guha, Sheerin Aswat, her parents Fasila and Mohammed, who extended the finest hospitality, and the inimitable Wodehouse Society of Bangalore. For China, I had the seasoned advice and support of Ed Gargan, Rob Gifford,

Martin Jacques, Tamara Sharp and Kathy Flower. Other crucial bits of research were done by Rosie Rickett and Richard Rogers.

Globish is another outing for the Anglo-American team of W. W. Norton and Penguin. I am delighted to pay tribute once again to my editors Star Lawrence and Mary Mount. My agent Binky Urban and her London deputy Karolina Sutton have been wonderfully support-ive. Sadly, Kate Jones, who negotiated the original contract, died before I had completed the research. I still miss her wicked sense of humour and bracing realism. Another nice element of continuity has been the eagle eye and sharp literary intelligence of my copy-editor, Elizabeth Stratford, who has saved me from many egregious errors. Any that remain are, of course, entirely my responsibility.

Finally, a heartfelt thanks to my family: Sarah, Alice and Isobel. Words, said Samuel Johnson, in one of his loveliest phrases, 'are the daughters of earth'. My wife and my girls, equally, are children of words, a delight and an inspiration.

Index